WORLD WISE

World Wise

What to **Know** Before You **Go**

Lanie Denslow

FIDM/THE FASHION INSTITUTE OF DESIGN & MERCHANDISING

CARTOONS BY MARY NADLER

FAIRCHILD PUBLICATIONS, INC.
NEW YORK

Executive Editor: Olga T. Kontzias

Development Editor: Sylvia L. Weber

Assistant Acquisitions Editor: Jaclyn Bergeron

Art Director: Adam B. Bohannon

Production Manager: Ginger Hillman

Production Editor: Elizabeth Marotta

Copy Editor: Vivian Gomez

Cover and Interior Design: Adam B. Bohannon

Cover photograph: Erin Derby

Cartoons: Mary Nadler

Cartography: Alice Thiede

Intern: Yelena Bromberg

Library of Congress Catalog Card Number: 2005931393

ISBN: 1-56367-359-2

GST R 133004424

Printed in the United States of America

TP12

CONTENTS

PREFACE

Thanks to the size and diversity of the United States, Americans, more so than people from other countries, have remained within their own borders for work and play. Although we are a nation built by people from many places and many cultures, we have prided ourselves on being a "melting pot," creating one American way.

However, that inward-looking pattern no longer works. Saturated markets, consumers' demand for low-cost goods, and the need for speed to market that drives companies to 24/7 operations push our activities around the globe. In today's economy, whether you stay at home or travel the world, your business is global. Employees of Amazon in Seattle manage teams in Ireland as well as Boston. A Chinese company buys the PC division of IBM and moves its managers to the United States to operate the company. Federated Department Stores, based in Cincinnati, sells its private label merchandise in Japan. Basic T-shirts are made in Africa, East Asia, and Latin America for sale in the United States.

At the heart of this world economy are individuals striving to communicate across differing cultural heritages, surroundings, and experiences. If they don't understand the range of values, attitudes, and definitions of appropriate business behavior, these businesspeople invite misunderstandings. Their misunderstandings may make it difficult to build the connections that are the foundation of all commercial activity.

The purpose of this book is to enable readers to learn about the variety of our world and thereby be prepared to engage with colleagues, customers, partners, employers, and employees, regardless of their backgrounds or locations. It is not intended to change people's behavior but to expand their knowledge. It is hoped this book will serve as a reliable reference, even a traveling companion, for quick reading on a journey to a new destination. It isn't targeted to a specific industry but is an overview, intended to provide some fundamental insights useful no matter what your profession. The text provides facts about various countries as well as revealing experiences and perspectives of business-people from around the globe.

A Look at the Contents

The book begins with the basic issues that relate to how we view our lives. The first four chapters cover the concept of time; the organization of society, whether around groups or individuals; styles of communication; and relationship building. The next three chapters change the focus to business, looking at corporate cultures and related issues. In the the following ten chapters, globalization, trade, and regions of the world are discussed. The last four chapters cover practical matters such as topics of conversation, travel, and protocols for dining and gift giving. At the end is a resource section with suggestions for additional reading. Following is a more detailed look at each group of chapters.

The purpose of Chapters 1 through 4 is to enable readers to understand that people's behavior, while varied and sometimes surprising or puzzling, is based on reasons that are obvious to them, stemming from the culture in which they are reared. Cultures vary throughout the world, but they all seek to answer people's question: What is the appropriate way for me to behave, to lead my life?

These four chapters deal with the questions about organizing one's life from the aspect of whether schedules or relationships must be considered first. We then move to styles of communication, the focus on groups and individuals and follow with the topic personal connections, the formation of relationships and friendships.

The attention in Chapters 5 through 7 shifts its focus from individuals to the business environment. The material here looks at elements of corporate cultures, types of advisers involved, and attitudes toward innovation and achievement.

Next we turn the readers' attention to the global environment where business takes place today. The purpose of Chapters 8 through 17 is to add to the readers' knowledge about global trade and alliances, providing a historical perspective as well as a contemporary outlook. In addition to Chapters 8 and 9, on the history of global trade and current international trade agreements, respectively, there are eight individual chapters on specific world regions, presenting information about geography, history, trade, and the business environment of each region.

The last four chapters spotlight practical tools to deal with day-to-day situations ranging from shared meals, topics for informal conversations, and gift giving to travel planning.

I Couldn't Have Done It Without You

This book reflects more than the work of the author whose name is on the cover. There were dozens of people who contributed in an extraordinary variety of ways. Naming everyone would create a list that would fill as many pages as this book is long. There were friends who left messages, expecting no reply while the chapters were evolving. Others read and reread the work in progress, offering advice, insight, and encouragement. People provided introductions for the interviews that fill the book, and interviewees gave generously of their time and willingly shared their stories. To each of them I offer my sincere thanks. The following reviewers, selected by the publisher, provided valuable advice: Charles A. Braithwaite, University of Nebraska—Lincoln; Gary Christiansen, North Iowa Area Community College; Leslie Davis Burns, Oregon State University; Debi Forse, Holland College; Sally Harmon, Purdue University; Soyoung Kim, University of Georgia; Cynthia Lockhart, University of Cincinnati; Suzanne G. Marshall, California State University, Long Beach; Theresa Mastrianni, Kingsborough Community College; Joan McKenna, San Diego Community College District; Lynda Gamans Poloian, Southern New Hampshire University; Tana Stufflebean, University of Central Oklahoma; and Richard Wilkins, Baruch College, City University of New York.

Special mention must go to my editors at Fairchild Books: to Olga Kontzias, executive editor, for the opportunity to write this book; and to Sylvia Weber, development editor, whose good humor and patience guided me through the process. Her suggestions always improved the manuscript. More thanks go to production editors Beth Cohen, who helped begin the process, and Elizabeth Marotta, who saw the project through to its final stage. For overseeing the design of the cover and interior, I thank art director Adam Bohannon.

Special appreciation goes to Mary Nadler, who created the cartoons that light up the text, and most of all, thank you to my family for allowing me to become a hermit so I could do this work. Finally, I dedicate this book to Talia and Noah, with hopes that they will travel far and often, discovering new places and making new friends.

WORLD WISE

CHAPTER 1

The Clock
and the Calendar

I Wish I'd Known

I always thought that the past was something to study and the future was pretty much all that mattered. I learned that's not always the case. My business activities in Europe would have been easier, especially at the beginning, if I'd studied some history as well as customs regulations. Not only did conversations refer to events I didn't recognize but also I would have had a better understanding of their meaning. Past and future seemed connected in ways I couldn't grasp.

→→ *American consultant*
working in the food industry in Poland

I Wish They Knew

If the business delegations that come here would just leave their watches and calendars at home, it would be so much easier to get business started. It would help if they understood that a two-hour meeting, even combined with lunch, isn't enough to start a productive connection. Here in Spain, as in Pakistan and Korea (all places I've worked), it's relationships that count in business. I wish that all the Americans I work with could grasp that before they arrive. Relationships can't be built when you're watching the clock; they evolve over time, and without them, there's no business.

→→ *American with the United States Department*
of Commerce in Spain

Is the Clock King?

As businesspeople begin to work with professionals from other countries, they rapidly discover that not everyone considers schedules, deadlines, and the clock to be the focus of their lives. In some places

3

people and their relationships rule; in other places the clock is indeed king. Grasping how time is understood, valued, and organized from place to place is key to building successful experiences, at home and abroad.

It's Obvious: Time Matters

Before we learn to talk, we develop a sense of time—we understand the rhythm to our days. Light and dark. People coming and going. Eating. Playing. Sleeping. Awakening. Time shapes our lives before we know what the actual word is or means.

We seldom ask what this thing called time is that so influences our lives. We time a runner in a track meet, set aside time for a meeting, and check a clock to see if it's dinnertime. It's as much a part of our lives as breathing, but what is it?

No matter how real we believe it to be or how concrete the message conveyed by the hands moving on our watches seems, time is a concept to which people have given meaning—multiple meanings, in fact. It is not a tangible commodity that can be molded, shaped, saved, or spent.[1] Time is an idea.[2]

Different people in different places understand it differently and thereby comes the challenge. In spite of the difficulty, understanding the varied meanings of time is necessary because the concept of time is important everywhere. Jeremy Rifkin, president of the Foundation on Economic Trends, says, "All of our perceptions of self and world are mediated by the way we imagine, explain, use, and implement time."[3]

We learn about time from the people who guide our lives, from our families to our teachers once we're in school. They communicate their interpretation, their cultural understanding, of time. That common knowledge allows us to coordinate activities and to work and live together. We rely on and expect a shared understanding of the meaning of time. What we don't generally realize is that each culture has its own ways of explaining, imagining, and organizing time. Read the following sayings to get a sense of these differences.

- American: Time is money.
- Spanish: He who rushes arrives first at the grave.

- Japanese: The more haste—the less speed.
- Arabs: Haste is the devil's work, and patience is from the Merciful (Allah).
- Chinese: Feather by feather the goose is plucked.
- Ecuadorian: Little by little one walks far.
- Ethiopian: If you wait long enough, even an egg will walk [the chicken will hatch].
- Indian: Time is free.

When we encounter people whose interpretation of time differs from our own, it often surprises, puzzles, and disturbs us. First of all, we think our way should be the only way, for it is, we're certain, the "right way" to interpret and live with time. We become annoyed and frustrated when other people don't operate as we do.

When we're called on to work with people from other places, we encounter the differences. If our joint venture partner is across the world, our team is scattered over ten countries, or we're transferred from Atlanta to Paris, or from Des Moines to Mexico City, differences related to time abound. Even if we expect the differences, we think, no matter what we've read, that it will be simple to learn, to adapt to another form

"Oh, goody—Greenwich Mean Time."

of scheduling. After all, we all wear watches, and they look alike. Can't we simply adjust a little bit and "get on with it"?

No, we can't. Because our sense of time shapes our views of the world, when we learn a new version of time, we have to relearn everything we know about the world. It changes our understanding of how things (and people) function. We actually have to relearn the very rules of life. Peace Corps volunteers and businesspeople report that the most difficult part of their adaptation to other countries is the adjustment to a different view of time. It's more difficult than learning another language.[4] However, it's possible to develop an understanding and to be prepared, simply by knowing how these differences may present themselves.

Time: Scarce or Plentiful?

Our first indication that things related to time are different in different places may be when we travel and discover, for example, that we can't have dinner at 7:00 P.M. because restaurants don't serve before 9:00 P.M. In business this realization occurs when people don't arrive at the announced starting time for meetings, when agendas aren't adhered to, and when interruptions are accepted during meetings. Our response to these situations may range from mild annoyance to raging anger. We interpret the delays and interruptions to mean, "They don't value my time, therefore they must not value me or my business. How rude can they be?"

Yet, no insult is meant. It's simply people acting out of a different perception and organization of time, one that is defined by their answer to the basic question: How much time is there? A lot or a little? Is it scarce or plentiful?

Edward and Mildred Hall named these two views of time—time being scarce and being plentiful—and the related behaviors as monochronic and polychronic time.[5] People who answer that time is scarce often prefer to do one thing at a time, in sequence, with a focus on schedules and tasks, and thus fall into the designation of monochronic. People who answer that time is plentiful can be involved in multiple things at once and focus on people and relationships, and thus fall into the designation of polychronic.[6]

Those of us who operate within U.S. business culture are certain there's little time, that it's a scarce commodity. We bemoan the fact that we can't add two hours to each day or a day to each week.

Along with the United States, Great Britain, Switzerland, Germany, Canada, and Australia fall mainly into the monochronic category, with everyone else in the world in the polychronic group. (This does not suggest that every person and every culture fits exactly into each definition. But the preferred behavior, the tendency for a person raised in a monochronic or polychronic culture, will generally follow the corresponding pattern when conducting business as well as in their personal lives).

It is important to keep in mind the key difference between the two concepts of time. The monochronics focus on time, schedules, and tasks. They conceptualize time as a scarce resource. In this chapter we'll refer to this as clock time as well as monochronic. The polychronics put people and relationships ahead of schedules and tasks. Their view is that there is an adequate amount of time available for everything. To them time continues without end. It is when both monochronic and polychronic viewpoints encounter each other that challenges emerge.

Most often, differences are expressed as complaints. A businessperson in an office lobby in Mexico City might say, "They're never on time; don't these people know the meaning of 'on time'? They made the appointment, picked the time, and I'm here. Why aren't they?"

On the contrary, an Italian might say, "Why are our American partners so focused on the clock? I was only 15 minutes late. I knew they were coming. We had an appointment. Why are they so rigid? How can you do business with someone who only cares about the schedule—what the clock says—and doesn't even trust that I'll keep an appointment?"

From a monochronic perspective, we believe each minute is important. Our general American culture focuses on accomplishment and personal achievement. Completing tasks leads to realizing goals. Americans have an expression: "Don't just stand there. Do something. Get on with it."

It would be simple but inaccurate to think that polychronics don't value time. They do. For example a Chinese businessperson may thank you for your time and even arrive early; however, the meeting may extend beyond the designated completion time. The emphasis is not on finishing an agenda by a set time but rather on finishing what must be done in a way that is appropriate and recognizes the people involved. The emphasis is on people and relationships, not on hours and minutes.

Events or Clock, Sequential or Simultaneous?

When people are the focus, your schedule is linked to the events involving people rather than tasks, deadlines, and time.

A German international business student at a U.S. college relates a story of lunch in Barcelona and laughs at her frustration. On a recent visit to Spain, she and her friends scheduled just two days in Barcelona. They had a list of places to see and a schedule to follow. Their plan included time for lunch with their friends who lived there. One hour for lunch and a visit. "Imagine," she said, "how frustrating it was for us, so organized, so scheduled, when we realized that lunch was going well past our one hour—in fact, it went [on] for three hours!" There was nothing to do but enjoy the people, the lunch, and laugh at themselves. The event had a time of its own. They missed a museum visit, but it was important for the friendship to allow the event to control time, not their watches.

The differences between polychronic and monochronic isn't only about schedules but also about how tasks and activities are organized. Must things be done sequentially, one action following another, or can multiple things happen at once? Guided by clocks, the monochronic considers time as linear as well as scarce. One activity follows another. Each must be completed in its turn. If I'm in a meeting with you, I expect you to finish our business before starting something else.

Contrast this with the polychronic viewpoint that allows simultaneous or synchronous activities. (Some researchers call these people multi-actives.)[7] Interruptions are not seen as problems. People are able to move between activities without losing the thread of conversations or focus.

Monochronic people approach this when they talk on their mobile phones while driving from one meeting to the next, trying to eat a sandwich from the nearest drive-through. But these people feel rushed and impatient. Contrast this with a Brazilian person who may stop a tennis game to talk on the phone with a client, fill out an order while talking, and munch on a snack all at the same time. The difference is that this is the order of life—a pattern not considered stressful.

In a world where human interactions are considered the best way to invest your time, interruptions are allowed. People expect to be acknowledged. If a group is meeting and one of the people in that meeting, who is returning from a trade mission to Costa Rica, arrives early, he or she may join the group immediately. There will be talk about the trip, which completely changes the topic of the meeting. In fact, the meeting may be interrupted several times, but each time the group returns to the matters that brought them together. It just may take a little longer than originally planned.

When a situation like this occurs, monochronic people tend to get angry or feel insulted. If this happens to an American architect in Mexico City who is waiting for his new joint venture partner, he will feel angry about this perceived rudeness. If he expresses frustration to his partners it will simply be a reminder of Americans' concern about time. While Americans see such a concern as efficient, for others the constant focus on schedules "makes Americans seem arrogant, rude, and untrustworthy."[8]

Past / Present / Future (Near and Far)

In addition to our clocks, our calendars help to regulate our lives. The large amount of calendars that sell at year-end proves how much people use and depend on them. Paper calendars aren't the only form of calendars people use. Now calendars are on watches, computers, and PDAs.

A calendar, however, is more than a device we use to set our schedules. It creates an awareness of past, present, and future. Of these three stages of time, our business activities are most often directed toward the future. We schedule meetings and product launches. We select dates as production targets and delivery schedules. We enroll in yearlong seminars to learn about exporting. We schedule vacations weeks or months in advance. We always look to the future, the time yet to arrive.

As with all matters related to time, the understanding of the three calendar elements—past, present, and future—is subject to varied interpretations. Culture and community influence our views and related actions, just as they do with clock time. Because these views have an impact on schedules and responses to deadlines, it's useful to understand something of the differences. One source of information is Fons Trompenaars and Charles Hampden-Turner's book entitled *Riding the Waves of Culture*. It includes results of their study that indicate how people around the globe perceive the relationship between past, present, and future.[9]

They determined that differences exist in several ways. Some people see past, present, and future linked to one another, and others do not. There are differences in which stage of time is considered most important. Some results of their study indicate that most people in Japan and Malaysia see past, present, and future as linked to one another. By contrast, people in Venezuela, Russia, and Hong Kong regard these as separate stages with the past being the most important. In Mexico and China, people regard these as three unconnected segments, all of approximately equal significance.

The United States differs from all of the foregoing. U.S. results show the past linked with the present, and the present with the future, but the future does not touch the past. In level of importance, for Americans, the future is the most important, and the past the least important.

A casual conversation may reveal how these attitudes show themselves in our daily lives. If you ask natives of Hong Kong to describe their families, they may begin with their ancestors (the past) while a native of the United States is likely to talk about children or grandchildren (the present and future).[10]

It's not only where we focus, forward or backward, but also the duration, the length of time we ascribe to past and future, that can influence our business lives. Looking again at Trompenaars and Hampden-Turner's study, we note additional differences. Hong Kong, China, and Israel have the longest definition of future, while Singapore, Russia, Italy, and the United States have the shortest.[11]

The U.S. perspective of its business world is shown in the focus on quarterly profits. We look for immediate results. The future is near and short. Contrast this with the story of the Japanese creating a 250-year business plan when they were bidding on the operations of Yosemite National Park.[12] This equates to 1,000 quarters—almost incomprehensible to Americans, for whom 5 years, or 20 quarters, is a very long time!

How much does tradition influence our activities? Does it focus on past or future? In attempting to understand the difference of focusing on past or future, it's useful to think about the history of some of the countries of the world. Relatively speaking, the United States is a young country with a limited past. It has existed as a country with 50 states since only 1959, less than fifty years. (The addition of Hawaii in 1959 marked the completion of the United States, as it is today.) Because of such a limited past, and because it is founded on the idea of creating a better future, we continue that focus today. We concentrate on the present and the future, the immediate future.

The relatively limited history of the United States stands in sharp contrast to the histories of its major trading partners. China has a recorded history that extends more than 4,000 years. Canada and Mexico trace back to times that predate the arrival of the Europeans in the 1500s. The United Kingdom and France can trace their roots to periods before the first century B.C. In the United States, we don't acknowledge our beginning as the start of the Native American population but rather begin with the colonial period and date our founding as 1776, a little more than two hundred years ago.

While these dates may have concrete meaning for historians, they may not have a strong impact for the rest of us. It is easier to understand how the past can be part of the present by thinking about the past in terms of buildings, a physical reality and reminder. What do you see frequently that reminds you of the past, the history of your city and country?

When members of a group of pension plan managers from the United States and the United Kingdom were asked to identify the oldest building they see daily, the responses were revealing. Those based in London said the Tower of London (built 1,000 years ago) or St. Paul's Cathedral (dating back close to 500 years). New Yorkers mentioned St. Patrick's Cathedral (built 120 years ago), and one person from Los Angeles said it was his house (built in the late 1920s—old at 80). How old is old? How much collective memory, sense of shared time, and past experiences are there to be shared and used to guide the present? What's old in one place is not in another. Once more, we can see a different meaning to time: past, present, and future.

Now We Know

Time as defined by the clock or calendar is viewed in many ways. People's thinking and actions reflect the variety. It's not just the clock but also the calendar and the perceived importance of the past, present, and future that shape our conduct. Time matters everywhere, and knowing the differences, whether people or deadlines come first, is a necessity when conducting business around the globe.

I'm Glad I Know

I consider myself very fortunate. Thanks to the United States–based representative of my Mexican joint venture partner, I knew how to begin our venture. Not with two days of tight schedules, watching the clock, scripted meetings, and discussions of contracts. What a mistake that would have been!

No, thanks to her advice, I met my new partners at the airport, took them to the hotel and then to lunch. We toured the city and our offices, met the staff, enjoyed a leisurely dinner. The next day we had some exploratory talks, found areas of agreement, and [encountered] no obvious obstacles. We scheduled my visit to see them in Mexico City, and I returned them to the airport for their flight home.

That was two years ago. We began our relationship with little discussion of business, no clock watching, and no rushing. Since then we've created and operated a profitable (and pleasurable) joint venture. They're even planning to attend my daughter's wedding. I'm glad I know when it's important to create and follow a detailed schedule and when it isn't.

↣ *American manufacturer*
headquartered in Salt Lake City, Utah

CHAPTER 2

Write *or* Call

I Wish I'd Known

While I realized that every industry had its own language, I never thought that it would vary from country to country. The differences in labeling the same functions or activities can sometimes make discussion a bit murky as people from throughout the company, which is spread around the world, come together on a project. It is both challenging and fun to learn to communicate about a common interest, a shared business around the world.

→→ *American COO of*
a global real estate company

I Wish They Knew

I was raised in Japan and Paris and went to graduate school in New York. I like to think I'm open and global. But I am still sometimes surprised by Americans' lack of understanding of the value of ceremony and protocol. I'm here because I love the directness, being able to speak my thoughts, but sometimes I miss the formal, slow approach.

→→ *A French investment banker*
working in New York

Speaking, Listening, Reading, and Writing

Just as there are differences in understanding of time from place to place, so too are there varied ways of communicating. As businesses expand their operations throughout the world we are often required to connect with people whose communication styles differ from our own. In a team of 30 people maybe only 5 speak English as their first language. It isn't only the words that may be different but also the form and delivery of information. No matter how skilled you are at speaking, writing, and connecting in your own environment, getting the message across in another culture can be challenging. The material that follows provides some insight to the differences you may encounter and adds to your communication skills.

The What and Why of Communication

Although we know that communication has two elements—the sending and receiving of messages—our efforts to improve our abilities generally focus on the transmission portion. We work to select words carefully, to create the perfect speech, and to design PowerPoint slides exactly right. Do all that, you are told, and you'll be assured that the message will reach the listener. We'll be good communicators. Although we know the importance of listening, of receiving information, the emphasis of our efforts tends to be on the message and on us, the speaker.

But communication is even more than speaking and listening. Whether we recognize it, communication is making something known "to release the right response."[1] We are trying to obtain the reaction we want from the intended recipient of the message. The goal is the response, and the message is merely a vehicle in pursuit of that goal. When we turn on our computers, televisions, or radios and an ad pops up or comes on, we experience an example of that concept. But communication isn't always a call to action or an exchange of information. It may be a way to establish a connection and cement a relationship (a bouquet of flowers sends a message) or even to obtain a "feel for what people are thinking."[2]

While we can agree across cultures that communication is the act of delivering a message to obtain a response, the actual delivery, goals, and methods will differ. The style of delivery and purpose reflect our ways of thinking, life, and culture. To be effective, to obtain the responses we wish, and to understand what is requested of us, we must understand the varied methods of communicating.

Two Ways in the World

We think of messages in terms of how they are delivered (phone, e-mail, snail mail) and as spoken and written language. But sending a message involves a complex set of elements. Broadly considered, communication combines language (spoken and written), physical expressions (using our hands, eyes, and faces), levels of formality expressed, and allocation of space.

As we explore the issue of communication, it may be useful to think first about the model, the overall form and elements of the process. The beginning is an idea to be shared. Whether it's a greeting or a corporate plan to be presented, regardless of place or purpose, an idea is the first step. The sender then gives the idea form, whether spoken or written. The way of sending the message varies. It can be spoken, conveyed with a letter, or by way of a PowerPoint presentation. The transmission is then received, decoded, and interpreted by the receiving party. Within the stages of the model, from the beginning idea to the final step, the interpretation or understanding are opportunities for both confusion and connections.

Today much of our interaction, both business and personal, takes place via e-mail and voice mail. We seldom have the luxury of a one-on-one conversation, much less a face-to-face meeting. The result is communication with limited inputs, few nonverbal clues, and not even the sounds of our voices to hint at emotion and intent; it is critically important to be aware of the differences in how people send and receive messages.

Overall communication patterns throughout the world fall into two categories: high context/implicit or low context/explicit. The key idea is context—that surroundings, background, or environment shape a message as much as words. For example, are the people attending a meeting senior managers, the president of a company, a key client, or a preliminary group of colleagues? Context can be the knowledge you have about the internal corporate environment, knowing who favors a proposal or is against it. In a high context culture, all these elements impact the presentation of a message, the method of presentation, and the entire process of sending and receiving messages. Moreover, the context provides additional meaning, understood by participants and not voiced directly. These can be difficult to catch if you are not prepared for this form of communication.

Alternatively, in a low context environment, the words and data rather than the background are the key elements. The meaning of the message is less likely to be shaped by the surroundings and known background. You can imagine a high context listener hearing a low context message may be puzzled while looking for a subtle meaning where none exists.

Below, Table 2.1 shows the contrast between the two forms.[3]

We quickly recognize that much of the business conversations in the United States fall under the low context/explicit category. The American preference is for data and facts. We favor bullet points in memos and sound bites of conversation. We want specific information, including details, and we want it quickly. With our monochronic focus on schedules, our preference is for conversations that are brief and direct. We exchange pieces of precise information rather than subtly explore ideas.

It isn't only our focus on time that shapes our style of gathering the knowledge we need but also the nature of our connections to other people. We are unlikely to have extensive intertwined networks that are more common in polychronic cultures. Our connections tend to be compartmentalized. We have relationships at our office, the gym, or organizations we support. Information is shared within each group, but what you learn in one area may have little relationship to the details you need in another. The only way to learn what you need may be to ask directly.

In high context cultures, groups tend to be connected by extensive, ongoing networks. Without the monochronic focus on the clock, there

TABLE 2.1   CONTRASTING COMMUNICATION PATTERNS

HIGH CONTEXT/IMPLICIT	LOW CONTEXT/EXPLICIT
Rely on context for the meaning	Rely on words for the meaning
Listener has previous knowledge gained from extensive networking	Direct passing of specific information; assumes little previous knowledge
Nonverbal messages relied upon	Little use of nonverbal communication
Emphasis on maintaining harmony	Emphasis on data and facts
Communication is subtle, inferred	Communication is direct, brief
Polychronic (people are the focus)	Monochronic (schedules, time are critical)

is time for people and sharing of information. People do not link into networks to share information for a specific purpose such as to find a job. Rather, they are connected because it's their way of life. In these circumstances, people share and obtain information regularly. When a question arises, they already have the background needed. As a result, the ongoing communication may be subtle, with the meaning suggested rather than stated bluntly outright. Just as high context people can have difficulties in a low context environment, the reverse is also true. Low context communicators in a high context environment may feel puzzled and frustrated. When they are unable to understand the messages and the form, they may feel people are "sneaky, devious, and possibly worst of all, time-wasting."[4]

Some of the frustration people feel arises because of differing interpretations of the overall purpose of communication. For explicit communicators, especially Americans, the purpose, as stated, is to convey information. However, in an implicit structure the same is not necessarily true. The purpose of communication may be to explore the reaction to a proposal, without creating divisions within the group, rather than provide details for analysis. If you are mindful of that goal, it's easier to understand why conveying the exact truth in a blunt manner may not be the appropriate way to deliver a message. An indirect technique leaves open the possibility of a change in plan or opinion. Yes, no, and maybe may all be said in a variety of ways, which allows harmony to continue if you disagree with a statement or decision.

Today's Challenge: How Much Context, and How to Deliver

It's so simple to rely on e-mail. No need to figure out what time is it in Paris if you're in Los Angeles. No need to worry what day is it in Tokyo or Sydney. No need to worry that you're going to interrupt people. They'll read it when they choose. Just send a note, and the reply will come.

However, before we select a technology or method of communicating, we should first assess the message we are sending, the type of response we desire, and the existing relationship between the parties. Do we have a long-standing partnership in Argentina? Is a crisis brewing with a customer in Canada? Are the people involved native English speakers, or is English their second or third language? Is the message routine enough to rely on e-mail?

Above all, the most important question may be: Is the communication taking place between high context and low context people? The answer to that question is key to your approach. These are questions you should ask within your home territory, but they assume critical importance when you deal with people across geographic boundaries. Each situation will benefit from a different form of delivery. Knowing the preferred methods of sending and receiving information will increase your options and success. (We'll look at some practical details on this topic in chapter 18.)

Elements of Communication

The process of communicating is composed of several elements. There are an idea, a sender, and a receiver. An idea is encoded, put into a form to be received and interpreted. In this section we look at the encoding of a message and the elements of communication that form this section of our model.

The Purpose of Language

Language, whether spoken or written, is a set of sounds and shapes that we combine to form a code of communication. Each language, or code, is made up of widely shared meanings and sets of rules (grammar) that allow messages to be constructed, delivered, and understood.[5] Beginning at birth we each learn a set of symbols, meanings, and rules that constitute our mother tongue. So fully is this original language integrated into our beings that it is said no matter how many languages you learn, you automatically revert to your mother tongue to count, dream, and swear.

Although English is the language spoken by the largest number of people in the world, Chinese (Mandarin, Cantonese, and other lesser known dialects) ranks number one as a mother tongue.[6] But as widespread as these two languages are, they represent only two of the nearly 2,800 distinct languages spoken throughout the world.[7] Spoken by few or many, a language isn't simply a useful way to send and receive messages; it is more. Language shapes ideas, helps us organize our thinking and our view of the world, and reveals what's important in a culture.

Each culture creates words for what's considered important. Whether it is food, wine, trees, or cows, the selection of words can indicate the critical issues within an environment. Learning a language provides insights to the thinking patterns and communication styles of people. Through learning the vocabulary, you may quickly grasp what's considered significant in a particular environment.

English Everywhere

English is considered a global language, with almost 500 million native speakers and triple that amount of people who use it in some capacity. It is considered the language of business. For example, India has a national language, Hindi, that is one of 14 official languages but uses English for politics and commerce. Switzerland has 3 languages set by the constitution (French, German, and Italian) but English is becoming the second national language. The European Union recognizes 20 official languages but works in only 3: German, French, and English. It's estimated that one-third of the European Union speaks English as a second language.[8]

It isn't simply a matter of formal policy. English becomes the language of business in many ways. A staff member at LVMH Moët Hennessy–Louis Vuitton commented that when U.S. fashion designer Marc Jacobs first arrived as the designer for Louis Vuitton, the French staff had to learn to speak English. "He's the boss, and he speaks English, so we are all learning."

Because English is spoken so widely, it's easy to assume that everyone speaks it and that everyone speaks it well. However, their vocabulary is often limited to what they need for work. When we try to have an extended conversation, we are surprised and perhaps somewhat uncomfortable to learn that we aren't understood. A German professional once commented to an American colleague that English had too many words. It was difficult to understand all the subtle meanings attached to each word, and therefore she couldn't always fully follow a conversation. However, we live in a world where people increasingly understand English even if they aren't prepared to speak it, so it's important that you be cautious about what you say.

Even when everyone speaks English, common understandings aren't always shared. A word as simple as *yes* may have many meanings. We get into trouble when we assume that *yes* means *I agree*. It can mean *I hear you* rather than *I agree*.[9] After spending nine months working and studying in Brazil, a California woman confirmed *yes* can mean *Yes, I hear you, and I don't care*.[10] To know the exact meaning of *yes*, you need to understand the environment and the total process of communication wherever you are.

Style: Formal or Casual?

Americans are famous, and sometimes infamous, for their informality in speech and action. We move quickly to the use of first names and ignore titles. This pattern is a symbol of the American ideal that all people are equal. We address one another without titles, as colleagues. When asked what surprised her most about the United States, a Belgian woman working in the United States for a French company said it was the informality. She was not only startled by the interaction between superiors and subordinates in her company but also that the same informality existed in all the client companies she visited.

It is often a surprise to discover that informality is startling and even offensive to other people. We listen to people who have lived in the United States for two decades still discuss their initial shock when being addressed by their first names immediately after a brief introduction. "No one ever called me Jean-Pierre before [in business] much less JP!" Moreover, for Japanese businesspeople, moving to first names is not a common tactic. It is reserved for "intimate members of the same group."[11]

The American focus on time and schedule makes them move rapidly to business matters so they don't participate in formal ceremonies to mark important events. However, the majority of the world prefers initial formality to a casual welcome. One of the teachings of Confucius is that "use of ritual, etiquette, and ceremony form the foundation for all good relationships."[12] When we rush ahead and skip the rituals, some of the underpinnings of a connection are omitted. Without that foundation, regarded as necessary throughout much of the world, it can be difficult to extend the initial relationship.

Conversely, people who are accustomed to a casual approach often find formal patterns constricting and puzzling. When our goal is to exchange information quickly we are impatient with the formal rituals.

"Thanks for coming, Bob. May I call you Mr. Klein?"

The security experienced by others when following the rules of protocol is not evident. Directness and clarity are what are important in a relationship. We believe that a level of informality helps get the work accomplished but through other eyes, it be seen as a lack of focus.

Can We Show Our Feelings?
The Affectives and the Neutrals

People add emphasis to their oral communication by displaying emotion. As with the other elements of communication, there are differing interpretations of what is emotional and what is an appropriate amount of one's feelings that should be displayed.

The labels for the two approaches to emotions and their display are *affective* and *neutral*. The affectives are those who show their emotions, and the neutrals are those who are more likely to be controlled and who will avoid demonstrating their feelings.[13] While there are no general patterns by continent, there are general tendencies that are associated with specific countries.[14]

For example, it is said that the Finns are not emotive, the Italians are effusive, and the French are intellectual. The Japanese, Chinese, Americans, Germans, and British are generally classified as neutrals.

To the affectives, emotions are persuasive and valid and not to be suppressed. Affectives may not be concerned with the precision of communication but place importance on the presentation of an idea.[15] We talk about the flowery language used by the Arabs and of the impassioned Spanish. While neutrals may describe themselves as cool and composed, the affectives may experience them as "unfeeling and one-dimensional."[16]

Watch Those Hands (Eyes, and Feet)

We are often cautioned to watch our gestures lest we embarrass ourselves or insult our colleagues. Stories are told of the U.S. president who waved what he thought was the "V" for victory hand signal in Australia and caused an international uproar because that gesture, in that place, is interpreted as a wish for failure.

If we limit our thinking to the narrow perspective of trying to avoid errors rather than observing and learning, we will miss critical elements of conversations. Studies indicate that "at least 75 percent of all communication is nonverbal."[17] As valuable as it is to learn the spoken patterns (some words of a new language), it is also critical to learn the nonverbal language (the eyes, hands, space, and posture).

The ability to interpret these indirect messages becomes especially important when you operate in a culture where communication is implicit rather than explicit. Not only will you understand what's happening around you more clearly but also "people who know the nonverbal clues will be better liked."[18] And no matter where you are, people prefer to do business with people they like.

For example, it's important to be aware that a smile may not be used to signal friendliness, approval of an idea, or acceptance of a suggestion. In some places a smile may seldom appear. A young Russian woman reports that she was taught to not smile at people she didn't know but to instead smile only at friends and family. A smile may also be used simply as a polite mask to hide frustration or lack of comprehension. A smile, like the word *yes*, can be interpreted in many ways.

I See You

Is a direct gaze respectful or rude? The answer depends on where you are. The directness of a look can be respectful (United States) or rude

(Asia). Even in cultures where direct eye contact is appropriate, the length of the gaze varies. For example, an American accustomed to being looked at with a direct but brief gaze may feel uncomfortable in France or Spain where the gaze may be longer. Winking, glaring (to show anger), raised eyebrows, even tears may be used to emphasize the points being discussed.

Movements

Admonitions to keep our hands still, but not in our pockets, restricts our ability to communicate. Gestures provide a way for us to emphasize our words, indicate flow in the conversation, or quickly deliver a message. The more emotional the affective culture, the more gestures you'll find.

As tools of nonverbal communication, hands are most famous for creating potential misunderstandings. According to author Teri Morrison, a simple American wave used as a means of greeting (hand raised vertically, fingers spread apart, palm out, and moving from right to left at the wrist) in Chile can mean *you're stupid* and in parts of Africa, *you have five fathers*. In parts of Asia and the Middle East it is critical to know that you only use your right hand to eat and to hand items to people because the left hand is considered unclean.

It's useful to know that in Brazil our circle made by the thumb and forefinger to signify *okay* is obscene; in Greece the head nod that usually means *yes*, means *no*; and snapping the fingers of both hands in Belgium may be seen as rude.[19] Italians are so well known for their extensive use of gestures that there's a Web site that includes a section to help translate them (www.italian.about.com). At the other end of the spectrum, the Chinese, who seldom gesture, may find it extremely distracting if you do.

The Dance of Distance

We each operate within a bubble, an amount of space that separates us from other people. The dimensions of the bubble vary from culture to culture and person to person. The size that is comfortable varies according to our relationships with the people around us, the activity we're engaged in, and our own personalities. These bubbles, distances between ourselves and others, provide comfort and a sense of safety.

We stand close enough to communicate and far enough to avoid a sense of threat. Problems arise when people with differing dimensions to their personal territories connect. If my comfort level is 2 feet apart but yours is only 6 inches, we'll both be surprised. Without thinking, we each seek our own comfort zone. As you approach me to speak and cross my 2-foot boundary, I'll back away. You will, of course, continue to move toward me, and I'll back up again. We'll be dancing the dance of distance.

Should we be close enough to smell each other's breath or far enough apart to avoid touching but still be able to hear? If you are too far apart, the person you're talking to may feel as though you're yelling across a chasm, but if you're too close, you may feel the urge to flee. Either way, the potential for misunderstandings exists. The dance of distance can be observed at almost any gathering that brings together people from different cultures.

Now We Know

How people receive and deliver information is shaped by culture as well as personal style. To communicate effectively, you need more than a common language.

You must bridge differences in formality and balance a preference for directness versus reliance on subtlety to ensure a harmonious environment. In addition, you must be mindful of your display of emotions and the use of gestures to quickly convey meaning. Communication within and across cultures is a complex activity.

I'm Glad I Know

It took some time to learn, but I now know to be patient, to listen. It's often frustrating. I want to say what I think, ask a few questions, and move on. Get something accomplished. I tried it that way, and nothing happened. No answers, no business. After several years, I'm more successful. I even know when not to approach someone directly. I can send my message via someone else in the organization and wait for a reply. Suggesting rather than directing—listening and watching. It's amazing what I've learned. My business is growing, and I think this new way of acting is a large part of the reason.

↦ *American designer working in Italy*

CHAPTER 3

Who Am I? Respect
for the Individual *and the* Group

I Wish I'd Known

How surprised I was that people wanted me to make the decisions. In our company, especially where I was based in North Carolina, everyone wanted to have his or her opinion, a say in whatever we decided. Here, people still prefer the manager to decide and tell them what should be done. I have hopes of encouraging more participation, but the beginning would have been easier if I'd known I had to be more directive than at home.

→ *American manager of a denim factory in Mexico*

I Wish They Knew

I do so wish that the people in the [United] States who plan corporate visits to learn about doing business in South Africa would recognize that Christian holidays are not the only important holidays. They don't seem to realize that many religions and many types of belief systems are represented here. There are holidays associated with each one and businesses that observe these holidays. It would help them get started if they'd just ask what days are businesses closed and not just assume it's Easter, Christmas, and the Fourth of July, U.S. Independence Day.

→ *Official with the United States*
South Africa Chamber of Commerce

We're the People

Billions of people dispersed around the globe are connected to one another in a variety of ways. Each individual is certain they know the best way to relate to others. What they may not realize is that two key points of organizing societies operate. One form places emphasis on the individual and the other on the individual's participation in a larger

25

group. The different focus shapes the actions and understandings of people.

The Fundamental Question: Who Am I?

According to the Population Reference Bureau, in 2003 there were more than 6.3 billion people in the world. Whether they are single or part of a group, they live in more than 283 countries.[1] People discuss the way these individuals behave in terms of the global economy, trading blocks, weather, and population shifts. However, in all these analyses of the world's people, there is little discussion of the two distinctly different ways societies are organized.

The form of organization discussed in this chapter is not that of political or economic groupings. Rather, it is the way individuals consider their relationships to one another. From this perspective there are two organizing principles that can be identified as individualistic and collectivist. These groupings differ in their responses to the following questions: Is the individual the key building block, or is it the group? Is individual achievement or group cohesiveness the goal toward which

people strive? In an individualistic culture, an individual's answer to the fundamental life question "Who am I?" is likely to be "I am me: a separate and unique individual." In a collectivist culture, the response is more likely to be, "I am me: part of my group." It is these dissimilar points of emphasis on either one person or many people that lead to differing interpretations of how to conduct your personal and professional life.

Whether they come from an individualistic or a collectivist culture, people belong to groups. They are members of families, companies, and political parties, and they share social activities and religious affiliations. However, fundamental to their lives is the question of which comes first: me or we?

Although people who would respond to that question both ways (me or we) are found in every part of the world, specific countries generally represent one or the other of these two perspectives. Countries that are generally categorized individualistic include the United States, United Kingdom, and Germany. Countries that are considered collectivist include Indonesia, Mexico, and Saudi Arabia.

Individualist/Collectivist

A look back at people's history tells us that a person's group is originally only the family, the tribe, and the nearby village. Over time societies changed and for multiple reasons living patterns altered. People moved to cities, where the size and complexity of the group expanded to include classmates, neighbors, and eventually work colleagues.

But a group, as considered in this book, is not simply a few individuals who live, study, or work in the same environment. In this section the group is bound together by more than physical closeness. It is a set of individuals with an emotional attachment to one another, who hold common expectations about how they and the others will behave.

In fact, training for that environment begins at an early stage. It is said that children in a collectivist family learn that personal opinions are not appropriate, that the group establishes beliefs for all, and that to speak out on your own is to display bad character. The opposite holds true for children in individualistic families. If you do not have an opinion of your own, you risk being labeled as having a "weak character."[2]

While originally a group and its rules of behavior related only to family and local customs, in modern society the emotional connection may extend to a person's workplace. Until relatively recent times, individuals throughout the world worked for long periods of time for a single employer. It was not considered unusual for a person to begin working with a company after completing their education and retire many years later. People's loyalties and emotional connections to their companies were reciprocated with the promise of lifetime employment. Until recently that promise was a guarantee. While this is no longer always true, especially in the United States, the concept of an ongoing connection to a business group is still critically important. Especially in a collectivist culture, a person joins a company knowing that the group will likely be in place over an extended period. Productive, harmonious relationships, therefore, are of significant importance. People learn ways to build a consensus to avoid causing embarrassment or friction within the group.

As companies expand, teams are created that bring together people from different parts of the world. These divergent teachings may come to life in the contrasting ways meetings are conducted among people from both individualist and collectivist cultures. When meetings include people who are trained to speak out and voice their opinions and people who have learned that consensus is critical, frustrations and misunderstandings may result. Through awareness of the differences, people can adapt methods to achieve desired results.

Another aspect of group membership, beyond identification and attachment, is protection for the members. Historically, protection may have been from physical attack, but now the group may shield members from financial want or problems. A group of Chinese immigrants formed a group in Los Angeles to support one another in their new homes. One component of their approach was to offer monetary aid to one another. Every time one of them was paid, a deposit was made into a group account. One man borrowed money to buy a new car to replace his old one. His American-born colleagues were astonished at his approach. Americans believe that money is borrowed from a bank (or perhaps from a parent) but not from friends. William Shakespeare's "Neither a borrower nor a lender be" is an often quoted line. Individualists pride themselves on being self-reliant and able to take care of themselves. They'd rather borrow from a bank (a stranger) than bother, and be beholden to, a friend.

Universalist/Particularist or Rules vs. Relationships

Another difference between individualists and collectivists is found in the response to the questions: Are the rules more important than relationships or vice versa? How are people to be treated? Are there special circumstances or special treatment required based on who is involved? The responses to these questions are formed by what can be called the universalist/particularist differentiation.

The universalists favor one set of rules that cover all circumstances applied in the same way to everyone, hence, universal practices. Particularists look to the specific situation as well as the rules. The parties involved and the relationships are as important as the rules. They look at the particular circumstances. (In general, individualist cultures tend to be universalists and collectivist cultures tend to be particularists.)

Imagine that you overhear a conversation between people who represent each of these two viewpoints. Both sides are talking about a decision made by one person from each side concerning a mutual friend's violation of stated policies. You can sense from their conversation whether the decision favored the friend. The collectivist says, "They won't even help a friend." The individualist says, "They always adjust things to help a friend, and that's not right." Collectivists are likely to adjust their response given the relationships involved and the particulars of a situation, while individualists prefer the idea of fairness and that the rules are the rules without exceptions.

The debate surrounding which approach is correct is not only about how friends are to be treated in personal situations but also in business. There are serious implications for human resources planning in global corporations because it influences people's decision-making and affects everything from production and product planning to advertising. Think of the frequently heard slogan "Think globally. Act locally." From the particularist view the emphasis is on special treatment (product modification and advertising) for their local environment. The universalist looks at the economies of scale in advertising and production and wants to create a global product, policy, or procedure. According to Philippe Rosinski, author of the book *Coaching Across Cultures*, the challenge is that to blend and balance these approaches you must adopt a consistent yet flexible approach.

Equal or Not?

We could reframe the question "Who am I?" to read "Who am I, and are you an equal of mine?" Is everyone essentially equal, or is inequality based in nature? Depending on your country and your culture, the answer is both: yes, equal, and yes, not equal.

In the United States the idea of equality is key to the general individualistic, achievement-oriented culture. It is a revered idea, a value that is at the heart of the legal system. Although it can certainly be debated whether the daily reality of life is that everyone is equal, the concept that all people are created equal has broad implications for the conduct of people's professional lives. It shapes the informality of communication as well as corporate policies.

This is not to suggest that the United States is without hierarchy of relationships and roles that go along with people's places in that hierarchy. This is true whether you look at roles of parent and child, among friends, or among people in a corporate structure. But as one international export consultant explains, American hierarchy has flexibility to it, and that's a key to what makes it different. It's as if the idea is an ability to move across the boundaries. In many corporations, the appearance is that the relationships are equal on a day-to-day basis. But to make processes more efficient there is a structure, a decision-making hierarchy. The form can shift, stretch to accommodate what is necessary. This, she explained, can be very confusing for newcomers.

The reverse can be true for people who are accustomed to flexibility and limited hierarchy. In many cultures, the idea of equality for all is foreign. In countries such as Saudi Arabia, India, and Mexico, a person's place in society is established at birth.[3] It is accepted that some people will have more power, authority, and privilege than others. Furthermore, it is accepted that the order of things will not change. Those who believe that people are all equal are likely to feel strongly that power inequalities are largely artificial and may find the structure uncomfortable. However, as one French businesswoman says, "It's necessary to respect the tradition, the hierarchy, in order to accomplish anything."

As with the other concepts, there is a range of interpretations and preferences along a scale from all equal to not equal. It's interesting to note that according to the Center for Creative Leadership study, France ranks almost as individualistic as the United States on the individualist/collectivist scale.[4] However, France ranks closer to Brazil and Mexico on the orientation toward inequality as a fact of life. On that scale the United States, Sweden, Germany, and Canada are at the opposite end of the spectrum. The French look to the corporate hierarchy for decisions but want their individual intellectual talent recognized and the ability to do things their way once the overall direction is set.

Beliefs Have Economic Impact

Family, culture, school, work, friends, and individual personality have all been identified as elements that influence behavior. Another aspect of life that can shape people's thinking and actions is their religious affiliations. Whether individualist or collectivist, particularist or universalist, people may also adhere to the tenets of a specific religion or belief system. Religion can be defined as a system of beliefs and commitment to observance that is shared among a group of people.

These shared beliefs, the key concepts of a religion, become the values that guide and shape individual behavior. But it is not just a private, individual matter. Religions can have an impact on economies and legal and political systems throughout the world.

According to the 2001 World Christian Trends, there were 8,400 religions as of the year 2000. Approximately 4 billion people, nearly 74 percent of the world's 6 billion people, are counted as adherents of one of these religions. (The remainder were classified as agnostic.)[5] Of these thousands of religions, four are dominant: Christianity, Islam, Hinduism, and Buddhism. Confucianism, which will be covered in this section, is often referred to as a religion but is actually an ethical system rather than a religion. Of the four religious groups, Christianity is the largest with 2 billion adherents, followed by Islam with 1.3 billion, Hinduism with 900 million, and Buddhism with 360 million. Judaism, the second-largest religion practiced in the United States, is statistically small, with only 14 million adherents worldwide. However, its historical, cultural, and even political influences place it among the ranks of the major religious and belief systems.

Although we associate certain religions with specific parts of the world—for example, we associate Hinduism with India—adherents of the major religions can be found worldwide. Islam is noted for its many followers in Indonesia and the Middle East, and it is also the fastest growing religion in North America. In contemporary society, as in the days of the ancient Silk Road, as people move from place to place they establish places of worship, spreading their beliefs to new areas.

While the major religions are defined in four major categories, it is important to recognize that there are variations of belief and interpretation within each group. Christianity includes two major divisions, Catholicism and Protestantism, and within Protestantism there are thousands of denominations. Islam also has two major segments, the Shiites and the Sunnis. Given the number of religions and variations of thought and practice within each, it is not possible to cover any in detail in this text.

Although not a religion but an ethical system, Confucianism is considered as important as the major religions in shaping people's views of the world and their personal and professional conduct. It is the smallest of the major belief systems, with approximately 150 million followers located primarily in China, Korea, and Japan, but its influence reaches throughout the world. Because of its emphasis on loyalty, reciprocal obligations, and honesty in dealing with others, Confucianism is regarded as having a beneficial economic impact.[6] It has been suggested that companies will be more willing to commit resources and sign contracts when they see that all parties share the same ethical code.

Countries where the Confucian influence is strongest also have cultures that are generally collectivist and reflect its emphasis on respect for authority and hierarchy. However, a characteristic of a collectivist culture is its strong, ongoing group affiliation. It is therefore difficult to be certain which of these two has the strongest impact, the Confucian teachings or the learned importance of cohesive behavior within a group.

Economic impacts are not limited to Confucianism. All religions influence economic development by shaping individuals' attitudes toward ethical behavior, work, achievement, and material wealth.

Historians, economists, and religious philosophers have examined the influence of religions in depth. One of the best known studies was done in 1905 by Max Weber, the historian and social scientist. Weber asserts that Protestantism contributes to economic development through more than the attitude toward work. His work *The Protestant Ethic and the Spirit of Capitalism* looks at the economic implications of Protestantism and Catholicism. He concludes that Protestantism is more supportive of and most closely associated with the idea of economic progress. His thesis is that Protestantism promoted the rise of modern capitalism by "sanctioning an ethic of everyday behavior that conduced to economic success."[7] That behavior includes hard work, honesty, seriousness, and the thrifty use of money and time. While accumulating material wealth was not the intent of early Protestantism, it has been interpreted that wealth resulting from business activities indicates or suggests that a person is living a good life. Over time, the phrase "Protestant work ethic" has become an expression employed to describe a serious approach to work.

A 2004 study entitled "People's Opium? Religion and Economic Attitudes" was done by 3 university professors from the United States and Italy.[8] They took a broader look at the question, considering 6 major religions: Catholicism, Protestantism, Judaism, Islam, Hinduism, and Buddhism. Their work is based on the results of the World Values Survey conducted in 66 countries, during the period of 1981 to 1997.

Their conclusions are that people who follow a specific religion, regardless of the faith, are more trusting of legal and political systems overall. As far as the individual religions are concerned, Buddhism and Christianity rank highest as supporting attitudes that promote economic growth. The teachings of Islam and Hinduism promote attitudes that are less favorable to economic growth. According to their work, it is possible to link the primary religion in an area to those with the most advanced economies. For example, Buddhism is prevalent in the Far East, and Christianity is prevalent in Europe and North America.

Trends to Watch

Religion influences behavior and, in turn, can be affected by broad social changes.

An article in *The Futurist* magazine identified some trends to note:

- Religions will continue to exist and grow, spread by immigration and technology.
- Conflicts based on religious differences will continue, and religion will play a role in national and international politics.
- Religious individualism and blended faiths are gaining popularity. Society in the developed world is becoming more fragmented and individualist. There is an increase in evangelical Christian denominations that focus on personal change and personal spirituality.[9]

It also appears that globalization and economic advancement may be changing some elements of the individualist/collectivist distinction. Economic advancement reduces the need for social and material support structures built on collectives, whether the collective is the extended family or the paternalistic company.[10] People are able to take care of themselves and are more mobile; these shifts reduce the ties people have to their groups.

Conversely, technology, travel, and globalization create new groups. John Micklethwait and Adrian Wooldridge in their book *A Future Perfect* label one such group the Cosmocrats.[11] These are professionals whose education and occupation take them around the globe. They create connections wherever they work and travel. A wedding in India with the groom from India and the bride from London via Los Angeles and New York brings guests from four continents.

Technology, especially the Internet and e-mail, allows people to share information and create new groups and online communities. While there is some evidence that groups move from online to in-person connections, the impact of this pattern is not yet known.

One significant change in social behavior is evident in Japan. The number of young people from ages 24 to 44 declined 7 percent in the 20 years from 1980 to 2000.[12] Furthermore, of this group more men and women are electing to stay single. Aside from the economic implications, the social changes will be important to follow. In the traditional structure, women marry and care for their families and their husbands' parents. How will these relationships evolve when there are more single people and fewer extended families? How will this affect the collectivist nature of the society?

In China the question is not "What will evolve as marriage patterns change?" but "How will the lives of the little emperors and empresses develop?" Little emperors and empresses are the single children, ranging in age from infants to young adults, born to parents as a result of China's one child policy. In an effort to control the population in 1979 China instituted a policy stating that each family, with some exceptions, could have only one child. While this policy is no longer enforced, it created a variety of complex issues. In addition to issues of indulgence, it has resulted in an imbalance in the male/female population, discussed in Chapter 15. Historically, male children were preferred because it was sons who cared for parents as they aged. Therefore, male children were more highly valued than female.

Studies on the impact of this policy, including the practice of giving up infant daughters for adoption in the hopes that another child would be a son, are still under way. Stories of the impact of the policy are varied. One Chinese college student reveals that his family came to the United States in part to have the freedom to raise a second child. However, as he was the "little emperor" in his family, his parents asked his opinion as to whether a second child should be added to the family unit. Asked to make this decision at the age of ten, it's not surprising that his reply was, "No, no other children are needed." To this day, at 22, he is still an only child.

From the labels little emperor or empress, it is clear that these children are indulged by parents and grandparents since they have no siblings.[13] Their lives are shaped by more than attention and indulgence. They are also the focus of the family, expected to bring honor to their families. With all the pressure and all their demands granted, how will these children grow and build their lives in the future? Again, how will these individuals, highly focused on themselves rather than their groups, impact the collectivist culture that is already being changed by China's participation in the global economy?

Now We Know
Whether you consider yourself an individual or a member of a group, your affiliation shapes words and actions in all aspects of life: personal

and business. This distinction creates communication patterns that emphasize either presentation of personal opinions or maintenance of harmony in the group. While the *me* or *we* foundation shapes multiple actions and attitudes, religion is also of importance in business as well as personal life. To be able to effectively work together globally and build the connections that build the business, it's necessary to consider all these elements that shape people's outlook and behavior.

I'm Glad I Know

A recent assignment was for the North American division of a Japanese company that is now doing business in Mexico. My assignment was to help them improve their safety record in Mexico. It was key to the successful outcome of the project to understand that the cultures of Mexico and Japan are similar. If one looks at only the geography, one wouldn't make that assessment. But they both place importance on the harmony within one's group, loyalty, and respect for authority. Knowing these basics allowed me to structure a program that was appropriate for the participants.

↠ *Consultant based in California*
who is a workplace safety expert

CHAPTER 4

Friends Old *and* New
for Business *and for* Pleasure

I Wish I'd Known

How complicated it can be and how much time it takes to make friends. For me, it's always been easy. Friends came with projects I worked on or places I lived. They'd be part of daily life for a time, then some slip off to the Christmas card list. Others [last] forever. But either way, the beginnings, to start off, were easy. Not so in France, where I just spent two years. What a surprise. I barely made the move from stranger to acquaintance before I left.

>> *American who studied and worked abroad,*
now living in the United States

I Wish They Knew

You have to take some time to get to know people if you want to do anything. Share a meal, coffee, and some conversation. You don't necessarily need days or weeks. Simply spend five minutes chatting before you ask questions. We'll get to the business and do it right, but first, let's enjoy a cup of coffee.

>> *A German professional working*
for a U.S. agency, based in Germany

Business Is People More Than Products

No matter what your industry, product, or service, business is carried out by people drawn together by common commercial interests. In most companies the focus is on price, quality, product, and brand image. Less time is spent on thinking about the relationships that drive the business than is allocated to delivery schedules. But it's the connections between people that make all the activities possible. In this text you will learn how developing relationships differs from place to place and culture to culture.

Relationships Matter

Relationships, friendships, and connections to people are key elements in our lives. The need to connect to people begins at birth when it is an issue of survival. A newborn's existence cannot be sustained without help from at least one other person. Notwithstanding this fundamental need for another person's help, babies and young children have little awareness of others as entities separate from themselves. Only over time does a child develop a sense of mother, father, and caregivers as individuals. Later, the world opens and extends to include siblings, grandparents, aunts, uncles, and cousins.

People eventually recognize that relationships matter more than physical survival and basic learning. They satisfy the needs for companionship, intimacy, identity, and belonging. A person's world expands from the extended family to include teachers, friends, parents of friends, coaches of teams, leaders of groups, business colleagues, and even friends of friends.

Relationships Differ

Although the need for personal and professional relationships is universal, the ways they are created varies from place to place. Because these patterns start at the beginning of people's lives, they seldom reflect on how they link to others. They don't analyze the process or ask questions such as, "How do I bond to these people?" "How do I behave?" "Where do they fit in my life and my view of the world?" Only if they are establishing connections may these questions come to mind.

One generally learns how to form relationships through observation, by example, and from subtle instructions. The basic rules are defined by the experiences and opinions of people's families, later modified by personal knowledge and feelings. However, the foundation from which all the patterns and rules evolve is the societal culture and one of the most important aspects in the orientation of the culture as individualistic or collectivist.

As discussed in chapter 3, most societies in the world are collectivist, where people are part of ongoing groups that begin with family connections and expand to school and work. Up to this stage the pattern is similar for individualists, including most Americans. However, the difference emerges as time goes on. In a collectivist culture, groups tend to stay together once created and additions come slowly. People become friends over time.

A Frenchman living in New York says his French friends stay together. They've known one another since childhood and although many left home to study, most returned to Paris to work. He observed that in the United States everyone seems to go out to meet other people. "That's not for us, even the part of our group in New York," he said. "We go out to be together. We're already friends. We don't need to meet more people." Imagine how this attitude might shape an American's experience if transferred to Marseilles for work.

Even the language may distinguish levels of closeness in a relationship. For example, in French and Spanish there two forms of the word *you*, one used for family and intimate friends and the other used for all other people. Simply by listening to a conversation, you can learn something of the relationship between the people speaking. Are they professional colleagues or close friends? Forms of address provide useful information.

This approach contrasts with the general style encountered in the United States. Although the culture in the United States varies from group to group and place to place, the country is known for having a highly individualistic culture. It is the dominant American style of relationships that will be considered in this text.

Americans have relationships where ties are loose, contractual, and flexible. Connections expand and contract as lives evolve and interests change. These changes may reflect new life stages: student, parent, and retired person. People move to various places for school, work, and new opportunities. Friendships change, expand, and contract, reflecting this movement.

Americans may think about how relationships are created in the context of their business experiences. They tend to think of building relationships and friendships as projects, things to be created with a to-do list and a set of guidelines and practical steps. Who is in your network? How do you create and manage a network? This is surprising for many in the world for whom relationships simply exist. Rather than being cultivated, relationships develop as part of the life process, almost without thought. It is understood that connections will develop and be maintained, as they are vital to people's lives. Nothing gets accomplished without a relationship in place.

Benefits, Rights, and Obligations

Americans have multiple connections, most of which have limited focus and which form the network of their lives. People enjoy and value each of these connections, each of which contributes something special to their lives. Most of these relationships entail relatively few obligations: show up on time, be available occasionally, keep in touch, and participate in shared activities. Even familial relationships may be loose, flexible, shaped by busy lives, and limited by distance. This structure reflects the independent and self-reliant aspect of the culture.

The concept of mutual obligations, benefits, and responsibilities is an essential component of relationships in a collectivist culture. For Americans and others in individualistic cultures, where relationships are flexible, the accountability and commitment that come from belonging to a group in a group-oriented culture may be surprising. Be-

"I'll call you back when I'm off-line."

cause each relationship may mean work (in the sense of duty and responsibility) as well as a long-lasting commitment, it is easier to understand why people move cautiously before establishing or expanding
their friendships.

It isn't that Americans lack a sense of obligation or responsibility in
their relationships. Rather their bonds are looser, and so too is the sense
of commitment from one person to another. Given that relationships
may be temporary and terminate, there is an effort keep the obligation
"books" balanced at zero. For example, if you take me to dinner, I will
reciprocate in short order. The idea is to keep the books balanced, and
never be in debt, even with your friends.

Another factor that shapes the definition of mutual responsibility in
an individualistic culture is that people are raised to be independent and
self-reliant. The need people have to demonstrate that they can take care
of themselves may shape the pattern of behavior in their relationships.
It may be difficult to accept help from someone else, to ask for assistance, to risk being seen as dependent. For individualists it's important
to be able to abide by the saying "stand on your own two feet."

Neither the idea that relationships are temporary nor the demonstration of self-reliance exists in the same ways in group-oriented cultures.
Their ties are often strong, ongoing, with the good of the group placed
before the needs of the individual. In return, the group provides many
benefits to individuals.

Beyond providing assistance and identity, networks serve as sources
of information, providing business intelligence where formal systems
are shaky or undeveloped. Plus, in an environment where the legal system is not transparent, working within a network may provide more security than a written contract. In companies, corporate news is not
passed via an Intranet but through the grapevine. It is *les bruits du
couloir* (chatting in the halls, hence the grapevine) that provides the key
to knowing what's going on.[1] While this informal system does exist in
U.S. companies, it is not as vital a method of communication as elsewhere.

But the commitment within a group entails more than sharing information; it entails helping one another. Whether you consider the
friendship, networks, or connections in France, Eastern Europe, Japan,
or Latin America, the core idea is that within the connected "in-group,"

people trust and help one another. They can rely on one another for assistance and support over time. Help provided today may be repaid next week or next year. Moreover, the friend you helped may help another of your friends rather than you, and that third party will then assist you in some way and at some time in the future. Because the group is together and stays together over time, people can trust that assistance will always be forthcoming.

As part of the group you not only receive information and assistance but you are also committed to give it. It is your obligation and responsibility. Because you recognize this aspect, often a direct request for help isn't required. It is just implicitly assumed that a member of the group will help another member who may be in need.

Harmony: The Key to Maintaining Relationships

Because all relationships and connections are integral to our personal and professional lives, especially in a collectivist culture, people learn methods to sustain balance within the group.

A skill developed to support this effort is the art of speaking indirectly, to avoid confrontations and potential embarrassment. There is a story that says there are 120 ways for someone who is Chinese to say "no" without ever using that word. Communication can be subtle and ambiguous to allow room for further discussion. Some common phrases include the following:

- It will be very difficult.
- That is probably not necessary in these circumstances.
- Conditions at present are not favorable.
- Yes, but . . .
- Let us just discuss this other topic.

Such caution in communication can cause confusion and friction in business situations. Americans, who often pride themselves on directness and clarity of speech, often express frustration when they seek a definitive response to a business question. An engineer who works in Brazil asks, "Why won't they just say *no* instead of temporizing? I finally get the message but a simple 'no' right away would do it easier!"

What this engineer and other individualists do not understand is that for the speaker, saying *no* directly is too direct. It may lead to a confrontation, which would be extremely rude. It would be disrespectful and destabilize the harmony within the group.

From the perspective of the individualist engineer who is taught that "speaking one's mind is a virtue" and presenting varied viewpoints is a benefit, the hesitation and circumspection are puzzling and frustrating. The idea that it is better to say what is polite rather than what is accurate to guard the harmony is foreign to any individualist. Whether you are sending an e-mail to a distant colleague or participating in a conference call, you need to consider how to frame a question or comment. Is directness required, or would a subtle approach encourage a better response?

Friends or Friendly?

None of the matters discussed above seem to fully explain the frequently posed questions: Why do Americans think of themselves as friendly and open when others consider them superficial and cool? Why do Americans return from trips abroad and claim people are hospitable but not friendly? Plus, if they live abroad why do they have difficulty making connections, except with other Americans?

Misunderstandings about American friendship often begin with the initial greeting and extend to other elements associated with building relationships. The informal casual introduction of many Americans puzzles people from other countries. Further challenges stem from another more subtle matter: our emotional organization of personal connections.

Kurt Lewin, a German American psychologist, called this organization of relationships a matter of emotional (not physical) space. He said that "all people have private space and public space, in their lives and that they assign others to these spaces."[2] Through understanding his observation regarding the different types of space we gain a deeper understanding of the actions we observe.

To clarify the concepts of public space and private space, it's useful to think in terms of a familiar physical environment. In this example, consider two offices in the same urban high-rise. One office has a large open work space with a few partitioned areas and one relatively small private conference room. The other has a small open area and a large conference room with a door to be closed.

The first office with the large open public space and small private conference space is the American's. The individualist Americans want to be liked and are eager to make friends. When first encountered they may appear open and warm but they are actually very private. Deep friendships come slowly but Americans have many casual acquaintances. Connections start easily and may either last for years or evaporate in months. The title of friend is given to many people although the level of closeness varies significantly.

There is a need for lots of space to accommodate the many acquaintances. It is easy for someone to be invited into this open space. There are some semiprivate spaces, too. These are not so much to allow special intimacy but rather to allow groups to stay together in one place. The friends from the gym, school, or work may each occupy a special area. This is the idea of Lewin's public space.

The conference room—the private area—is relatively small. This is the space for our closest friends. These are the people who share holiday celebrations, joys, and sorrows. Access to the private space is not given easily or to many people.

In a collectivist culture the building design is reversed. It is the private conference room that is large and the public space that is relatively small. To receive an invitation, a person must be introduced. New friends are added with caution. A Russian student studying in California says she remembers being told, "Don't smile. You don't know those people." For her smiles are shared only with good friends.

The ability to move within the public section may offer more freedom than in the American office, but the space itself is small. The conference room—the private space—is large enough to allow everyone from the close-knit, ongoing network to enter. It is the reverse of the American design; it is the largest space, built to accommodate a well-formed group that will often be gathered there together.

How Different: Trends?

Most studies of cultural differences present strong contrasts between the numbers and types of friendships in individualistic and collectivist environments. However, a study of the friendship patterns of 1,410 university students reported in 2001 revealed some differences from common expectations. The study done by researchers from the United States, Korea, and China included students from 5 countries: China, South Korea, United States, France, and Romania. The participants were from urban and rural areas, men and women from 18 to 26 years old.

While it was anticipated that U.S. students would report the highest number of friends and the collectivist South Koreans would report fewer, the reverse was true. Also there was no significant difference reported in the duration of the friendships; however, the U.S. group had more contact with their friends than the other groups.

The latter observation may link to the more individualistic perspective that people select their friends. Accordingly, direct communication and work are necessary to maintain a sense of friendship. On the contrary, studies suggest that "people in collectivist cultures tend to see all relationships as phenomena over which one has less control than is assumed in individualistic cultures."[3]

While one study may not be sufficient to indicate that traditional patterns have shifted entirely, it does remind the reader that behaviors may change in cultures as well as individuals. It is also wise to remember that all studies provide insight to the dominant traits in a culture. Individual actions may vary based on personality, education, and experience.

Building the Connections

For Americans who endeavor to build connections, whether business or personal, the largest barrier to success may be their own impatience. In chapter 1 we discuss the differing views of time in the world. Is it a vanishing resource or an endless supply? The contrasting views are significant in the process of building relationships. Are you in a hurry, or is there time for something to develop?

When doing business, Americans tend to want to focus on tasks, to achieve a goal, even one as simple as getting through a meeting's agenda. When we believe that others aren't working in that same direction we become frustrated. Accordingly, the time spent getting to know someone, the shared meal, and the casual conversation can seem like a distraction from the purpose at hand. We think business first, pleasure (dinner or a conversation) later. But for Southern Europeans, sharing a meal, even in the midst of a negotiation, can indicate that they are serious, that they want to develop the relationship knowing that the relationship is the key to a successful business endeavor.[4] Allow the time for conversations so the relationship can grow. Enjoy the experience and reap the business benefits.

Now We Know

Although the definitions of friends and space are sometimes conflicting, satisfying personal and professional relationships can be created. Friendships can be formed, experiences shared, lives enriched, and business goals achieved. It simply takes awareness and patience.

I'm Glad I Know

That it's going to take time to make friends. It's not that they don't like me. I realize people are busy. It isn't that they are ignoring me; it's just a different pattern in their lives. I can issue an invitation and build a different group than I have at home. It's just hard to keep track of many different people, rather than just having a few close friends. The variety is interesting, but this is still different for me.

↦ *An Austrian woman,*
living and working in the United States

CHAPTER 5

The Companies

I Wish I'd Known

It took some years of experience for me to realize that all multinational companies reflect the culture of their founder[s] and of the countr[ies] where they are headquartered, whether the company is from Switzerland, Great Britain, Japan, or the United States. No matter how many countries they cover, the home culture has a significant ongoing influence.

→→ *American working for*
a global consulting company based in Paris

I Wish They Knew

People move upward in companies based on time spent, longevity rather than skill. The United States is still a meritocracy and other countries' companies are not. Being young and skilled does not mean advancement. Wouldn't you think in trying to increase shareholder value you'd move forward people by what they can do best, learn fastest?

→→ *French investment manager working*
for a French company based in New York

Global We Will Be

Corporate leaders agree that "the shift from a local to a global marketplace is irreversible and gaining momentum."[1] Business activities leap geographical boundaries and, in so doing, become increasing complex. For employees the change can be challenging. Working globally requires that connections be across continents, time zones, and cultures.

As corporations seek new markets and resources, they pull their staff into new locations, both physical and mental. A manager at Dell Computer may lead a team based in India one day and a team based in the southern part of the United States the next. The manager must deal with different languages, time zones, cultures, and experiences. When your company is global, suddenly you are, too.

This isn't a phenomenon peculiar to the United States. Companies in India look to Germany and Australia as markets to which they can provide services. Thai department stores plan to market their private label merchandise in China and Japan. Toyota, IKEA, H&M, and Pret A Manger travel across the world to open the U.S. market. Headquarters are located in one country, while staff are distributed around the world. Teams are diverse and spread apart, global and local simultaneously. This is the corporation of the twenty-first century.

Corporations Live On

We seldom think about what defines a corporation. Our efforts are focused on studying their marketing campaigns and their use of technology. We debate the benefit or harm caused by their expansion. We assume that the multinational, global corporation is a modern creation.

However, the *Merriam-Webster* dictionary reveals that the first definition of a corporation dates back to the 1400s and defined it as "a group of merchants or traders united in a trade guild."[2] Individuals came together to do business and according to history, their trade was often across the continents in Europe, the Middle East, and Asia.

Over time the form of the corporation changed and made the original definition obsolete. It evolved from one based on individuals to one that was less personal and more bureaucratic. It was no longer dependent on one individual for its existence and ability to conduct its activities. The current definition is a "body formed and authorized by law to act as a single person although constituted by one or more persons and legally endowed with various rights and duties including the capacity of succession."[3] This basic description is appropriate whether a corporation's business is conducted in Antigua, Mexico City, Vladivostok, or worldwide.

Is Your Corporation Multinational, International, Global, or Transnational?

The dictionary definition captures the legal distinction that a corporation is many people acting as if it were one. Moreover, it captures the idea that success rests in the concept that the corporation is ongoing without regard to specific individuals. In a sense, it does not die. Thus people can rely on contracts and plans made by corporate representatives knowing that the entity will honor them whether that specific individual is there.

However, as companies continue to extend their activities throughout the world, the basic definition has been expanded to reflect the ways they organize their businesses. Following are the most common descriptions.[4]

Multidomestic or Multinational A portfolio of multiple national entities where each formulates business strategy based on perceived market differences. The modern multinational entity emerged in the seventeenth century (1600s) in the shape of the Dutch and British East India companies.[5]

International Transfers and adapts parent company's knowledge or expertise to foreign markets. The parent company retains considerable influence and control but less than in a classic global company.

Global Treats world markets as an integrated whole, views the global operating environment and worldwide consumer demand as the dominant unit of analysis. It has centralized capabilities and headquarters-based decision-making. For example, Jeffrey Immelt, chairman and CEO of General Electric, stated, "GE is a global products company with technologies, factories, and products made for the world, not just a single nation."[6]

Transnational While each of the previously defined forms has worked well for some companies, the corporation of the future must combine elements of each of them. This evolved form is the transnational corporation. It combines global competitiveness, multinational flexibility, and worldwide learning capability simultaneously. The organization is dispersed, interdependent, and specialized. The national units contribute to integrated worldwide operations and jointly developed knowledge.[7]

Global People

No matter the type of corporation or the product or service it delivers, the reality is that business entails that people do things together. While research indicates that multinational corporations are becoming more similar in their structures, it also tells us that people within them are maintaining their specific cultural identities.[8] Therefore, people skills, especially cultural understandings, are essential to success in today's corporations. In fact, the ability to understand and communicate across multiple cultures is one of the key management competencies for the twenty-first century.[9]

On the surface it may seem surprising that people working in multinational, multicultural companies are maintaining their individuality rather than becoming more similar. However, the way people learn about their own culture is generally by contrasting it to other cultures. Multinational companies offer the opportunity for that experiential learning. When people examine the similarities and differences between their culture and other cultures, the strengths and special attributes of their own culture are revealed. Knowing about the cultures of others does not demand personal change but does increase understanding of yourself as well as that of other people. In some instances people are able to adapt other ways of problem solving that may add to their managerial flexibility. In addition to observation and discussion, it can be valuable to read basic references on the subject of cultural differences. The resources and recommended reading sections later in this book contain some suggestions.

Awareness of cultural differences leads to the understanding that culture influences what people hear and see. It shapes what they perceive is happening around them. National culture, gender, age, education, and personal ethnicity are components that shape people's views of the world and their behavior in business environments.

Building Connections Across Cultures

Communication and relationship building, two key activities in any business, are strongly influenced by people's cultures. The key points presented in chapters 1 through 4 are as follows:

- Flow of information. Is it direct or indirect? High context or low context?

- Organizing principle. Focus on time and tasks or people and relationships?
- Is equality valued or hierarchy respected?
- Individualistic or collectivist? Which is emphasized, the individual or the group?
- Universalist or particularist? Do the rules apply equally to all, or are they adjusted based on the relationship?

These key differences in approaches to communication and relationships shape how people handle all business matters. They are the foundation for corporate policies from the structure of meetings to hiring, promotion, and compensation. If part of your group is in Germany, part is in China, and part is in the United States, the styles of thinking and problem solving will vary. The answers to address these issues are not obvious or universal. They will evolve as is appropriate for both the company and the individual people involved. What is important is first knowing that these issues exist.

The Emerging Global Manager

Signs of a global manager are appearing, according to Michael Marks, CEO of Flextronics, a Singapore-based company, who says there is "more uniformity among young managers around the world. Today's 30-year-old grew up with travel and education abroad and is familiar with technology."[10] Managers who are raised in one country, go abroad for part of their schooling, and work in yet other countries have experiences that are vastly different from those of their peers who remain at home.

Stephen Green, group CEO at HSBC, a worldwide banking and financial services firm that hires people from 38 countries, says that "a British manager with international experience will tend to identify more with a Japanese manager with international experience than with another British manager who has worked in only his or her home country."[11]

Reading the Corporate Culture

While a person's ability to work with other individuals is of paramount importance to succeed, it isn't sufficient to only understand the culture

of individuals. It's necessary to recognize the culture of the corporation. Whether you are an employee, a supplier, a consultant, or a com-
petitor, the culture matters. Is it a law firm where formality is required
or a design firm where the environment is casual? Is it similar to Wal-
Mart where the day begins with the required Wal-Mart song or does the
daily routine vary? Each corporation has a history, policies, and procedures that are both formal and informal. Culture is to the organization
what personality is to the individual—a hidden yet unifying theme that
provides meaning and direction.[12]

The way people work within an organization is shaped by the culture. It guides their behavior with internal and external colleagues, plus
it tells employees what actions are grounds for dismissal or for promotion. Is all company information secret, or can procedures and thinking
be widely shared? The corporate culture defines the personality of the
company and how it conducts its business.

But it is never simple to read the culture and especially not in a company whose operations exist in multiple locations. Corporate culture
can be simultaneously global and local. The attitudes, visions, and
values set by headquarters are interpreted and influenced by the local
culture and further shaped by the individuals who operate in the environment. Everyone has an expectation of how things will operate in a
business setting and how roles will be defined. The culture of the enterprise can vary from place to place and may render inaccurate preconceived ideas.

For example, by looking at one cultural dimension, "uncertainty
avoidance" (discussed in chapter 7), it is possible to understand the idea
of cultural influence on the structure and procedures of a business. Uncertainty avoidance deals with the desire to reduce anxiety connected to
the unpredictability of events and situations. Countries such as Singapore and Germany demonstrate a high level of uncertainty avoidance,
and this is evidenced by a preference for formality, use of contracts, and
written procedures. A manager who is accustomed to strict protocols in
Germany who moves to a different location of the same company in
Venezuela or India may be surprised by the local culture. Both of these
countries score low on the uncertainty avoidance dimension; furthermore, local procedures set by people in the region may show more flex-

ibility and vary from those in the German headquarters. Although it is the same company and the same core culture, there are local variations.

Sources to Guide You

To understand the corporate culture and how it operates, you can read the annual report, if one exists, or the employee handbook. These two documents describe the interior environment. To add to the picture check the external environment as well. Read press releases, articles in trade and consumer publications, and search online sources. See how the company presents itself to the outside world.

For a global company, you'll need to look broadly at a variety of places. What are the regulations, legal systems, and politics in the home country? Where else are offices located? How do employees work within these countries? What does the local and international press say? What are the key industry issues that affect their business in their various locations? How is the company's sense of social responsibility regarded?

Always look for involvement where a company operates even if it's not global. Are they active in their communities? For example, McDonald's has taken not only their golden arches symbol around the world but also includes the Ronald McDonald Houses charity programs in many locations. Look at the people, their offices, and the location of their operations. Engage your senses. Then reflect on all the data. What's your opinion? What do you understand from your research?

One Aspect to Consider: Doing or Being?

One important element of corporate culture that people should understand is how status is earned and how the hierarchy is organized. All companies have a hierarchy. How it's organized and how levels of status are achieved differ by size, tradition, and culture. One key question is how success and thereby advancement is measured. Are success and status based on personal achievement, or are they ascribed, given for certain characteristics? In a culture where personal or individual achievement is the key to what someone has accomplished, achievement is a measure of success. In an ascribed status culture, qualities such as age, gender, and social class are the important measures.[13] In a sense, an achievement culture places the emphasis on doing, while from an ascribed status culture's perspective just being is sufficient.

One indicator of which culture exists in a place is the level of formality. Are people addressed by their first names or by honorifics (Mr., Ms., Dr.)? For someone who is accustomed to the informal American business environment, to suddenly be called Mr. Lee instead of Chris can be surprising. But the reverse can create an insult where none is intended. To move from Mrs. Bordeaux to Francine without an invitation risks ending a productive relationship before it begins. Are titles used extensively? Titles are an important indicator of status within a hierarchy, and in an ascribed culture titles are often used so that status can be quickly understood. In this environment roles are generally well defined, and the hierarchy is likely to be rigid. Further, this show of respect for seniors in the hierarchy is not only a form of politeness but also seen as a measure of your commitment to the organization and its mission.[14]

The status and role of a manager are quite different in the two cultures. In an achievement environment it is often more important to get the job done than to observe the hierarchy. In fact, there may be fewer levels to the hierarchy, fewer positions between entry level and head of the enterprise. If a traditional hierarchical structure resembles a pyramid, then one with fewer levels is often defined as being "flatter." In an organization that is considered relatively flat, the role of a manager is as a mentor, a "resource" for subordinates. Within that relationship it is possible to admit errors, pose questions, and explore solutions, communicating with others as needed.

By contrast, the manager in an ascribed status company is expected to know all the answers. Subordinates look to him or her for solutions to problems. This is a more traditional, paternalistic role.[15] Further, communication follows the hierarchy, manager to manager, down— not up—the hierarchy. In this environment people support the status of others who may then achieve the goals that are set.

This difference is likely to reveal itself in the human resources policy areas. It will affect the structure of promotion and compensation. Is seniority the critical issue or personal accomplishment? As one considers this issue it's easy to see why creating policies that satisfy all the perspectives in a corporation that reaches around the world can be extremely difficult.

Meetings, Meetings, and More Meetings

It isn't unusual to hear managers express frustration about the number of meetings they must attend. A frequent complaint is that they are unable to do any meaningful work because their days are filled with meetings. Books are written and seminars are conducted to improve the effectiveness of these gatherings.

Given that conducting a productive face-to-face meeting of attendees who share a common culture, is difficult, the challenge of organizing a meeting for people spread across the globe is enormous. The practical aspects alone can be daunting. Where will people meet, and what form will the meeting take? In person or by phone? Video conference? Who will travel, and who will get up at 3:00 A.M. for the conference call?

In ideal circumstances, everyone gathers in the same place to allow the most effective communication. Only in person can you rely on all the senses and all the ways people communicate: voice, gesture, and facial expressions as well as the words themselves. Because it's in meetings where cultural differences show themselves most clearly, it is ideal to have the broadest choice of communication inputs. Meetings can be intimidating even in your own environment. People don't want to look foolish, make an error, or show lack of knowledge.[16]

To complicate matters, all the cultural dimensions are evident in meetings. People's attitudes about time, their styles of communication, and ideas about hierarchy and rules are evident. What does being on time mean? Does it start at the exact hour, or is a starting time more flexible? Will the American participants arriving a few minutes early be frustrated by the later-arriving Brazilians? These issues influence the flow of conversation and the decision-making process.

Whether it is acknowledged, one of the activities of meetings is relationship building, especially in a culture where relationships are the key to doing everything. Allowing time for the informal conversations that support the connections can frustrate some participants and be the most important activity for others.

Possibly the most difficult matter to define and manage is context.[17] How much information is enough? Is this an American group where precise clear data and lots of related particulars are typically preferred, or is this an Italian group, where much of the background is known? Will the detailing of much background be seen as useful or boring? Will people tune out? Will the low context members miss the contextual clues of gesture and tone? High context cultures (such as Japan and Saudi Arabia) tend to be well informed about the people and events affecting them. The farther apart people are on the high context/low context scale, the more difficult it is to create a productive environment.

Almost every decision, large to small, involves some level of negotiation. Since this is a vast topic and the subject of many books and articles, we will not cover it in this text. We will, however, remind the reader that the skills and attitudes brought to a negotiation are also culture driven. Did the negotiator grow up in a culture where barter was part of the daily economy? Have their skills been honed since childhood? Consider what you know about their view of time. Is there a preference for short-term results or long-range growth? For example, Henry Kissinger, a former U.S. secretary of state, said, "Americans think in terms of concrete solutions to specific problems. The Chinese think in terms of process that has no culmination."[18]

In addition to considering the individual negotiating counterparts and their cultures, it's valuable to understand their external business environment. What are the government and legal structures? What about the banking and taxing systems? Issues that are obvious when all parties are operating within one country can bring additional challenges to cross-border negotiations. Know the person and the place to gain insight to the process.

Now We Know

Culture, tradition, rules, and organization vary for nations, people, and business enterprises. Whatever a person's business—pharmaceuticals, food, or fashion—its culture will vary, influenced by geography, history, and the people within the company. To work effectively with a company, whether on its staff or connected in other ways, you need an understanding of the specific culture. The culture influences hiring, promotion, formality required, definition of appropriate dress, and even conduct at meetings. By learning to read the culture, a person can be successful in a variety of environments, building connections whether they're local or global.

I'm Glad I Know

You have to be flexible. You can't expect to do things the way you always have. Every place has different rules, practices. You have to adapt, and flexibility is critical.

>> *American manager who has worked in Ireland;*
Washington, D.C.; Los Angeles; and South Africa

CHAPTER 6

Advisers All

I Wish I'd Known

It takes some time to understand how complicated it is to do business outside the United States. The more companies I work with, and the more countries that are involved, the more complex business gets. Don't get me wrong, it's still fun, and there is lots of business to be done. There are just so many things you have to know about and take into consideration. Lots of learning all the time.

↦ *American with the United States*
Department of Commerce in New Jersey

I Wish They Knew

Listen well before you talk. Really focus on hearing what people are telling you, how they're sitting, [and] what they're not saying. But most of all listen. We Americans tend to hurry, to want to move the discussion along, [to] get things finished. Listening and patience make a big difference.

↦ *American senior vice president, international banking*
for a global bank based in California

A Variety of Advisers

The complexities of doing business globally go beyond the issues of culture and communication. Each country has its own legal and banking systems. There are distinct and complicated rules for taxation and regulations covering import, export, sales, and creation of goods and services. Beyond knowing how the government operates and becoming familiar with the tax structure, basic knowledge of the legal system is critical. How transparent and predictable is the legal system? Are attorneys common and available, or are there others who handle legal matters? How are property and intellectual property rights protected? The

"I was always the go-to guy, and it got to me."

legal system is key, as it forms the foundation for banking, capital markets, and business operations.

Learning the answers to these questions isn't a matter that must be handled alone. There are skilled and knowledgeable advisers who can provide the answers and guide people. These advisers are people who understand the issues in your home country and in the country where your business is conducted; they are professionals who can provide insights on how to create procedures and products that are acceptable in both places. Key among this group are attorneys, accountants, bankers, and trade organizations that are skilled at bridging the differences: advisers all around.

The Law Is the Law

When they think of law, Americans often first think of attorneys. Many of the questions about what can be done are best answered in terms of what is legal and what isn't. We are known as a country with many attorneys. In 2001, the United States was home to 70 percent of the attorneys in the world.[1]

Contrast that with China, which has the world's largest population, almost four times greater than that of the United States, and which had only 120,000 lawyers as of 2002.[2] The influx of foreign firms has no doubt added to that total, but it's still not a large number compared with the United States. As the legal system in China develops, partly as a result of joining the World Trade Organization, requirements for attorneys are shifting. One firm advertises that it is looking for people who have "modern" minds, speak English, are computer literate, and have foreign contacts.[3]

While the number of attorneys in a country offers an insight to the legal system, we must look beyond this to develop an understanding. The form and traditions of a country's legal system affect all activities within a country. They dictate the form and activities of businesses and the structure of a country's financial systems. While today's legal systems continue to evolve, they can be traced back to Mesopotamia in 2350 B.C. That is the date historians give to the first consolidation of ancient law called Urukagina's code. Among other things, it confirms that the gods appointed the king and that citizens are allowed to know why certain actions are punished.[4]

While all legal systems have changed through the years, they are all considered to have evolved from this common beginning. Today the legal structures throughout the world can be identified as common, civil, or religious law.

The United States, the United Kingdom, Hong Kong, India, and Canada are among the common law countries. The common law tradition dates back to 1066, although the Magna Carta signed in 1215 by King John of England is sometimes referred to as the "blueprint of common law."[5] One important element of this document is that it was the first time a king allowed that even he could be compelled to observe a law. (We express that idea today, when we say, "No man is above the law.") The distinguishing characteristic of common law is that it is based on tradition and prior rulings. Lawyers and judges look to earlier decisions that set precedent to make decisions about current cases. Additionally, lawyers and judges have the power to interpret the laws and even to create new laws through their interpretations.

Civil or code law is considered to be the "world's most common form of legal system."[6] The original code, the Napoleonic Code, dates back to 1804. That was the first civil law code, but it is based on Roman law and can be traced back to the Code of Justinian in 529.[7] It is a detailed set of written laws and codes that tell what is and is not permissible. Civil law does not rely on precedent to the same extent as common law but rather is based on what is written.

In most countries religious law applies to individuals who choose to follow the dictates of their beliefs. As in the United States, there is a separation between the laws of the church and those of the state where the system is either common or civil law. However, many Muslim countries do not make a distinction between secular and religious law. An often cited example is the banking system in Pakistan. Because the Koran forbids collecting interest, banking regulations had to be adapted to be consistent with religious laws, while still meeting the need to make a profit and stay in business.

Knowing the basis for the legal tradition isn't sufficient. The questions to answer are: How is what's written interpreted? How does the system work? How will the laws be interpreted and enforced? Can you tell what the government is trying to achieve? Is the system strong or weak? In today's rapidly changing environment it is important to know how predictable the business environment is.

After a recent visit to Russia, Janet Elliott, the executive director of the International Visitors Council of Los Angeles, offered the following observation: "There's no predictability in the people's lives. They are in a state of anxiety all the time, although they don't really understand the source. Every time anyone new comes to power, all the laws, all the rules may change. The laws are so loose that when you're driving and you pull up to a corner, it's impossible to be sure which car should go first across the intersection."[8]

Rule of Law

In the United States business relies on the rule of law, that is, the predictability of the legal system. Companies create detailed contracts to spell out the rights and obligations of the parties involved. They endeavor to explain how problems will be solved if they arise. Each contract identifies what the governing law will be (which country and state). If the contract doesn't adequately deal with a problem that arises, the parties know that through the courts a solution will be found.

However, not every legal system may offer that same level of certainty.

For example, the legal system in China is still, from a Western perspective, "skeletal, and rule of law remains subjective."[9] Traditionally Chinese leaders ruled by virtue rather than law; legislation and regulations had little relevance. Today's system reflects this tradition. Some claim that Guanxi networks are a substitute for the legal system. (These networks are connections between people, developed over time, based on shared interests and mutual obligations. See chapter 12.) It is claimed that these relationship-based networks can be more important in helping to enforce agreements between businesses than the Chinese legal system.[10]

The Rules Are the Rules Unless They're Not

The universalist/particularist cultural dimension presented in chapter 4 is important to consider when you talk about legal systems and the application of laws and regulations. Some of the countries considered universalists are the United States, the United Kingdom, Sweden, Canada, and Germany. Some of the countries considered particularists are China, Chile, Saudi Arabia, and Singapore.

Universalists believe that there are general or universal principles that apply to all people. The rules take precedent over the particular details of a given situation. Truth telling is more important than loyalty if a choice has to be made. In contrast, particularists believe it's the details of the specific situation that count. "Who's involved, and what is my obligation to the parties?" they ask. The difference is that in the first the focus is on rules, while in the second the focus is on people. Where's the emphasis? Rules versus relationships.

Consider the difference in the matter of contracts. As described above, universalists attempt to set forth the entire agreement in the contract document. For them, the conclusion of the negotiations and everything needed for the transaction are included. If there's a problem, they look to the contract for resolution.

Particularists may feel insulted by a detailed contract. They look to the relationship to solve problems when they arise. According to Gordon Reese, a consultant who has experience in Asia, for particularists, a contract marks a beginning point not an end. Its purpose is to express the intent of the parties and may be modified to fit events that cannot be foreseen at the time of signing.

No matter where you operate or what the systems of other countries are, if you are a U.S. company you must abide by U.S. laws. Two laws that deserve special mention in the context of global operations are the Foreign Corrupt Practices Act and the Sarbanes-Oxley Act of 2002.

Remember the FCPA

"Don't forget to talk about the FCPA," an attorney told the author. "Everyone needs to understand it; it's a tough one!"

The United States has what is considered the most restrictive anti-bribery law that exists. It is the Foreign Corrupt Practices Act of 1977, commonly known as the FCPA. The act came about because more than 400 U.S. companies had made questionable or illegal payments to foreign governments, officials, and political parties in an attempt to gain or retain business.[11] This act prohibits corporations and their employees to make such payments. It prohibits direct bribes and those paid by intermediaries. Further to companies not being able to make payments, it is a violation to know that a portion of a payment will be used for that purpose. You can get charged with "willful blindness" or "conscious disregard."[12]

Penalties can be significant. The Justice Department can fine a company up to $2 million per violation and impose five years of imprisonment in criminal cases, according to John Davis, a partner in a Washington, D.C., law firm who specializes in the FCPA.[13]

Obeying the FCPA when operating abroad can become a problem because "bribery is culturally ingrained as an acceptable business practice in some countries such as Mexico," said Margaret M. Gatti, an attorney in New Jersey.[14] This practice is not only an issue of paying to get a contract signed but may also affect daily activities. An American who lived in Mexico City tells of having to pay a policeman every time she reached the stop sign near her home. Every day, at least once, a small sum had to be paid. There was no ticket, and she paid him directly, a fee for being able to move through the intersection. Although there is no legal standing, a payment was required. When she realized this situation applied to everyone, not just the Americans in the area, she began to question people about it.

"These people don't make enough to live by working at their jobs," she was told. "They need the money to live." If the problem was that the policeman's salary was so low he couldn't live on it, why didn't people just pay a bit more in taxes, raise the salaries, and eliminate the daily aggravation? One reason is that it is cheaper to pay these small amounts daily and directly to the policemen in their areas than it is to pay the additional taxes that would be required to pay decent salaries. Who knows whether the money would get to the local person, or whether people would just pay taxes and pay at the stop sign, too.

More Than FCPA

The FCPA isn't the only law that touches issues of corruption that U.S. corporations must now consider. Whether local or global, all companies are affected by the Sarbanes-Oxley Act of 2002. This piece of legislation, also known as SOX, was designed to protect investors by creating a new "transparency" (or increased reliability) in the way companies create and communicate their financial data. In some areas, it dictates corporate behaviors and in others it requires companies to create their own policies and procedures.[15] This law will not only influence the composition of corporate boards, establish auditing oversight, and determine requirements for potential board members but also stretches into the technology departments as it specifies the time periods for record retention. To ensure that the law is followed, there are stringent reporting requirements paired with significant penalties for corporate officers who fail to comply.

What's the Corruption Ranking of That Country?

It isn't just the United States that is concerned about bribery and corruption. In 1998 the FCPA was amended to implement the Organization of Economic Cooperation and Development Convention on Combating Bribery of Foreign Public Officials in International Business Transactions.

To learn how a country is rated in terms of corruption, you can look at the Transparency International (TI) annual Global Corruption Report. Transparency International was founded in 1993, and according to the *Guardian* (UK) TI is a "kind of travel guide to the jungle of various standards and practices in different world regions."[16] The annual report presents analysis and information on what is happening in various countries and regions. According to TI the reports are written by academics, journalists, and local experts.

For a quick look at countries' relative standings, consult the TI Corruption Perception Index that ranks countries according to perceived corruption. The 146 countries included in their 2004 list are ranked from a high of ten that they call "squeaky-clean" to zero or highly corrupt. For that year Finland ranked highest ("cleanest") at 9.7 and Bangladesh and Haiti were at the bottom of the list at 1.5. (The United States moved from 7.6 in 2001 to 7.5 in 2004, with 5.0 considered the minimum to be considered clean.)

But it isn't only through legislation that corporations are being asked to monitor their behavior. According to Professor Lynn Sharp Paine, author of *Value Shift*, throughout the twentieth century jurists in the United States and Europe have come to accept the idea that corporations have moral responsibilities to constituencies beyond their shareholders. They are responsible to employees, consumers, and the general public. At the same time that this legal concept was evolving, new regulations have been enacted covering everything from product safety and discrimination to anticompetitive business practices.[17]

These concerns are echoed in the actions of investors big and small. Representatives from around the world of major pension plans meet to discuss socially responsible investing. While not a new approach, socially responsible investing is becoming better known. It dates back to the eighteenth century when religious groups in the United States placed restrictions on their investments and avoided companies in the production of tobacco and gambling.[18] Investors today look for a balance between financial returns and the responsible actions of companies in terms of the environment and labor issues. For today's corporations it's not enough to obey the precise reading of a law. They must be perceived to be ethical in their ways of doing business.

People are the Key

People can advise you on any issue, from taxes or accounting regulations to product, corporate, or environmental laws. Want special insight to operating in Sweden, Brazil, or Cambodia? You can find people to provide assistance.

Attorneys are not the only source of information or the only advisers you need. Bankers and accountants also provide valuable insights. An experienced international trade banker points out that problems can be unexpected. She recently met with a company that was excited about the potential market in China until they learned that it would be extremely complicated to move their money from China back to the United States, no matter how successful the business became. The laws regarding portability of money vary from place to place. An experienced banker can also be a valuable adviser.

You will constantly hear, "It's difficult to appreciate the importance of personal relationships. They are the key to doing business wherever you go." But how do you find the people who may be the key? Is there a network that broadens your understanding of another place or system? In addition to the advisers discussed above, other organizations to consider are the chambers of commerce, French American or Polish American chamber, or the American chamber of commerce in Hungary or Hong Kong.

When looking for assistance and information, don't forget the Department of Commerce. This is a government agency that works with exporters and importers who wish to develop their businesses, whether large or small. Whether you are in Boston, Beijing, or Barcelona, there is a commercial service officer who can answer your questions and give advice. These are friendly and knowledgeable people who understand the complexity of global business.

Search for People and Information

To find an attorney you can look at a Web site such as www.hgexperts.com. Type in the name of the country you're interested in to get names. You should search for a firm in organizations such as the International Bar Association and specialized groups such as the Customs and Trade Bar Association.

According to a partner in an international law firm based in Washington, D.C., it's best if you can find a U.S. attorney who is already representing clients in the area that is important to you. She says they will not only have an understanding of legal issues but also make suggestions regarding a local adviser. They will know the people there.

Because they understand this need to build expertise in many places, law firms in the United States and other countries have expanded, formed organizations, and built alliances. One indication is that some of the largest U.S. law firms, according to the *National Law Journal NLJ 250* for the year ending September 2003, all operate in at least 10 countries. The largest of the firms, with 3,200 lawyers, is present in 36 countries.

Search on your own, talk to a variety of advisers, and build relationships, and you'll develop your own view of the laws, banking systems, and the country's business climate.

Now We Know

Although cultural understanding is fundamental to global business success, it isn't sufficient to ensure that a company can operate in all locations. This knowledge must be paired with an understanding of the business environment, including a country's government structure and legal and taxation systems. To acquire the specialized information pertaining to your locations and specific business it's wise to seek out advisers, people with experience and expertise who are able to provide current and practical information. Advisers need to know U.S. laws that affect global operations as well as those of the applicable country. What's legal in one place isn't in another. One person's gift is another's bribe. Do your research in advance, find advisers to assist you, avoid errors of ignorance, and build successful operations.

I'm Glad I Know

You have to be able to cope with changes. You think you've got everything set and then, a law changes—a new regulation appears. The goods are in [a] country far away, and you have to figure out how to get them through customs to your customer. Yesterday the rule that blocks them didn't exist; today it's there. You can't panic. You just have to figure it out and work around the problem. Things change without warning. That's just how it is.

>> *American attorney specializing in customs issues, based in Los Angeles, with clients who import and export around the globe*

CHAPTER 7

Change

I Wish I'd Known

It took me a while to understand that all the formality I encountered in my assignments existed for a reason. It isn't simply a matter of being old-fashioned, out of date. The greetings, seating according to status, waiting for the oldest person to speak before you talk, all can be very useful. Once I stopped being annoyed, I realized it helped me understand the relationship between the people I traveled to work with and actually made me comfortable.

↠ *American consultant to*
U.S. companies doing business in Asia

I Wish They Knew

Underneath the differences you notice and experience, people are alike. People in other countries have the same worries and hopes we do. They're trying to cope with their business, families, and health issues, too. No matter how different the environment, the language may be, it's just people like you and me.

↠ *American banker who specializes*
in international trade based in Los Angeles

The New New Thing, or No New Thing?

The United States is a country built by people who are acting out their willingness to try something new. Immigrants changed their lives to come to this place, believing that opportunities awaited them. This attitude was one of the factors that created the highly individualistic culture that the United States is known for: independence, achievement, change, and innovation. All these words are associated with the American culture. But everyone in the United States, and in the world, is not excited about change. Regardless of people's attitudes, avoiding change today is almost impossible.

"It's death if you stop trying new things," said Carleton (Carly) S. Fiorina, then chairman and CEO of Hewlett-Packard, during an interview with the *Financial Times* in November 2003.[1] This statement captures the prevailing attitude in U.S. business culture that ongoing change is an essential element of corporate survival. Overall, Americans regard change as indisputably good and linked to development. New things are necessary and good.

Although this mind-set is seen as an integral part of the U.S. culture, the same cannot be said for all people or all cultures throughout the world. Some see change as a beneficial process leading to new ideas and new opportunities. For others it merely disrupts existing processes and creates unforeseen problems. Is change good, or is it bad?

Geert Hofstede, emeritus professor at Maastricht University and noted author on intercultural behaviors, identified attitudes toward change in his well-known study of more than 40 countries. He considers this issue to be one of the key dimensions in a society's behavior.[2]

To understand his point, it's useful to realize that the response to change, even just the idea of change, varies considerably. Reactions can be placed along a scale that moves from comfort to consternation, from curiosity about what may evolve to dread about what may be different. Something new, whether it is a product or procedure, may be approached with ease and eager acceptance or panic and resistance.

The underlying difference along this scale is tolerance for uncertainty. Change creates uncertainty because it introduces something new and different. It leads to the anxiety that comes about in new situations. What will happen? What will my role be? How must I now think? Act? It is the uncertainty, the resulting anxiety, that troubles people.

Recognizing that it was not change but the ensuing anxiety change causes, Hofstede called this characteristic "uncertainty avoidance." How much uncertainty is acceptable, and further, how does society cope with the anxiety? How strong is a culture's desire to avoid uncertainty? In her book *International Dimensions of Organizational Behavior*, Nancy J. Adler renamed this trait "anxiety avoidance" that captures the core of the matter.[3] Regardless of how we label this idea, it as important to understand it as it is to understand a society's attitudes toward time and relationships.

Whether you use uncertainty avoidance or anxiety avoidance to describe this dimension, the question "Is change good?" is still not answered with a simple affirmative or negative. In his book *Coaching Across Cultures*, Philippe Rosinski captures the variation in attitudes well. He says, in part

> Cultures on the high end of the change dimension welcome changes that are nonlinear, innovative, and turbulent. What is different causes curiosity. Ambiguity is acceptable. Rules are limited to what is necessary. However, some cultures value stability and are anxious about change that is too substantial or turbulent. They prefer incremental, orderly change. Familiar risks are acceptable, and rules are welcome.[4]

The attitudes vary according to country and culture. Sweden, Singapore, the United States, the United Kingdom, South Africa, Poland, and India score low on the anxiety avoidance scale, indicating that people in these countries are more likely to accept uncertainty or ambiguity as a natural part of life. Even countries whose uncertainty avoidance rating is relatively low may find it beneficial to use others as agents of change. This is a point made in a *Newsweek International* article about the role of American women in the British business community. Two Americans, Laura Tyson, who now heads the London School of Business, and Rose Marie Bravo, the CEO of Burberry, are cited as "change agents" at their respective posts, as outsiders who are able to stimulate change.[5]

Countries that score high on the uncertainty avoidance scale and that value stability include Japan, Chile, France, Spain, South Korea, Brazil, Chile, and Mexico. Their efforts to reduce anxiety include creating rules, policies, and regulations. It's helpful to note that not every country rests at the extremes of the range. Germany and Egypt are examples of two that fall in the middle range, slightly toward the dynamic.[6] Each place, like each person, will have its own dominant viewpoint.

Not Just a Big Picture Issue

Uncertainty avoidance in cultures may sound as though it is something that concerns us only when we contemplate issues such as where to move a factory or how to restructure a compensation policy. But it isn't just a policy or place issue. It can be about something that touches us more immediately. According to Aaron Marcus, writing in the magazine *New Architect*, it's important to consider uncertainty avoidance in Web site design. He says in part that when designing for users from a high uncertainty avoidance culture, a designer must limit choices and make things clear. The objective is to make the experience as easy and error-free as possible. When designing for the opposite group from a low uncertainty avoidance culture, it's better to provide lots of choices and let the users discover surprises as they go.[7]

Avoiding Anxiety

As stated earlier in this chapter, change today is almost unavoidable. Globalization is responsible for some of that. Stress and anxiety come from its relentlessness, the creation of new corporate forms, and new competitors.[8] For managers today, learning to tolerate the resulting uncertainty is one of the ten strategies for success abroad.[9]

The necessity to cope with change, uncertainty, and related anxiety is not new. Throughout history, people have sought ways to reduce their concerns. They have looked to religion, laws, and technology to provide predictability and safety. Religion defines what is right or wrong, what is acceptable, and what is prohibited. Technology makes the environment safer. Laws ensure the security of the food chain and of products and to regulate gubernatorial, corporate, and personal behavior. All of these provide structure and make daily lives more comfortable.

Rules and regulations are another means to cope with change. These are welcome because they provide predictability, a structure for the ways people and companies will behave in given situations. Rules not only foretell how people around you will behave but also provide a guide as to how *you* are expected to behave. Follow the rules, and you will have done the right thing. Uncertainty avoidance cultures shun ambiguous situations.[10]

In the business world, avoidance of ambiguity may translate to structure in organizations with a preference for a clear hierarchy and chain of command. Authority is well defined. For example, decisions can be voiced only by the most senior people. The rank of the parties in a delegation are checked to ensure that each person will meet with someone at his or her own level. Titles, often including schools, appear on business cards.

It has even been reported that a manager was outraged about not being awarded a promotion simply because he graduated from school six months before his colleague who was given the post. In his eyes, graduating earlier gave him the edge. All of these measures help to make events interpretable, behavior predictable, and uncertainty reduced.

Rules with Flexibility

While societies that score high on the uncertainty avoidance scale may be distinguished by numerous rules, there is often some flexibility in how they're followed. Countries such as South Korea, Mexico, and Chile, which rank high on anxiety avoidance and prefer stability, are also counted as particularist, adapting rules to people and situations rather than applying them universally. Be cautious, however, in assuming that one dimension always connects to another. France, which also ranks high on the anxiety avoidance scale and is known for hierarchy and tradition, is very individualistic. A French woman working for an American firm complained not about the rules but about the expectation that she follow all the procedures. In a French company she and her colleagues could find their own way to get things done.

Learning and Failing, Failing and Learning

Innovation and *entrepreneurship* are two words associated with ideas and things that are new and different. The words bring up images of struggles and failures as well as excitement and successes. Mixed in there somewhere, too, is the anxiety factor. *New* and *different* likely equate to some level of change and thus uncertainty.

Attitudes toward failure, like those toward uncertainty, are shaped by both an individual's personality and culture. The following two quotations below give a good idea of the U.S. attitude:

Failure is an event, never a person.

—William D. Brown

I have not failed. I've just found 10,000 ways that won't work.

—Thomas Edison

These two quotations reveal important notions held about failure. Further, children are taught the saying "If at first you don't succeed, try, try again." This saying conveys the idea that returning to something that didn't work and repeating it is a good idea. It now implies that you can learn something in the attempt and apply it later. Edison's quote gives new meaning to the idea of trying again.

While consultants give examples of companies where this attitude is not the reality, where caution outweighs creativity, the notion of failure being a stepping-stone continues to draw people to the United States. "I can't believe that people think it's okay to start a new business when your first one didn't work out. That I can try something new when I'm almost 40," said a European woman now working in Los Angeles. A British woman said, "I just wanted to try [to] see what I could really do!"

A recent article in the *Economist* magazine regarding innovation made a point that "to be successful companies need to tolerate failure."[11] This is true no matter where they are located. But to adopt that viewpoint, it is helpful if the culture where the company operates is accepting of failure as part of learning.

If the culture adopts a punitive attitude toward errors, the results can be significant. According to Dr. Carol Craig, that is the case in Scotland. A Scot herself, she writes, "we are so frightened of failure that we avoid taking risks. In America the belief that everyone is equal translates into the notion that everyone is special. The Scottish variant feeds into the idea that no one is special. [The] biggest Scottish fears are failure and making mistakes." One outcome according to her is a lack of entrepreneurial endeavors. In a Global Entrepreneurship Monitor survey 40 percent of Scots agree with the statement "fear of failure would deter you from starting a business," a figure 10 percent higher than for the rest of the United Kingdom.[12]

Entrepreneurs Everywhere

It isn't only attitudes about change and anxiety avoidance or accepting failure as a component of learning that are necessary to support entrepreneurship and innovation. To create the necessary environment a country must have legal systems and financial markets to support business creation. India and China are examples of two countries whose economies are growing rapidly and yet have taken different approaches to that growth. China has encouraged foreign investment, and India has created infrastructure to support private enterprise.[13]

People can't predict the place or form of entrepreneurship. To expand their entrepreneurial community, Britain's Department of Trade and Industry set up a program to import entrepreneurs.[14] Originally looking to bring back British expatriates, it evolved to a broader program eventually luring Russian and South Korean businesspeople to relocate to the United Kingdom.

With or without sophisticated levels of support, entrepreneurs appear around the world. For example, in some Bangladeshi villages, women have gone into business as phone service providers. They buy cheap cell phones and sell phone time to their neighbors, making a profit on the transaction.[15]

To obtain more insight about the entrepreneurial culture in a variety of countries, consult the Global Entrepreneurship Monitor's (GEM) annual reports (www.gemconsortium.org). GEM is a research program started in 1999 that covered 10 countries and expanded to cover 37 by 2002. According to the 2002 annual report, the United States ranked as the country with the highest entrepreneurial activity, with Denmark, Finland, Japan, and France holding the lowest rankings. Not simply a numerical reporting system, the individual country reports provide useful background information.

Now We Know

What's new makes me happy. What's old makes me happy. Depending on who you talk with, each statement can be true. From the macro-level of national behavior to individual, personal preferences, the views about change, experimentation, failure, and innovation vary. A new procedure, technology, or idea is exciting for some, while the same thing frightens others. By understanding that newness isn't always eagerly welcomed, that attitudes and coping mechanisms vary, we are better able to create connections across cultures and distances. Simply remember: What's new makes me happy. What's old makes me happy.

I'm Glad I Know

You have to take some things slowly. I had a vision, what I thought was a terrific idea and it meant changing a few (to me) things. I was in a hurry and didn't listen well enough. No changes. Much aggravation. Lucky for me, I got to stay, to learn. Next time I had a great idea, I took some time, had some conversations, [and] listened. Took things step by step. Suddenly, it worked. Change sometimes has to be done piece by piece over time.

→→ *American quality manager*
in a denim mill in Tajikistan

CHAPTER 8

Trade Isn't New

I Wish I'd Known

A little more knowledge of geography would be useful. What country is next to another? I was never good at that in school. It didn't seem important. It's important now and still changing. New countries and new connections keep emerging. When we're on a conference call, I can't pull out a map to figure out the placement of cities (and countries) exactly. They're talking about shipping rates, and I'm still wondering exactly who the neighboring countries are.

→→ *American insurance agent specializing*
in international trade based in Los Angeles

I Wish They Knew

People don't realize that they can learn about trading relationships between countries, openness of markets simply by looking around when they travel. What are the hotel chains in a city? What makes of cars are on the roads? In Barcelona, you don't see the Ramada name but you do in Shanghai. Mercedes [Benz cars] seem to appear on the road in every country but not a Kia. Look on the streets as well as in the shops to build a picture of trade between nations.

→→ *American Department of Commerce*
official posted in Spain

Placement and Connections

Our early geography lessons teach us about continents, countries, mountains, and seas. We look at flat and round maps to see where these things are located. What we see are landmasses separated by bodies of water. With the exception of the boundary lines that separate countries, or rivers that run from one place to another, these images don't even hint at the connections that exist. Moreover, the depiction of the continents and countries doesn't provide an indication about the importance

76

of place, the fact that where a country rests on the globe shapes economic development.

In reality, geographic placement and ongoing connections among places are the basis for world trade. Geographic placement influences development of regions and nation-states. Historic and modern connections are at the core of trade today. Moreover, it is the expanding links that often grow out of trade among places, countries, and people that we refer to as globalization.

Globalization: An Ongoing Process

The friends and foes of globalization strive to convince us that it is the best or the worst of occurrences to befall modern life. Advocates for globalization point out advances in standards of living and the creation of new jobs. Foes of globalization speak of debt, environmental damage, and sweatshops. With all the passion that surrounds the topic, people seldom take time to consider the meaning and origins of the concept that is globalization.

Globalization is often presented as a movement of jobs from one place to another. Manufacturing moves from the United States to China, Eastern Europe, or Mexico. German and Japanese cars are made in the United States; McDonald's restaurants open around the globe. But looking at globalization simply as a shift of jobs and profits is an oversimplification.

According to Thomas L. Friedman in his book *The Lexus and the Olive Tree,* "globalization is a dynamic, ongoing process that involves the integration of markets, nation-states, and technologies. It is one that enables individuals and corporations to reach around the world, farther, faster, deeper, cheaper than ever before."[1]

The International Monetary Fund, an organization of 184 member countries established to promote international monetary cooperation and to foster economic growth, defines globalization as "a historical process, the result of human innovation and technological progress. It refers to the increasing integration of economics particularly through trade and financial flows; to movement of people (labor) and knowledge (technology) across international borders; with cultural, political, and environmental dimensions."[2]

After you read multiple explanations about the subject, you realize several points of similarity emerge. Globalization is about worldwide connections and speed; it is an ongoing, continuous process. While the global trade has historical roots, the current stage of the process is something different, "it is an economy with the capacity to work as a unit in real time on a planetary scale."[3]

We communicate more broadly and quickly. Originally people delivered messages on foot, then switched to riding horses and camels. Later, inventions such as the transatlantic cable and telephone carried the messages and began to connect traders who were far from one another faster. Today we've moved to webcasts, e-mail, and video conferencing. Information is transmitted in fractions of seconds from New York to London, to Dunshabe in Tajikistan, to Hong Kong, to Hilo in Hawaii. What took months for early traders to communicate now takes an instant. Events that were once significant only within a 20-mile radius of their occurrence now have an impact across the world. The movement of ideas has shifted from local to global, allowing people to trade and work together to create products and services not imagined a few years ago. We are connected quickly with benefits and costs. We see problems and opportunities. Globalization keeps moving.

Looking Back to Look Forward

To better understand globalization and today's interrelated world of business, finance, and culture, it's useful to look back in time. Globalization as broadly defined to include the movement of goods, people, and ideas isn't new. According to historians, trade beyond a person's local area existed even before the nation-state.[4] Kings drove trade, goods were moved by traders, and travelers spread their religions and culture. Although communication was slow and transactions were limited to goods with high value to weight ratio (spices, jewels, medicinal herbs), there was still trade.

Our purpose isn't to review in detail the history of world trade but to obtain a sense of its ongoing nature. With that in mind, here is a brief look at some significant points from the past.

It does not seem possible to identify a clear beginning, a first event of trade, or the beginning of globalization. What is clear is that it was part of early history. One of the earliest aspects of globalization can be traced back as far as 8500 B.C. with the movement of food and seeds for new varieties of crops.[5] As farmers selected the best growing plants to use to start new crops, varieties emerged that were particularly suited to their climates. The development of more reliable crops, the domestication of wild animals, and the exchange of these new sources of food were important in the development of the world. As food supplies improved, it was possible to support community activities other than hunting and gathering. Other specialties evolved, including trading.

If we consider food as a foundation of early trading, it's interesting to note that food plays a major role in trade agreements today. In 2004, the subject of government subsidies for agriculture was a key and volatile issue among the trading nations. Disagreements about the issue blocked development of complex trading agreements that had clear benefits in other areas. An old matter is thus a modern one, too.

Another important point in trade development came about in 325 B.C., when Alexander the Great negotiated peace with Candra Gupta, the dynastic founder of the Mauryan empire credited with uniting most of India. This event opened an eastward line among overland routes among people from the Mediterranean, Persia, India, and Central Asia.[6] While this is what we might call regional trade, it marked a change in previous patterns and made it easier to reach some markets.

About A.D. 100, a time known as "archaic globalization," evidence of broader links emerges. It is at this time that merchants and travelers went from England to China and Japan.[7] Further, the Silk Road, which connected Europe, the Middle East, and Asia, appeared. The Silk Road wasn't a road by current definition; it was a combination of different caravan tracks. From west to east went metals, wool, and glass and in return came spices, silk, and ceramics. Its importance as a trade route lasted until the late 1300s. Along with physical commodities, culture in the form of religion moved along this route. Both Buddhism and Islam spread with travelers and traders who used the Silk Road.

Moving forward through the centuries we come to the Holy Roman Empire, established in the ninth century, which "propagated not only religion but [also] trade and knowledge."[8] People traveled, and Latin became a common language. During the tenth century, the Song Dynasty (960–1279) came into power in China. In part, this is known as the period of the revival of Confucian thought and traditions (which had been replaced by Buddhism) and the expansion of trade by sea that

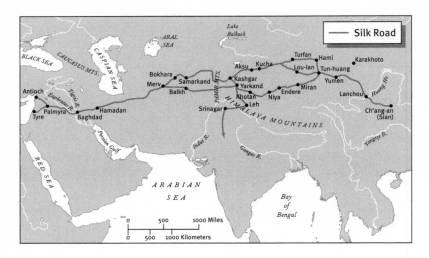

increased China's link to Europe. At the same time, African trade expanded both within the continent and externally with Europe and China.

As trade expanded, organizations of traders came into existence. There were specialized groups of merchants taking commodities from one port to another, creating networks. In the 1300s, two early multinational groups that formed in Europe were the Hanseatic League, based in northern Germany, and the Merchant Adventurers of London.

At that time, the 1300s trade was increasingly important, and China was a significant trading partner of many European nations. This was the period of the rise of the Ottoman Empire that spanned North Africa and the Middle East and connected Central Asia and India. (The Ottoman Empire lasted from the thirteenth to the twentieth centuries, ending in 1924 with the founding of the Republic of Turkey.)[9]

The rise of power of the Ottoman Empire not only expanded trade with Europe but also increased costs of trading in Asia for Europeans, which helped to drive the merchants of Spain to look for another (Western) route to the Indies and resulted in their discoveries in the Americas.[10] One well-known name from that period is Christopher Columbus. The 1400s are also known for the spread of Islam into Asia and the Viking ships that carried trade into northern Canada. In the 1500s, Italian banks began to dominate international commerce. The

Medici family in Florence had at least eight trading and banking branches across Europe. This is a reminder that finance is always an important component of trade.

In addition to precious jewels and metals trade also brought plagues that sprang up, diseases likely carried from place to place through the trading network. In Europe, from the 1300s to the 1500s, plagues reduced populations and thereby changed the ratio of people to land. Although the devastation was horrible, the changed ratio did allow some surplus production of food that could better nourish the population and be used to extend trade.[11]

Closer to modern history, the period from the 1600s to the 1800s was identified as proto-globalization. Europe, Asia, and Africa saw the emergence of the power of sovereign states with expanded taxation, military organization, and preindustrial manufacturing. State-sponsored trading companies supporting the colonial system provided the first type of international investment. In the early 1600s the Dutch led the world in commerce, and Amsterdam was a trading hub. In North America companies such as the Hudson's Bay Company, chartered in 1670, came into being. This company became a major figure in the development of Canada and is still active in the twenty-first century with 500 locations throughout Canada.

The 1760s are considered a globalizing decade in Western society, characterized by commercial expansion, imperial acquisition, and a knowledge revolution. Explorers surveyed and mapped the world; multilateral trade in consumer goods expanded. Further, tobacco became the first product to reach consumers worldwide and is still sold throughout the world in the twenty-first century. The next decades brought revolutions in the United States (1776) and France (1789) and saw the creation of the modern state and alliances based on military and business interests.

Modern globalization came about in the 1800s with the spread of industrialization, the move from trade in raw materials to manufactured goods, and the emergence of new states with specific legal and tax systems. The changes in this century, including the advancement of science and the emergence of new technologies, set the stage for the upheavals of the twentieth century.

The 1900s was a period that encompassed two world wars, multiple regional conflicts, and the Cold War. There was worldwide depression between periods of astounding growth. International expansion vied with isolation and protectionism. Astonishing technological advances included the telephone, telegraph, television, automobile, airplane, and computer.

By 1944, Webster's dictionary had added the word *globalization*, and the multinational corporation (MNC) gained importance in the world economy. Advances were made in building construction, medicine, and food production. Communism rose and fell. Countries split, and new ones were created. The European Union came into being, created the Euro zone, increased workforce mobility, and has poised for expansion. The world moved through stages of connection, isolation, free trade, and protectionism. Barriers to trade were lifted, revised, abandoned, and added. (See chapter 9 for more on this topic.)

Growing recognition of the importance of worldwide connections, threats, and opportunities led to the creation of new nongovernmental entities. The United Nations came into being in 1945, the World Bank in 1944, the International Monetary Fund in 1979, and the World Trade Organization in 1995. In response to increased concerns about the impacts of global growth, other organizations such as Amnesty International, Human Rights Watch, Sierra Club, and Greenpeace went from local entities to important participants in the global economy.

Geography Matters

Location matters. This statement is a fundamental fact for real estate businesses and for all types of businesses that are searching for the right place to operate. Where should we be? You'll often note a group of retail stores or restaurants gathered in the same area. They form a cluster in and around a location that they think will bring the economic benefits of revenue and profits.

Restaurants and retailers select locations that they believe will propel their economic development. If they are wrong, they can close and move to another place. Location matters for the economic development of countries, too. Unfortunately, unlike retailers or restaurants, countries cannot move. Although globalization, with its speed of communication, may possibly eliminate the constraints of geography, there are limitations because a country's location is fixed and immutable.

Two factors tied to geography, among others, stand out as major contributors or limitations to economic development: climate and water. Countries nearest to the equator, where the climate is the warmest, fall into the lowest ranks of economic development. Based on gross domestic product (GDP), tropical countries are poorer than temperate ones. It's not simply a matter of speed, as one author wrote: "The pace is slower in hot climates, one takes long lunches."[12] The implication may be that less is accomplished. While arguments can be made about perception, there are more measurable impacts.

First there is an impact on agriculture: Extreme heat, weak soil, droughts, and floods cause difficulty with growing sufficient food to feed the population. Additionally, the continuous warmth, not offset by frost and cold, allows the development of insects and disease-bearing parasites. Accordingly, there is a high risk of infectious diseases, which develop new strains even when treated. If the population cannot be properly nourished or healthy, the possibilities for broad, strong economic activity are limited.

Location matters from another standpoint: Where is the country in relation to water? Is it near the sea? Does it encompass navigable rivers? What are its water resources? Water is necessary for development as transportation, to grow food, and as a draw for economic activity. "There is no precedent for a country developing without harnessing its rivers and utilizing its water resources," says David Grey, the World Bank's senior water adviser.[13]

Countries whose access to waterways is limited by mountains or whose boundaries don't extend to the sea often suffer from limited economic development. Rivers serve as points where populations congregate, providing water for irrigation, thus leading to the availability of food. As transportation pathways, rivers open the surrounding area to travelers and traders.

An Invention That Made a Difference

If asked to name inventions that changed the world as it was known, people are likely to mention the airplane, telephone, computer, and Internet. Looking farther back they include the water wheel, steam engine, and printing press. It is also interesting to note one particular invention, not often recognized, that made a difference in the development of the world and its economy: eyeglasses. Lenses used for eyewear were invented earlier but made usable for wearing in the late 1200s. The effect was to extend the working life of skilled craftspeople by as much as 20 years. Further refinement of the lenses led to the invention of other tools and precision measuring devices.[14] That one invention had an impact on people, jobs, and, ultimately, trade.

Now We Know

Trade, whether local, regional, or global, isn't a new activity. Its roots go back thousands of years, linking continents and people and allowing the sharing of goods, services, and ideas. Globalization, the process of the rapid and broad movement of ideas and trade, continues at what seems to be an increasingly faster pace in modern times. Both trade and globalization bring uneven problems and opportunities to the people of the world. People intensely debate regarding the benefits and costs. No matter what a person's opinion is, the connection of people across boundaries and the sharing of work and ideas make globalization a fact of contemporary business life.

I'm Glad I Know

To be successful today, you have to know world history. That's how you understand how business works. It helps you understand why Poland worries about Germany even as they enter the European Union and become partners in the organization. Looking at past relationships between countries can tell you how to plan your internal structure. Are there representatives from countries that are historic enemies? Do people from one area believe those from another are untrustworthy? Know history, and you'll have special insights to business possibilities.

↦ *Paris-based partner in a global consulting firm,*
who is French and formerly lived in Chicago

CHAPTER 9

Beyond *the* Handshake

I Wish I'd Known

I could have saved myself days of waiting and significant expense if I'd done some research about the history and culture of the country I visited. I thought I'd found a perfect niche for my product: little competition, big population of potential users. I finally met with a consultant who was kind enough to tell me clearly that the reason there wasn't any competition was that there wasn't a market. My product didn't fit the culture. If I'd read some history before I went, done my homework, I'd have known. The trip was interesting, but for my purposes, a waste of time.

→ *American businessman*
reporting on his experience in China

I Wish They Knew

We are not a completely unsophisticated country. We may not have the marketing know-how of the United States, but we are also members of the World Trade Organization. We are part of the global trading community bound by the same rules as the United States, France, and China. We are a small country and have yet to develop all skills, institutions, and knowledge to draw many active trading partners, but we are part of the club, committed to participation.

→ *Kyrgyz telecommunications consultant*
living in Kyrgyzstan

They Thought About Trade

Trade has evolved from a local activity to one that is global. A friendly handshake is no longer enough to establish an exchange. Complex written agreements control the process. However, conflicting attitudes about the benefits and limitations of trade exist today as they did in earlier times.

The writings of Greeks and Romans as early as A.D. 100 reveal strikingly varied attitudes regarding the sea and trade. Some people saw the sea as bringing benefits such as vines for wine, grains, and the alphabet. Other people such as the Roman philosopher Horace (65–8 B.C.), thought ships were "ungodly" and considered the strangers who came on them as a danger to the population.[1] But it was more than the means of trade that were in question. The attitudes toward the people conducting trade were just as complex. According to the Greek philosopher Plato (427–347 B.C.) merchants and shopkeepers were inferior people.[2]

Of the many philosophers, economists, and others who contributed to these deliberations, three stand out for their contributions on the subject. In the late thirteenth century the writings of the Englishman Richard of Middletown established the idea of mutual aid as an aspect of trade. This concept is key to trade agreements today.[3] Today this mutual aid can come in the form of reduced tariffs or providing assistance in developing a product category for market.

Almost 200 years later, Francisco de Vitoria, a Spanish Dominican theologian and international jurist, stated foreigners could carry on trade, provided they did no harm to the citizens.[4] His writings were interpreted as defining trade as a right of nations, another idea that provides a foundation for current agreements.

It is the Scotsman Adam Smith whose book *Wealth of Nations*, written in 1776, is perhaps best known and most often quoted. His clear presentation has been referred to frequently over the course of more than 200 years as providing a "coherent framework for thinking about the economics of trade policy."[5] This work set forth the idea of benefits for individuals and nations from trade and specialization. It advanced the idea that international commerce can increase the aggregate wealth of all countries that participate in trade.

However, not all people agree that trade is beneficial or even equally beneficial to the parties involved. The debate continues even as the world's economies enter into more agreements and build closer connections. One aspect that complicates things is that trade agreements may have political purposes as well as economic ones. (See Table 9.1 for a partial listing of the trade alphabet.) An example of an agreement considered to link both political and economic issues is the Free Trade Agreement (FTA) between Australia and the United States that went into effect in January 2005.

TABLE 9.1 CAN YOU TALK TRADE AGREEMENTS?

(A PARTIAL LISTING OF THE TRADE ALPHABET)

ABBREVIATION	NAME
AGOA	Africa Growth & Opportunity Act
ASEAN	Association of Southeast Asian Nations
APEC	Asia Pacific Economic Cooperative
CAFTA	Central American Free Trade Agreement
CARICOM	Caribbean Community and Common Market
CBERA	Caribbean Basin Economic Recovery Act
CEMAC	Economic and Monetary Community of Central Africa
COMESA	Common Market for Eastern and Southern Africa
ECOWAS	Economic Community of Western African States
EFTA	European Free Trade Association
EPA	Economic Partnership Agreement
EU	European Union
EUMFTA	European Union and Mexico Free Trade Agreement
FTA	Free Trade Agreement
GATT	General Agreement on Tariffs and Trade
Mercosur	Southern Common Market
Merceuro	Mercosur and the EU
NAFTA	North American Free Trade Agreement
PTA	Preferential Trade Agreement
RIA	Regional Integration Agreement
SADC	Southern Africa Development Community
SACU	Southern Africa Customs Union
TAFTA	Transatlantic Free Trade Association
WTO	World Trade Organization

The two countries have been close allies since World War II, when the United States helped defend Australia. But the creation of the recent FTA may be about a more recent conflict, the one in Iraq that commenced in 2002. Australia was one of a limited number of countries to join the United States in that conflict. This relationship founded because of conflict expands to a partnership in commerce and will benefit Australia by granting it more access to the U.S. market. But Australia isn't limiting its trade and closer ties to the United States. Like other nations in the region, it is also extending its connections to China, a country that is increasingly important as a trading partner. The emergence of China as a regional power adds a new dimension for trade and politics throughout all of Asia.

The Balance of Trade

The word *globalization* is often used to stand for the concept of trade and is often discussed narrowly, focused solely on jobs that are won or lost. Depending on whether your hometown is in California's Silicon Valley, the textile region of North Carolina, or Pakistan, Mauritius, or India, jobs may be increasing or vanishing. Either way, headlines are made. Jobs move from Italy to Cambodia or from Guatemala to China. The losses fuel passionate rhetoric.

But what isn't included in the discussions is acknowledgment that along with the losses there are benefits. A move of jobs reduces incomes in one area and increases them in another. Benefits may include reductions in poverty, improved women's rights, and new protections against child labor. Overall, increasing trade by reducing barriers is socially benign.[6]

In the United States, for example, foreign companies invested $29.7 billion in 2003. Foreign direct investment in ownership of factories and office buildings equals the $2 trillion dollars that U.S. companies have invested in other places.[7] French wineries invest in Chile, and fashion designers sell their products in Russia and South Africa. Business goes in many directions. Trade is a two-way street everywhere in the world.

No matter what people's opinions of world trade are, globalization is still complex, difficult, and subject to starts and stops. According to the WTO World Trade Report 2004 released in September of that year, countries need good infrastructure and functioning domestic markets to take advantage of the possibilities of trade.[8] There must be a foundation to support trade and that includes the items mentioned plus transparent legal and financial regulations and stable governments. Throughout the world countries are at different stages of development for all these elements. Trade is ongoing, complicated, and seldom evenly balanced between nations.

From Handshake to Contract (Casual to Contractual)

Whether you see trade as an unquestioned benefit, as an ongoing problem, or as a challenge to be managed, it continues to grow. Neither trade nor trading patterns are static. One statistic captures that dynamism: More than one fifth of today's global export market is now held by economies that had little or no international significance when the twentieth century began.[9]

They have evolved because of the growth of trade and efforts to promote its continued growth. Agreements between the parties have also changed from handshakes between individuals who knew each other to complex agreements involving multiple nations. In response to the fact that trade is between nations and not just companies and individuals, organizations have been created to facilitate the process.

Peace and Trade for All: GATT and the WTO

The effort to expand and formalize trading rules by creating worldwide institutions can be traced to 1947 and the end of World War II. At that time a political goal was to create a more cooperative, peaceful world. The plan was to encourage open trade among nations, and thus replace the protectionist environment that prevailed from the 1930s through World War II.

An outcome of that effort was the creation of the General Agreement on Tariffs and Trade (GATT), signed in 1947. This agreement was an outgrowth of the early work of the United Nations. The concept of GATT was "to provide an international forum encouraging free trade, [and] regulating [and] reducing tariffs on traded goods."[10]

Further, it was developed to be a provisional agreement, intended to be replaced soon after coming into existence. However, the institution envisioned to replace it didn't materialize, and GATT lasted almost 50 years.

Twenty-three countries signed the original GATT agreement. The United States, France, and the United Kingdom were among them, but Germany, Japan, Russia, and Italy were not. This perhaps reflects both the political and economic realities of the postwar period. Germany,

Japan, and Italy were defeated in World War II, and their economies were destroyed. Rebuilding rather than trading was the key issue for those nations. Russia played the role of both friend and enemy; as a Communist nation, it considered itself opposed to Western democracies in all matters.

During the years of its existence, GATT conducted multilateral negotiations in an effort to reduce tariffs and eventually other barriers to open trade. These negotiations were called "trade rounds" and took place over several years. They were named for the host city or country. For example, the Tokyo Round held between 1973 and 1979 was the first segment of negotiations to tackle the subject of nontariff barriers.

Perhaps the best known of the negotiations is the Uruguay Round held between 1986 and 1994. This was the last of the GATT rounds and the most extensive. It is noteworthy for several reasons. Best known may be the creation of the GATT successor, the World Trade Organization (WTO). This was created as a permanent organization that would be able to settle trade disputes among member nations and enforce the decisions by levying fines and trade sanctions. The goal in creating this permanent organization was not to punish countries that did not abide by agreements but rather to create a predictable environment that would facilitate trade flows.

The other important aspect of the Uruguay Round was the creation of the first agreements regarding trade in services and intellectual property. This underscored the reality that trade had become more than simply an exchange of tangible things with weight and shape. Now it involved ideas as well. In addition, this was the first time rich and developing countries participated in negotiations.[11]

As of October 2004, the WTO has grown to 148 members from the original 125, with 30 additional observer governments, candidates for membership. Countries that become observers commit to joining within five years. During that time there are ongoing negotiations to ensure that the nations are prepared to participate.

Although the number of members has increased in the years since its creation, as of 2004 the WTO is an organization that is deeply divided. The latest stage of the Doha Round held in Cancún in 2003 ended abruptly without any consensus to continue. The division between developed and undeveloped nations had split even further.

Another group formed called the "Group of 20," which includes Brazil, India, China, Indonesia, Thailand, South Africa, Mexico, and Argentina. These are "not-so-poor nations" that account for more than half of the world's population. They are resource-rich, have manufacturing centers of their own, and are "economically dynamic." The fact that they are not satisfied with their role in world trade negotiations creates significant challenges for the WTO.[12]

According to a Los Angeles consultant who has worked on many trade agreements, "This is a precarious time for the WTO." In a recent speech he suggested the possibility that the WTO's days of being effective are limited. It is possible that the turmoil and conflict will tie their hands. "They can't even get the next round of Cancún scheduled, much less make any decisions. It's disappointing."[13]

One World or Many Parts?

Make it bigger. Then make it smaller again. Try to keep the big and the small connected. That's the challenge for the WTO as member countries create new agreements with specific countries, generally within a specific region rather than the entire WTO membership.

While the WTO was established to create a structure that all countries could adhere to, it was also recognized that not every issue could be handled on a global scale. Some matters are better addressed in a more limited environment. Therefore, regional agreements that offer special benefits to a few countries are allowed. These agreements vary in type and details and are referred to as Regional Trade Agreements (RTA) or Preferential Trade Agreements (PTA). Two areas that are often mentioned in this context are agriculture and environmental issues. But the components in regional agreements are extremely varied and reflect matters of local importance.

For example, in 2001 the European Union announced a grant to Syria to enable it to modernize telecommunications infrastructure and to train archaeologists so that historical sites could be better preserved. In 2004 Afghanistan negotiated with Tajikistan and Uzbekistan to create closer cooperation. In these negotiations the Tajiks were offering 200 scholarships for Afghan students to study technical subjects and would build bridges across the Amu Darya River that divides the two countries.[14] Trade gets supported in many ways.

Having approved the concept of regional agreements, the WTO stipulates that it must be notified when countries plan to establish one. As of 2004, there are 170 RTAs in force. All WTO members except Mongolia are either party to one or negotiating one. Projections are that there will be 300 such agreements in place by 2005[15] accounting for 55 percent of world trade.[16]

Many Places, Many Agreements:
Regional and Superregional

One reason for these groups' special agreements is that WTO agreements are binding on all the member countries and can be difficult to achieve. To be able to create relationships with specific countries, WTO members are forming agreements with one another and with others outside the WTO organization. Some agreements cover a region while others are between individual nations. Further, some of these regional groups are creating agreements with one another and with individual countries. For example, the European Union is a regional agreement. As a unit the EU is negotiating with Mercosur, another regional group that includes Argentina, Brazil, Paraguay, and Uruguay. If created, the result will be Merceuro, the first biregional group combining PTAs from two different parts of the world.

Mercosur looks farther than its immediate neighbors. In November 2003, it was announced that talks were under way to create an FTA that included India, SACU (South Africa Customs Union), and Mercosur. This would be an agreement that spans three continents and multiple cultures, languages, and stages of development.[17]

However, as these regional agreements continue to increase, the debate over the benefits of their roles has also increased.[18] PTAs increasingly overlap one another. According to a recent article in *Intereconomics*, " one-third of PTAs under negotiation are among trading partners that belong to different world regions." This not only complicates trade for businesses with locations in multiple places but also creates conflicts within the individual countries and regions. What benefits one industry may present challenges to another.

Another aspect of the preferential trading agreements is the fact that some are moving toward Regional Integration Agreements (RIAs). While it is understood there are political considerations that influence their creation, these agreements encourage "deeper integration" among countries. The RIAs are not limited to eliminating trade barriers but attempt to harmonize other economic policies, including environmental and labor standards, capital mobility, and technical assistance. Two well-known examples are NAFTA, involving the United States, Mexico, and Canada, and the European Union, which now includes 25 countries.

Friends or Foes? It Depends

Another aspect to consider regarding regional agreements is the history of the relationships between the parties. Were the parties always collaborative, or were they once enemies? Old foes as well as old friends join together in the interest of expanding their economies through trade. The European Union (EU) includes France, Germany, and Poland, all of which were once passionate enemies and are now allies.

It's easy to find evidence of these old tensions being ignored. For example, Russia and Japan, who were at war 100 years ago, are now economically cooperative with each other. Trade is encouraged between Europe and Latin America. A shared culture is cited as the reason that trade should be easy to expand. However, little is said of their

"I'm pretty sure 'pillage' has two l's."

joint history with reference to the aspect of invasion and conquest, and the subsequent years of Latin American countries as colonies of European nations. Similar issues exist with the negotiations between the EU and the African nations, as the relationship between colonial rulers and their colonies now evolves into trading partners.

When assessing trade agreements, history is only one element to consider. Agreements can be shaped and their ultimate success affected by the differences in culture, political systems, and levels of social and economic development. The varied viewpoints reflecting the dissimilarities become obvious in the WTO trade expansion negotiations. Topics such as protection for intellectual property are of major importance to countries such as the United States but less so for Cameroon or even China. In the midst of developing basic infrastructure when attempting to craft a market economy, other matters are more urgent.

Agriculture is cited in chapter 8 as an early element of trade globalization. A 2003 WTO ministerial conference in Cancún, Mexico, ended in discord based on issues surrounding agriculture. Countries such as Brazil, China, and India joined with more than 20 other developing countries to stand against the industrialized nations of the European Union, Canada, and the United States on the matter of agricultural subsidies. Just as individuals have varied needs during stages of their personal development so do countries, and for them the issues come to light when creating agreements related to trade.

Will They Happen?

The trend toward regional agreements appears set to continue. Following is a brief list of some connections predicted for the future.

China and the ASEAN nations plan an FTA by 2010.

South Asian nations (India, Pakistan, Bangladesh, Sri Lanka, Nepal, the Maldives, and Bhutan) with one fifth of the world's population may start eliminating tariffs in 2006.[19]

The United States plans FTAs with Australia, SACU (Africa), New Zealand, Egypt, and Morocco.

Russia, Iran, and India signed an agreement in 2001 to develop the North/South Transport Corridor. This corridor connects Mumbai with St. Petersburg via Tehran and Moscow. This route links the Indian Ocean and the Baltic Sea. Neighboring countries Iran, Kazakhstan, and Azerbaijan support the project and may also create cooperation agreements of some form. This new route does not only benefit the contracting parties. Western Europe will gain access to Asia using the Russian network of roads and railroads connecting them through Eastern Europe.[20]

Just as trade is dynamic and constantly evolving, so are the agreements that shape the paths of exchange.

What Comes Next?

As of this writing, the question in the trading community is how will the end of quotas scheduled for 2005 affect manufacturers, consumers, and all the other members of the trading community. Will China take over all apparel manufacturing, ending activity in Africa, Latin America, and Asia? How will the new licensing regulations and export fees established by China and pending lawsuits in the United States affect trade? What new activities, services, and professions will arise from the changes, and what countries will benefit? Agreements made over ten years ago will come into effect in a world economy that differs significantly from the one that existed then. Trade has changed many times during the course of history. It is about to change again.

Now We Know

Trade has existed throughout recorded history. Today it is local, global, and regional. Once again, as in the earliest times, attitudes about its benefits and costs vary and the opposing views are passionately debated. What is certain is that it is ongoing, increasingly connected, and subject to a variety of restrictions. Free trade is only free within the boundaries of the global, local, regional, and superregional agreements. These agreements are shaped by nations' desires to reach new markets and support emerging economies and even political viewpoints. Trade is an ongoing, ever changing activity linking nations, companies, and individuals.

I'm Glad I Know

During 40 years of working in Korea, Mexico, China, and Africa, I've learned a great deal about trade agreements. No matter how good the agreement or who the countries involved are, I can tell you that if you don't understand the culture in the marketplace you can't do business! Before you enter a new market, in addition to checking on the trade agreements and financing, you must learn the culture. No matter how good your product or service, without understanding the culture you can't do anything.

>>— *California-based American business adviser*
specializing in textiles and apparel

CHAPTER 10

Canada *and the* United States

I Wish I'd Known

I could have used some history lessons and some geography, too, to understand more about Canada and Canadians. Growing up, Canada was a place for vacations known for great pastry and beautiful scenery. I was surprised to learn that it's as varied as the United States with regional differences in style, language, and history.

→→ *Protocol consultant based in California*
working with Canadian counterpart

I Wish They Knew

That Canada is not the United States. Please don't say "we Americans" one more time! We Canadians are North Americans in the sense of where our country is located, but we are not Americans, part of the United States of America.

→→ *Canadian businessman working with U.S. firms*

Connected but Separate

On the landmass identified as North America there are a total of 38 countries. Canada and Greenland, the world's largest island, are the two most northerly of these countries. At the southern extremity is Panama, bordering the continent of South America. It is the third-largest continent in the world, extending almost to the North Pole at its most northerly part and south to within 500 miles of the equator. (The largest continent is Asia, and the second is Africa.)

In this chapter we will focus on the two countries whose names typically come to mind when we say North America: Canada and the United States. Mexico and the other countries that are considered North America because of their location on the physical continent are discussed in chapter 11.

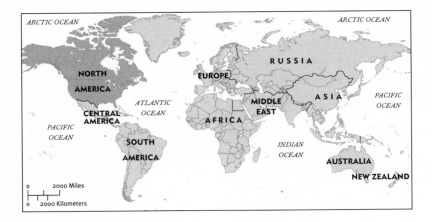

Both the United States and Canada extend coast-to-coast from the Atlantic Ocean on the east to the Pacific Ocean on the western extreme. They are two of the largest countries in the world, with Canada ranked as number five, immediately following the United States at number four.[1] It takes slightly less than six hours to fly from Los Angeles on the West Coast of the United States to New York on the East. During that flight people pass through four of the six time zones that exist in the United States and Canada.

Within the boundaries of the continent there are vast differences in climate and geography. Temperatures reach extremes of cold in the north and heat in the deserts. The northern part of Canada is not populated because of the extreme cold and frozen ground, which makes it uninhabitable. There are mountains, rivers, lakes, and streams. Both Canada and the United States began with rich mineral endowments and expansive forests. Both experienced the excitement and challenges associated with the discovery of gold and the ensuing gold rush. Today the challenge is not in managing the bounty of natural resources but in guarding the remaining deposits. The focus has shifted from freely consuming resources to managing them, using them properly to maintain and improve the environment.

More Than Shared Borders

It isn't simply the 3,987-mile shared border, the longest undefended boundary in the world, that accounts for the deep connection between the two countries. Nor is it that the only land border of Alaska, a U.S. state, borders Canada. At no point does Alaska have a physical connection to the rest of the continental United States. Its other boundaries, in addition to Canada, are three bodies of water, the Arctic Ocean, Bering Sea, and Gulf of Alaska. Even the daily trade that exceeds one billion dollars each day doesn't explain the intensity and

depth of the connection. It is instead the shared experiences, especially of early history.

There are shared roots as former British colonies, although Canada, unlike the United States, obtained its independence from the United Kingdom through treaties, not war. (However, Canada has had full control of its affairs since 1931 and adopted a constitution in 1982 that still connects to the British Commonwealth with the Queen of England as the head of state.) While Canadians did not have their own war of independence, some of them did participate in the U.S. Revolutionary War, fighting on the side of the British. However, it wasn't only the Canadians who supported the British but also residents of the thirteen colonies. While the revolution is taught "as [a] noble fight, a popular uprising against taxes and imperialism, it was also 'bloody civil war' where perhaps one of five Americans wanted to stay a British subject.[2] American Indians also fought independence, thinking it would lead to further encroachment on their land."[3]

Canada not only provided soldiers to the British but also offered a place of refuge for Americans who fled the war. U.S. refugees went to Ontario and Nova Scotia where they were among the British subjects who transformed Canada from its status as mainly a French territory to becoming predominately British. Today about 10 percent of the population are direct descendants of those refugees, the losers of the war.[4]

Although they fought on opposite sides in the U.S. Revolutionary War, the two countries have also been allies. They fought together in World War I and World War II. However, historical events were somewhat repeated in the sixties when young U.S. citizens went to Canada seeking refuge from the draft that required them to fight in the Vietnam War. Differences arose again in 2002 when Canada elected not to join the United States and Great Britain in the Iraq conflict. This was a reminder that Canada is a friend, connected by history, geography, and trade and an ally in *most* global activities, but also an independent nation with its own viewpoint.

The Beginnings

In a sense the roots of both countries are simultaneously similar and different. They are similar from the perspective that Europeans traveled great distances, on dangerous journeys, to start new endeavors in places that were almost entirely unknown. They were people willing to take enormous risks to follow their visions. Their motivations, however, were different. The first people to come to Canada were there to expand their commercial activities. They were fisherman, trappers, and traders. The first settlers in the 13 colonies were people looking primarily for religious freedom, the ability to speak and act according to their beliefs.

While their motivations as just described here sound noble and exciting, it is important to maintain some perspective. As one member of the U.S. embassy staff based in Asia said, "You have to remember the United States was founded by people that today we would call misfits."[5] There were people who didn't, couldn't, or wouldn't conform to the societies where they were raised. Some were good, and others were not. What they did share was a desire for change and a willingness to try something new in a new place.

What the people arriving in all parts of the continent both discovered was that the lands weren't entirely empty. In Canada there were Indians and Inuits (Eskimos) who had been there 10,000 years before the Vikings arrived in A.D. 1000. In fact, the name Canada originated from a Huron-Iroquoian word *Kanata,* meaning "village."[6]

The British colonists met the Indians, or Native Americans, upon arriving on the East Coast. (Native Americans is the term most often used to refer to the Indian tribes that inhabited the United States prior to the arrival of the colonists. More broadly this term can apply to all indigenous people of the Americas, including the Eskimos.) The story of the newcomers' relationship with the native population fills many books and is too complex to be discussed in detail. However, much of what is now the United States originally belonged to the Native Americans. Some was taken by force, some by treaty, and some was allowed to remain in the control of the descendants of the original tribes.

More than 200 years passed before either Canada or the United States reached its full size and independence. The United States fought multiple wars and paid millions of dollars to acquire all the land known as the 50 states. Creation of the United States can be dated from the confederation of states between 1775 and 1783. A little more than 100 years later in 1896 it had acquired territory from France, Mexico, Russia, and Spain and grown to 45 states. The last 5, ending with Hawaii, were added between 1907 and 1959.

After the Vikings the Europeans arrived in Canada, beginning with the French in the early 1500s. They were followed by the British in the late 1500s and the Scottish fur traders in the 1600s. Although seldom mentioned in recaps of Canadian history, the Scots were key to the fur trade for decades. Their descendants went on to create railways, banks, and universities and hold public office. Canada's first two prime ministers were Scots.[7] However, the influence of the British and the French is more obvious in modern-day Canada.

Canada acquired the land that makes up the majority of the country through the acquisition of what was known as Rupert's Land in 1870. This vast parcel, stretching from Ontario in the east to the Pacific Ocean in the west, and extending from the United States border in the south to the most northerly tip of today's Canada, was owned by the Hudson's Bay Company, granted to it when the company was a fur trading enterprise known as the Company of Adventurers of England. (Today the Hudson's Bay Company is still active. Founded in 1670 and in business continuously for more than 300 years, it is the largest retailer in Canada with over 500 locations and 70,000 employees.)

In 1867, prior to the acquisition of Rupert's Land, the British created the North America Act that created the Dominion of Canada, bringing together the existing provinces. They selected the name Dominion to avoid calling it a kingdom that would have annoyed the Americans. It took more than 80 years, until 1949, when Newfoundland and Labrador joined the other colonies and territories. But in 1931 Britain had granted control of its affairs to Canada. It relinquished the last of its control over Canada in 1982 when the Charter of Rights and Freedoms guaranteeing fundamental human rights to all Canadians was signed (except by Quebec).

Must We Stay?

In countries as large and diverse as the United States and Canada, it is not surprising to discover periods of internal strife. For most of their histories the people of the United States and Canada have expressed their political differences through impassioned speeches, peaceful marches, and vigorously contested elections. Words have been the weapons used in battle.

In contrast, when the United States was a union of just 34 states, between 1860 and 1865, its citizens fought in the bloody U.S. Civil War. At issue was the future of the union itself. Would the states, north and south, stay united, and if so, would slavery be allowed to continue? The issues were so closely connected, so fundamental, that more than a century and a half later it's difficult to separate them. The underlying question was how the new country would develop. Was it to be really a country where everyone was equal, where opportunity was open to all, or was there to be a rigid class system, another form of royalty and serfs?

The Union, the United States, remained intact and grew. Slavery ended, although the issue of equal rights for all regardless of color, ethnicity, religion, or now lifestyle continues to be a topic for discussion, legislation, and struggle. But since that time, most of the combat has been with words rather than guns.

While the question of breakup in the United States was resolved by the end of the 1800s, as recently as 1995 a portion of the Canadian population was considering the idea of secession. Should Quebec stay or go? Would Canada's largest province, one sixth the size of the United States housing one fourth of Canada's population, remain part of the country?[8] For them the secession issue was not linked to a fundamental right of freedom, as was the case with slavery in the United States, but rather one of identity.

Was Quebec French or Canadian? It is a part of Canada originally developed by the French. Quebec City was founded in 1608, and the region was named New France in 1663. Although French culture and language were dominant in the area, the French ceded the territory to the British in 1763. Although it has been part of Canada since that time, French is still the first language of up to 80 percent of the population. Signs in public areas are in both English and French. Even the legal system is French. Quebec uses civil law based on the Napoleonic Code while the remainder of the country uses common law from the British tradition (like the United States).[9] Culturally, Quebec is considered the most European of the regions in customs.

Notwithstanding its long cultural and historic ties to France, Quebec is a province of Canada and as such an integral part of the country and its economy. Although the efforts to create an independent Quebec continued for more than 30 years beginning in the 1960s, voters rejected a referendum in 1995. The challenge of competing alone in the global economy may have outweighed the desire for independence. Canada, like the United States before it, avoided a split and the union still stands.

Connected by Games

History and billion-dollar trade are not the only things that connect the two countries. There's a sporting link, too. The Canadian city of Toronto is home to a U.S.-based Major League Baseball team. Toronto also fields a team in the National (not International) Basketball Association. Of the 30 teams in the National Hockey League, 5 are from Canada (Calgary, Ottawa, Montreal, Vancouver, and Edmonton). International teams play in national leagues. Is it a surprise that Canadians think Americans don't know they are an independent, separate nation?

Safe, We Hope

Neither Canada nor the United States was invaded during any of the wars of the twentieth century. They were participants in the conflicts but at a distance. Many of their people died, overwhelmingly people in the military, but their cities remained untouched. Citizens of both countries believed themselves to be safe from foreign aggressors, secure within their borders, in their cities, and at home. It wasn't until the events of the twenty-first century with the attack in the United States on September 11, 2001 that this changed. That day destruction arrived within the North American borders.

Although Canadian cities weren't directly attacked, they felt an impact. In an immediate sense their airports became holding places when U.S. airports were closed. A passenger on a flight from Italy returning to Los Angeles spent 5 days in Toronto, unable to get home. But more important than the events in the immediate aftermath and the new regulations for travel and transportation are the changes in outlook. People in both countries lost the belief that they were safe and secure at home.

The People

Measured by population, the United States is the third-largest country in the world, following China and India. One quarter of its people are non-white and 12.5 percent of Latin American descent. Although the median age now stands at 35.8 years, one quarter of the populace is younger than 18 (see Table 10.1). Population forecasts indicate that by 2050 only 50 percent of the U.S. population will be Anglos and that the Asian and Hispanic populations will have tripled from 2003 levels.[10]

The Influence of Immigration

Judging by the immigration statistics, people from varied parts of the world consider the United States and Canada good destinations when seeking to relocate. Over the past two decades, the United States has absorbed approximately 20 million immigrants.[11] Canada has one of the world's highest immigration rates and is one of the most culturally diverse countries. One sixth of all Canadians are foreign-born, a number exceeded only by Australia.[12]

The reasons people move to new countries are widely varied. Some make the journey to join family who have already established themselves and sent for them. Others come for education or are sent by their employers. These people often decide to remain in the country after an assignment is completed. What makes a place attractive is an individual matter. For one professional woman raised in Hong Kong, Toronto offered something special. Her family liked Hong Kong but preferred living in Toronto. She explained it in terms of their lifestyle as follows:

> It was so much easier to live there. We have two children and our house was bigger. We could have friends to visit with their children. There was room for everyone. Entertaining could be done at home where we could relax and talk as long as we wished. In Hong Kong there's no room. You go out to dinner with your friends. Conversations are limited by the time spent at the restaurant. It's more formal, less relaxing. Life was just easier for us in Canada.

TABLE 10.1   POPULATION AND AGE

COUNTRY	POPULATION	MEDIAN AGE	15–64
United States	296,208,476	35.8	66.9%
Canada	31,846,900	38.2	68.7%

Source: CIA World Factbook 2005 and Internet World Stats 2005

While both countries have a long history of accepting immigrants, there have been differing opinions about how to best add them to their society. America has prided itself on being a melting pot, creating an "American" culture. Canada on the other hand has encouraged ethnic groups to maintain their distinct cultures and did not regard itself as a melting pot. In both places newcomers often clustered with others from the same area. There are large Chinese populations in Toronto, Vancouver, San Francisco, and New York. There are Cubans in Miami and Koreans in Los Angeles.

The first waves of immigrants arrived, learned English, sent their children to school, and became part of the melting pot of America. However, the concept does not fit the United States well today. The population is increasingly diverse, and that diversity is recognized and valued. (Depending on what one reads in the United States, either the Asian or Hispanic population is the fastest-growing segment within the country. In either case the numbers are growing, and the importance of both groups is increasing.)

Regional Diversity

The variety of people can be described not only by ethnicity but also by age, religion, and lifestyle. Furthermore, in the United States diversity differs by region. For example, there is a large gap between the average age of the five states with the youngest populations (Utah, Texas, Alaska, Idaho, and California) and the five states with the oldest (West Virginia, Florida, Maine, Pennsylvania, and Vermont).[13] There is more than a ten-year difference between the average age in Utah and that in Vermont. This difference in age may translate into varied viewpoints on national issues such as Social Security and education, affecting selections of elected officials and shaping local, state, and national policy. More often, people's experience of diversity is dictated by where they live, even within a specific state. Is home Sacramento, California, with a large Caucasian population, or San Jose, with a broader mix where a playground is filled with people from Asia, Central America, and Caucasians from California and Utah?

The diversity of population, age, and education create the regional differences within both countries. One easily observable difference is the styles of dress. According to one writer, what's fashionable depends on what part of Canada you're from. The appropriate style may be athletically sexy, internationally chic, or creatively expressive depending on whether you're in Vancouver, Toronto, or Montreal.[14]

Within the United States it's not only fashion but also how people live that is stereotyped through a regional lens. New York is known as a culturally sophisticated center where people rush frantically and are rude and impatient. Los Angeles is notorious for its freeway traffic and is envied for its weather and beaches. Long known as the film capital of the world, its residents have to work to overcome the image of being only interested in getting suntans. The competition between the two cities is ongoing. Dallas presents another view of the United States, with tall men wearing cowboy hats and women covered in sparkling jewels. While there is some truth in all these images, there is some fantasy, too.

What is true for cities in the United States and Canada is the reality that each one is different. From the look of the buildings to the sounds of the voices of their inhabitants, each place has a style, personality, and special culture. These are big countries with many cities, big and small, each one unique in some way.

People and Their Language

One element that allowed the United States to become the melting pot was the common language of English. English is often designated "the language of business," because you can find a person from France and a person from China speaking in English in Beijing because that is the one language they have in common. However, there is a wide variety of languages spoken in the United States. One person in seven speaks another language besides English at home.[15] English is still the language for business and government but evidence of the variety increases. Signs and voter ballots are printed in Korean, Japanese, Spanish, and Chinese as well as English.

The growing importance of Spanish in the United States is evidenced by the significant increase in the number of Spanish language newspapers. In 1990, there were 14 such papers nationwide. By May 2004, that number grew to 40. This expansion of newspapers matches the growth seen in magazines and radio and television programs targeted at the increasing Hispanic market.[16]

The Canadian government uses two languages, English and French, both accorded that official status in 1969. As mentioned before, French is the primary language used in Quebec. Visitors can find signs posted in both languages. Italian is considered a "strong third" choice due to the influence of Italian immigrants who arrived after World War II.[17] However, as immigration continues from Asia, Chinese grows in importance. Language choices expand as population diversifies.

Online and on the Phone

The United States ranks as number three, with 68.8 percent of the population, for most people using the Internet, slightly behind Sweden at 74.3 percent and Hong Kong at 69.9 percent. Canada ranks as number six with 63.9 percent. Both countries have millions of mobile phone users, with approximately 53 percent of the U.S. population and more than 40 percent of the Canadian population (see Table 10.2).

Linked by Trade

The trading relationship between the United States and Canada continues to grow in importance. According to a U.S. Department of State country report, the bilateral relationship between the two countries is perhaps the closest and most extensive in the world. In addition to the trade in goods and services, almost 200 million people cross the border each year. Trade with Canada is larger than the total U.S. trade in goods with the original 15 members of the European Union.[18]

Although the business and news reports focus on the United States trade with China and seldom mention Canada, the value of U.S.-Canada trade is almost three times that of U.S.-China trade, $393,936 billion versus the Chinese total of $180,798,000.[19] Canada sends 85 per-

TABLE 10.2   CELL PHONE AND INTERNET USAGE

COUNTRY	CELL PHONE	INTERNET USAGE
United States	158,722,000	197,895,880
Canada	13,221,800	20,450,000

Source: CIA World Factbook 2005 and Internet World Stats 2005

cent of its exports to the United States and receives 85 percent of its imports from the same source.[20]

But the numbers do not tell the entire story. The first formal agreement aimed at opening the two markets, the Canada-U.S. Free Trade Agreement (CUFTA), was signed in 1989. This was superceded by the agreement known as NAFTA, the North American Free Trade Agreement, which has three parties: Canada, Mexico, and the United States. This agreement led to much closer integration among the three countries. Raymond Chretien, Canadian ambassador to the United States, sums up the trade relations: "We are looking north and south far more than east/west as we did in the past."[21]

As it did when it was signed, NAFTA arouses strong emotions, both for and against. According to Jeffrey E. Garten, writing for *Business Week*, merchandise trade between the United States and Canada has grown twice as fast since NAFTA was signed as it did before.[22] While most analysts agree that trade has increased, the most passionate arguments surround the question of job growth. According to Garten, the impact has been "pretty much a wash." But lost in the rhetoric about jobs are several key items worth noting. This was the most extensive trade agreement between advanced industrial nations, the United States and Canada, and a developing one, Mexico. Further, it included the environment and labor in its provision establishing a standard for agreements that followed.

NAFTA also marked a commitment to a deepening integration within the continent that is being continued and extended through the work toward the Free Trade Area of the Americas. This agreement will involve 34 countries with widely differing sizes and levels of economic and political development. The stated goal is to reach accord in 2005.

Not everyone is enthusiastic about the addition of new trade agreements nor about the extension of areas they cover. While businesspeople praise additional protections for intellectual property, an article in the Canadian magazine *Macleans* presents another viewpoint.

> To Americans culture is a commodity and to Canadians it is the fragile essences of nationhood. We've become more citizens of a continent and less of a country; does the new free trade agreement include culture or not? Are intellectual property laws really

about culture and the right to other cultures to come into your world?[23]

But neither the United States nor Canada limits its trading activities or agreements to the Americas. Both are members of the WTO; both have extensive trading activities. Canada is the fifth-largest world trader after the EU, the United States, Japan, and China.[24] They both have agreements with Chile and Israel. The United States has recently added agreements with Australia and Singapore.

The ROW (Rest of the World)

People from outside the United States joke that if Americans drew a map of the world they'd show it divided into two sections, the United States and the ROW, the rest of the world. No matter how many trade agreements are inked, people in France, China, Chile, and Canada observe that Americans who come to do business don't know much, if anything at all, about their countries. Their complaint isn't that Americans don't know the proper form of greeting rituals or titles; it's more than that. Tim Walsh, a New Zealander who has worked in the United States, expressed the widely heard sentiment as follows: "I often wished that Americans knew more about the world and the people outside of America and that there [are] other quite different approaches to life and the ways of living life than the American ways."

Although some may take issue with these comments, the American reputation for being naive about the world beyond its borders has been earned over time. A December 2003 interview with Orin Smith, the chief executive of Starbucks, is revealing. His response to the question "What have you learned now that you've opened more than 1,000 stores outside the United States?" hints at the problems. He said in part, "The biggest lesson is not to assume that the market or the customers are just like Americans even if they speak English. They're not. This happened in the United Kingdom and in Canada. They are not Americans. They are different."[25]

This situation, America's internal focus, is not surprising given the development and size of the United States. It is a big place, and until recently, it was the largest single market in the world. No matter what the industry or service that an American company provided, there were buyers within the home borders. There was little need to confront differences in currency or culture to grow a business.

But it isn't only a matter of size that shaped the attitudes. It's necessary to remember that the United States is a country made up of immigrants. The people who founded the country and those who continue to arrive have always come to the United States because they seek better lives. Each has made a personal calculation that life in the United States is better than life in his or her own country.[26] Because of that, many immigrants seek to become "American" and to adapt to American culture. The United States produced the world's most varied and integrative culture.[27] Although the United States is no longer the "melting pot" of the nineteenth and early twentieth centuries where all traces of people's origins disappear, there is still a push to adapt to the new environment.

Further, the easy learning about people and places that comes through travel still doesn't occur for many Americans. With little vacation time, generally no more than two weeks a year, holidays are limited. Thanks to the variety within the country, people don't need to travel great distances or struggle with language and currency differences. International travel was something that was to be enjoyed upon retirement when there was time to take a grand tour. While there are signs that this attitude is changing, you can still find young adults in California who have never been to an airport, much less taken a plane to visit a foreign destination.

An Australian on assignment in California says the limited travel experience of American professionals always surprises him. "We all travel as soon as school's done. If you grow up in Australia or New Zealand you know you're headed for Europe, Asia, or the States for at least several months before going to work. It's just how it is. We go, and we learn about new people and new places."

The lack of travel experience, coupled with the scarcity of international news available in newspapers and on television, limits Americans' abilities to understand the issues of importance outside their areas. One way to change this pattern was suggested by a U.S. embassy official working in Asia. She would require all Americans not only to travel but also to spend their junior year of college studying outside the

United States. Even more specifically, that year would be spent in a country whose language and culture would take them out of their comfort zones. She believes this is one of the best things that could happen to promote long-term U.S. interests globally. Further, immersion in a new place will do more to help Americans understand the complexity of the world than all the books and articles they can read. Only then will the ROW be people and places with history and commerce, not just words on a page.

McDonald's: More Than a Restaurant

For American companies that want to begin their international expansion, Canada presents a logical first step. So it was for McDonald's, which opened its first international unit in British Columbia in 1967. In 2004 Canada had 1,300 McDonald's outlets employing 77,000 people.

McDonald's now operates 30,000 units in 119 countries throughout the world. It has come to represent the spread of American culture, and for many, it is the symbol of economic development and globalization. According to Harvard China scholar James L. Watson, "the start-up date for McDonald's corresponds to the emergence of a new class of consumers with money to spend on family entertainment."[28]

Thomas L. Friedman said in his book *The Lexus and the Olive Tree* that no two countries that had McDonald's in their borders had ever fought a war with each other. This was true until the 1999 war in Yugoslavia changed things. But Friedman's idea that when countries reached the stage of development sufficient to attract and support a McDonald's, them not being able to afford to go to war still makes some sense.

McDonald's is so much a part of the global economy and conversation that the *Economist* magazine, based in London, created a Big Mac Index. This is a tool used to compare purchasing power parity between countries. Using the price of a Big Mac, they attempt to decide the relative value of each currency. Is the euro overvalued compared with the real of Brazil or the zloty of Poland? Does the dirham of Morocco equate appropriately to the Canadian dollar? Check the price of a Big Mac, and you'll know.

Business Their Way

The similarities in the U.S. and Canadian business cultures are not likely to be a surprise. According to research done by the Center for Creative Leadership, Canada ranks closely to United States and the United Kingdom on scales that measure cultural orientation.[29] For both, time is linear, hence, punctuality is important and expected. Both countries are more individualist than collectivist where the efforts of individuals are valued and equality is important.

Not to suggest that they are absolutely identical. Canadians are more quiet and introspective than Americans, according to Steve Prentice, president of a Toronto consulting firm.[30] It's important not to appear boastful.

As with all generalities, we know that all of the characteristics will vary from person to person, influenced by ethnicity, education, age, and even regional patterns. The French impact in Quebec was discussed. However, in both countries there are many regions with distinct personalities. People from Ontario are considered fairly reserved when compared with those from British Columbia. In the United States people in the Midwest and Southeast are considered more conservative than their counterparts on either coast. Businesspeople in the Northeast are known for efficiency that some see as rude while southerners are noted for their warmth and hospitality. While people share similar underlying values, their speech, dress, and rules of protocol may differ.

When participating in a roundtable discussion about Canada's role in the world, the Canadian-born ABC commentator Peter Jennings made an interesting observation. He said, "Americans take action; Canadians influence. We make our way somewhat more subtly on the world stage than the United States has ever been obliged to do."

Another way to look for differences in the conduct of business is to review the Transparency International Corruption Perception reports. Their definition is that corruption is the "abuse of public office for private gain." The annual reports measure the degree to which corruption is perceived to exist among a country's public officials and politicians. The scores range from 10 (completely clean) to zero (absolutely corrupt). A score of 5.0 is considered the separating line between clean and corrupt. The 2004 Corruption Perceptions Index shows Canada with a score of 8.5, placing it as number twelve in the world. The United States scored 7.5, placing it at the seventeenth spot along with Belgium and Ireland.[31]

Now We Know

Neighbors are connected by history, language, geography, and trade. The United States and Canada are so closely linked that for some, it's difficult to remember they are two distinct countries with unique histories and cultures. No matter how similar they seem, they each are distinct and proud of their differences. When doing business in either place you need to remember these are not the United States of North America but two separate countries, linked but independent of each other. They are neighbors and friends, but they are not identical twins.

I'm Glad I Know

It's useful to be a little more formal when you begin doing work in Canada. Not as casual as you'd be in Los Angeles. People are friendly and helpful, but you have to be cautious about how you sell yourself and your services. Don't overstate your case. It's so similar sometimes you forget that you're not home!

→→ *California-based consultant*
working in British Columbia

CHAPTER 11

Latin America

I Wish I'd Known

Spanish doesn't count in Brazil. If I'd done some research, I would have discovered that translating all my materials into Spanish would be useless in Brazil. Worse yet, it revealed my ignorance. In Brazil the language is Portuguese.

→→ *American fashion designer*
based in California

I Wish They Knew

I wish people understood that you cannot generalize about countries in Latin America. Each one is different. People must understand that if they plan to do business in the region.

→→ *Chilean government official*
working in Los Angeles

Where Is There?

If you told your friends you were flying to Latin America, they would have to ask for more details; otherwise, they couldn't guess your destination. Latin America isn't a place, nor is it a continent, like Africa, that is divided into multiple countries. Rather it's a name, a definition of a group of countries.

The nations we know as Latin America are primarily Spanish-speaking and are geographically situated in North, Central, and South America. The French created the name in the late 1800s. For them, Latin America included countries that spoke Spanish, Portuguese, or French. They included countries occupying parts of North America and all of Central and South America. (This did not include the Caribbean islands and English-speaking countries of the Bahamas; Belize; Jamaica; Trinidad; Tobago; Barbados; or Suriname, originally a

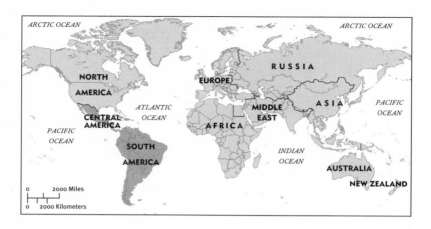

Dutch colony.) So Latin America is more of an idea of countries that are related to one another even if they are not physically adjacent.

The majority of the 22 Latin American countries are located on the continent of South America, the world's fourth-largest continent. Within its boundaries are the world's longest mountain range, the Andes, and the largest rain forest and river, the Amazon, with a water volume exceeding that of any other river in the world.[1] The other countries are technically part of North America, beginning with Mexico at the most northerly part covering the stretch of land that reaches to the South American continent. In some cases this area is referred to as Central America. To see where a specific country is located refer to Table 11.1.

The differences between the countries begin with their range in size. Ecuador (less than 110,000 square miles) is smaller than the state of Nevada. In contrast, Brazil, encompassing over 3 million square miles, is larger than the continental United States. Some nations such as Bolivia and Paraguay are landlocked. Chile's entire western border is the Pacific Ocean. (To this day there is tension between Chile and Bolivia over territory Bolivia claims, theirs but is now part of Chile. That area would have given Bolivia access to the ocean.) Some of the variations are startling. For example, there are parts of the Atacama Desert in Chile where no rainfall has been recorded, as well as the world's largest tropical rain forest in Brazil.

But the differences are not simply size and geographic endowments.

Today Latin America is known for its political and economic extremes and is thus among the world's most challenging regions in which to do business.[2]

Given the size and complexity of the region, this chapter will not attempt a country-by-country report. Rather, the focus is to provide an overview of Latin America along with some key points about three countries: Mexico, Brazil, and Chile.

When thinking about Latin America, it's necessary to keep in mind two opposing ideas. These are countries that have an enormous amount in common. They generally share the Spanish language, a growing

TABLE 11.1   WHERE ARE THEY? NORTH, SOUTH, OR CENTRAL

SOUTH AMERICA	CENTRAL AMERICA	NORTH AMERICA
Argentina	Costa Rica	Mexico
Bolivia	Cuba	
Brazil	Guatemala	
Chile	Haiti	
Colombia	Honduras	
Ecuador	Nicaragua	
El Salvador	Panama	
French Guiana		
Guyana		
Paraguay		
Peru		
Suriname		
Uruguay		
Venezuela		

middle class, and an increased outward focus and effort to update their economies and educate their populations.

However, one must also be alert to the reality that "differences that distinguish social, economic, and historical context cannot be emphasized enough."[3] No matter who you talk to about Latin America, the theme that emerges is that the differences are important.

Looking Back

It is important to remember that history throughout the Americas began long before the Europeans arrived in the 1500s. Aztecs, Incas, and Mayans created empires, built cities, conquered other indigenous tribes, and were overwhelmed by the Europeans. Their descendants and those of the many other indigenous peoples are today's Latin American population, as varied as the geography of the continent. In Mexico alone there are 56 different ethnic groups.[4]

While their history before the Europeans' arrival differs, the appearance of the Spanish, French, British, and Portuguese marked the start of shared experiences. Unfortunately, the commonality of their history for the next 300 years, from the 1500s to the late 1800s, was the reality of colonial rule. The European kingdoms controlled both North and South America during those years. These were turbulent years for the Europeans at home and abroad. The countries of Latin America felt those upheavals, too.

Close at hand was the American Revolution, wars that involved Mexico and the United States, and ones that were more regional. For example, Chile fought Bolivia, and Peru battled against Ecuador. In Europe, Napoleon's conquest of Spain and Portugal in 1808 briefly freed Brazil only to have the Portuguese royal family take control again. The American War of Independence from 1776 to 1783 along with the French Revolution in 1789 provided inspiration for Spanish America to revolt. The desire for freedom spread through the region, and the 1800s became a time of wars for independence.

By the beginning of the twentieth century, independence from colonial rulers was a reality. Rather than creating a time of peace and prosperity, however, it ushered in a period of additional troubles. From wars of independence many places moved to turmoil and civil war.

What these countries underwent was not so much a change of government, a new president or prime minister, but something daunting. To be independent, they had to do more than create a new structure. They had to overcome the traditions, beliefs, and patterns of behavior handed down over centuries by Indians and colonial rulers. Not everyone believed that independence was the best course of action. (The American colonists raised some of the same questions, as discussed in chapter 10.)

However, unlike the United States with its history as a British colony, the countries of Latin America had experienced more than 300 years of being ruled from afar by a distant monarch. That reliance on the monarchy and traditional society influenced the cultures and practices found today. The rigid inequality and hierarchy existing in the twenty-first century are a reflection of colonial experience. There is a concentration of wealth in a small portion of the population. As a well-educated Mexican woman explained to the author once, "The differences are okay. Everyone is comfortable with their role and place."

To have an idea of the difficulties countries had in achieving their goal of becoming independent and well managed, consider the example of Ecuador, which had 62 presidents in less than 100 years, from 1830 to

1948.[5] In Peru, during a 26-year period there were 4 military dictator-ships, 2 major coups, and 1 democratic government.[6] The histories of each country have similar tales of dictators, coups, elections, and internal strife.

But it wasn't only the internal and regional issues that affected these countries. Their economies were affected by world events, including the worldwide depression in the 1930s and both world wars. Not all the countries were aligned with the United States during World War II. Argentina, Paraguay, and Uruguay were supportive of the Germans, and many Germans immigrated there. The Cold War between the United States and the Soviet Union also affected Latin America. Each side endeavored to gain allies in the region, leading to support for various regimes and civil wars, all of which contributed to the ongoing turmoil in the region.

No, You Can't Go There from Here

Although the Cold War has ended and Russia is now a U.S. ally rather than an enemy, one Communist country still exists nearby. Cuba, an island off the coast of Florida, is still considered an enemy of the United States. Because of that, travel to Cuba, with few exceptions, is prohibited for U.S. citizens. According to a speech made by Treasury Secretary John Snow in February 2004, the travel ban is intended to "cut off American dollars headed to Fidel Castro."[7] This attempt to limit funds going to Cuba dates back to 1963 and President Kennedy's imposition of economic sanctions. The war is over, and the war goes on. You can't go there from here.

Trade Is Regional and Global

A quick glance at the list of trade agreements that include Latin American countries reveals the growing importance of regional and global trade for these nations. They are all members of the WTO, thereby linked to one another and the other 120-plus countries that are members. But following the pattern of the twenty-first century, they are not relying on just one entity to help expand their trading opportunities. There are regional agreements among Latin American countries and pacts among individual countries and those outside Latin America. For example, Mexico has more than 30 agreements, the most of any country. These include ones within the region as well as Japan, Singapore, and EFTA (Iceland, Liechtenstein, Norway, and Switzerland).

There are agreements within the Andean nations (Colombia, Ecuador, Peru, and Bolivia). There is CAFTA, the Central American Free Trade Agreement, connecting El Salvador, Honduras, Nicaragua, and Guatemala. Mercosur brings together Argentina, Brazil, Paraguay, and Uruguay. Best known of the agreements is the North American Free Trade Agreement (NAFTA) linking the United States, Canada, and Mexico. All of these may be joined by the FTAA, the Free Trade Agreement of the Americas, which will connect 34 countries from North to South America including Canada, the United States, and Mexico. Its Web site is translated into four languages: English, French, Spanish, and Portuguese.

These agreements among Latin American countries created regional markets that stimulate investment as well as trade. Notwithstanding the list of groups designed to expand trade in 2004, few Latin American companies earn more than 50 percent of the revenue outside their domestic markets.[8] One goal of the agreements is to change that statistic and provide an environment so that companies can expand within the region.

Along with the regional agreements and participation in the globally focused WTO, connections are being created with regional groups. Mercosur and the European Union (EU) are working toward a free trade agreement. When combined, both represent a market of over 600 million people. The European Union, with its expanded membership of 25 countries, has a market of more than 450 million people. The Mercosur countries consist of 230 million people and have a combined GDP of one trillion U.S. dollars. For the Latin American countries, the EU offers an enticing market for the agricultural sector.

The trade pact between Mercosur and the EU and bilateral agreements between the EU with Chile and Mexico are noteworthy when you consider the tumultuous shared history of the parties. These agreements bring together former colonies with their colonial founders (Spain, Portugal, France, and Britain are all EU members) whom they fought against to achieve their freedom. Now they work together to benefit both groups. In a recent interview, the trade commissioner from Spain in Los Angeles pointed out the deep cultural ties between Spain and Latin America. Because of the historical connection, he felt that Latin America is a natural market for Spain.

Even with the potential for trade due to cultural links and the size of the market, the benefits may not be easy to achieve. The Eastern European countries that are the newest members of the EU may challenge Latin America for opportunities in the EU market. For companies located in Europe, it will be easier to go to the new member states, such as Estonia or Poland, in search of less expensive land and labor. By locating a plant in the Czech Republic, a company can export duty-free into the 450 million EU, but distributing from Brazil it has access only to a "less affluent Latin American subregional market."[9] Even with trade agreements to create additional access, the challenges still exist for companies and countries alike.

In considering the regional agreements within Latin America, it is necessary to pay careful attention to determine which countries are participating in which groups. You can't assume a country is participating in an agreement with its adjacent neighbors. The factors leading to the decisions aren't always clear from reading the news nor are the issues of who makes the decisions. Two examples relate to CAFTA. The original negotiating group included all five Central American countries: El Salvador, Guatemala, Costa Rica, Nicaragua, and Honduras. However, Costa Rica, the richest nation in the group, dropped out, not wanting to open its telecommunications and insurance industries.[10] Eventually, at the urging of the United States, the Dominican Republic was added to the agreement although it doesn't belong to the customs union among the five Central American countries. In 2005, negotiations are still ongoing for the Free Trade of the Americas agreement that includes 34 countries. Among the group are the three NAFTA countries, the CAFTA nations, and others including the Bahamas and Saint Lucia. As of this writing, the future of that agreement is uncertain. Watch the news for developments.

Trade agreements aren't the only things that indicate the development of a country. A less formal indicator is the appearance of McDonald's, a sign of an emerging middle class with disposable income. In Latin America, McDonald's restaurants are located in Mexico, Argentina, Guatemala, Brazil, Chile, Colombia, Ecuador, Paraguay, Peru, and Uruguay.

Three Countries to Watch

While each of the countries within Latin America is important to understand, three stand out in this chapter. Mexico has a unique link to the United States. The two countries share a physical border, a historical relationship, and economies connected by extensive trade. Brazil is noteworthy for its growing influence in the world as one of the leaders of the developing nations. Along with China, India, and Russia, its importance in the formulation of world trade agreements is growing. Chile is the first country, aside from Mexico, in this region to have a Free Trade Agreement with the United States and as such occupies a special status with the United States.

Mexico

In 1929 the Institutional Revolutionary Party, or PRI, emerged as the leading political party of modern Mexico. It controlled the presidency and held national power for more than 70 years. With this nearly absolute power, the party became notorious for perceived corruption. Its power finally came to an end in 2000, when Vicente Fox, representing the National Action Party (PAN), was elected. In a sense this was a revolution, the overthrow of the oldest, long-standing ruling party by ballots not bullets. Fox promised reforms for the country, less corruption, more jobs, and a better life for the people. The next elections, in 2006, will reveal whether the Mexican people believe Fox's election and the change from PRI rule achieved these goals.

A change in the controlling party was not the only revolution that Mexico experienced as the twentieth century ended and the twenty-first began. The country moved from a poor country known as the neighbor south of the United States to a serious participant in the world economy, America's second-largest trading partner.[11]

The economic revolution focused on trade was propelled by the agreement known as NAFTA the North American Free Trade Agreement. "NAFTA got Mexicans to think forward and outward instead of inward and backward," according to Luis Rubio, president of Mexico's Center of Research for Development. No matter what a person's opinion of the costs or benefits, it is generally agreed that NAFTA brought significant positive changes for Mexico.

While Mexico may seem familiar to many Americans and is part of North America, it isn't like the United States or Canada, its NAFTA partners. Mexico is also different from other Latin American countries, notably in communication styles. Mexicans are more reserved and indirect. Mexico is much like Japan, where a "yes" may mean many other things besides "yes." Venezuelans complain because they don't understand the Mexicans' avoidance of parlaying unpleasant news.

On scales that rank countries on cultural dimensions, Mexico is shown to be collectivist with an emphasis on an in-group. This strongly contrasts it with its two NAFTA partners, who are among the most individualistic of countries. The same contrast appears when you look at attitudes toward time. The United States and Canada share a perspective that time is linear and scarce. Mexico, however, even more than Chile, Brazil, or Argentina, perceives time as plentiful and cyclical.[12]

NAFTA's supporters and opponents are equally passionate. One group is certain it has created great benefits, while the other is positive it has been extremely detrimental. Both sides present cases filled with statistics and examples to support their views. It may take another decade to resolve the issue, but meanwhile it's useful to know the points where the parties concur and the topics of disagreement occur.

NAFTA was the first agreement to bring together countries at dramatically different stages of development. The United States and Canada both have highly sophisticated global economies. Mexico, at the time of signing, was considered a developing country. The debates about the benefits of NAFTA started as it was being drafted. The differences today begin with the varied understandings of what NAFTA was to achieve. Was it a bill mainly to expand trade and investment, or was its promise broader than that? Was it to speed integration of the economies, create new jobs, and improve the environment? Our interpretation of the intent influences the perception of the results to date.

On the matter of the goal to increase trade, it is agreed that trade has grown dramatically. This facet has been a success. Mexico's exports are nearly double those of the rest of Latin America. Foreign direct investment grew from $3.47 billion to $13 billion.[13] Mexico moved its economy to the ninth largest in the world from its pre-NAFTA spot of 15.[14] (At one point trade was growing at $1.2 million per minute.)[15]

But the excitement about the increase, according to the opposition, is offset by what they see as faults in the area of job growth and environmental improvements. Although the final agreement contained special amendments to address these issues the results have still been disappointing. Although new jobs were created in Mexico, wages still fell and poverty rose. Furthermore, in some cases workers were not allowed to organize to present their grievances about working conditions. In the United States job losses to Mexico were substantial. At least 500,000 people qualified for retraining based on a provision in the labor segment of the NAFTA documents. It wasn't only Mexican factory workers for whom NAFTA was a disappointment. Small farmers, especially those who grow corn, suffered when that market opened to United States producers. (Consumers of products made from corn may have benefited by reduced product prices, but that is difficult to document.)

Unfortunately, the problems for Mexico with the creation of jobs continue to increase. Ten years after the jobs moved from the United States to Mexico, they have moved from Mexico to Asia. Mexico can no longer claim to be the lowest-cost producer in the world. In fact, some people thought NAFTA would reduce competition from Asia. One scenario had Chinese firms moving to Mexico, building factories, and training local workers to access the North American market. One group of investors created an impressive industrial park complete with golf course and housing for both management and workers. Their plan was to lure Asian textile companies to Mexico. They had ample supplies of land, water, electricity, and workers to be trained. Although there was some initial success, the results were not all that had been imagined. Instead industries shifted, communication became easier, and production continued to move to China.

Spending to improve the environment didn't grow as imagined at the onset of NAFTA. Not everyone faults NAFTA, however. According to a Los Angeles consultant with 20 years of working experience in Mexico, the problem with environmental protection has to do with lack of public spending. That, he says, can be traced back to lack of tax collection. Mexico has one of the lowest tax collection rates in the world. Although it is the world's tenth-largest economy, Mexico ranks with Sri Lanka and Ethiopia when it comes to generating revenue to pay for public services."[16] Without tax revenues, the government doesn't have money to spend on education, the environment, or other infrastructure to support job growth and trade.

In attempting to determine the success or failure of NAFTA, people point to a variety of related issues. Some point out that unlike the European Union when dealing with countries at differing stages, the planners of NAFTA did not include a "social protocol." There was no special allotment of resources to help the poorer nation, Mexico, adapt. Increased trade was expected to solve all the problems and provide all the benefits. Others look in another direction. "Mexican society at large has failed or refused to adjust to globalization," says Luis Rubio, president of the Center of Research for Development, a Mexico City think tank.[17] Others add that the government has not invested enough in education to create a vibrant, competitive workforce.

No matter what the reasons, current public opinion both in the United States and throughout Latin America is cooling toward the idea of expanded trade agreements. It's likely to mean that there will be opposition to the upcoming Free Trade Agreement of the Americas. Reflecting the limited enthusiasm in other countries, the current versions of the treaty is less extensive than originally intended.

Brazil

Although there's no written history before the arrival of the Portuguese colonists in the 1500s Brazil, like other countries in this region, was inhabited long before then. It, too, experienced hundreds of years of colonial rule, until 1822 when it won independence as the Empire of Brazil and later became a republic, in 1889. It is the fifth-largest country in the world with a population of almost 180,000,000. Its experience since independence is similar to that of other Latin American countries, filled with emperors, dictators, and upheavals. But today it is a democratic republic with a democratically elected president. Moreover, it is a country whose influence now extends beyond the borders of South America.

As mentioned earlier in the chapter, Brazil has joined with India, Russia, and China as a leader of the developing nations in the area of trade and trade policy. Although Russia is not yet a member of the WTO, it is associated with the other three countries of this group called the BRICs. Their influence has been evident in the Doha Round of trade talks, especially around the issue of agricultural trade. The three countries—Brazil, China, and India—present a powerful voice as they are home to two thirds of the world's farmers. They are the key players in a group crafting an agreement regarding agricultural subsidies and tariffs with the EU and the United States.

But Brazil is not only active within the WTO. Negotiations are under way with Ukraine to create bilateral agreements to open commodity and service markets. Additionally, President Lula visited Africa in 2004 and opened discussions of what was labeled an "economic superhighway" to link South Africa's Gauteng province to Brazil.[18] While details of how this will be accomplished are incomplete, it is a noteworthy discussion that is attempting to create a trading connection between two such different countries. Active also within the region, as the largest country within the Mercosur group, Brazil has been influential in creating the emerging trade agreement with the European Union.

While trade agreements are being debated and negotiated, business continues both locally and globally. Multinational companies identify consumer niches, and products are created or modified to meet a need. One such example is the new washing machine created by Whirlpool, the American appliance company, to be marketed in Brazil. Whirlpool spent over $30 million to develop a washing machine for the low-income consumer, women who never owned a washing machine before. It's smaller and less expensive than Whirlpool's typical machine. Consumer response has been good. For the women who use them, they not only get clean clothes but also some free time. "I no longer spend hours bent over a washing tub," says one mother of six. "Now I can tend to my children, cook dinner, and visit my sick mother."[19] (Small washing machines aren't appearing only in Brazil. At a recent visit to a Wal-Mart store in Dalian, China, the author noted a customer purchasing a machine with a maximum capacity of three shirts.)

According to Nelson Possami, manufacturing director of a Whirlpool plant in Brazil, the creation of products for specific markets such as Brazil, India, and China are the "second wave of globalization. These are products that appeal to the market beyond the well-to-do, the initial global consumer."[20]

Chile

To some Americans, Chile is known as the country that supplies fish, specifically the Chilean sea bass popular on menus and in markets. For others it's not fish that makes Chile a well-known place but rather the wine, often the inexpensive red wines. But Chile is important for the United States as more than a source of fish or wine.

In June 2004, *World Trade* magazine issued its annual report of the top 30 countries for trade expansion. The rating considered 23 factors including population, e-readiness, inflation, stock market capitalization, legal system, and government form. The highest-ranking Latin American country was Chile at number 27.[21] (The only other Latin American representative was Mexico at number 30). Number 1 on the list was the United Kingdom; China ranked twenty-fourth.

A Chilean trade commissioner for North America attributes the high ranking in part to the Chilean business community. He recently commented that in Chile the attitude of the people as well as the institutions promote doing business. Institutions, trade agreements, and tax codes are important. But most of all, people have to remember that business is about people.

In addition to its high ratings in the factors analyzed for the *World Trade* report, Chile scores in the top range for entrepreneurship in the Global Entrepreneurship Monitor's 2003 report. It is grouped in the top five worldwide along with Korea, Mexico, New Zealand, and Uganda.

Given these rankings, it may be no surprise that Chile was selected to be a party to a free trade agreement with the United States that was signed in 2003. But its activities are not limited to one country or one area. Chile has agreements with the European Union, Canada, Iceland, Korea, and Singapore. In addition, on a regional level there is a preferential trade agreement with Andean countries plus agreements with Argentina, Bolivia, Colombia, and Mexico. It is an associate member of Mercosur and started trade talks with India in 2004. Chile, along with Brazil and Mexico, is looking broadly to expand its opportunities.

As Americans seek to expand their connections to Chile, it's important to know that respect and courtesy are highly valued. One way to show respect is to learn to speak some Spanish. A California consultant working with American companies trying to set up partnerships in Chile noted that Americans assume everyone will speak English. People who come to the United States from Chile speak English, but Americans don't speak Spanish in Chile. Chileans want to be helpful so they all try to speak English. However, it isn't always easy for them. If Americans would just learn a little Spanish, they could create better business relationships. Relationships are the key to doing business in Chile and speaking the same language even a little bit definitely helps.

On the Phone and Online

As communication is the key to building relations, it's interesting to note that connecting with people in the region is becoming easier. Cell phones are increasingly common for business and personal use. One person in five in Latin America is now a cell phone user.

Mexico and Brazil have the largest number of subscribers, while in Chile 48 percent of the population have cell phones. Venezuela has seen a dramatic growth in cell phone usage, from 40 million in 1990 to 118 million in 2004. This significant change is driven in part by the emergence of prepaid services that enable lower-income users to have access to the phones.

Entrepreneurs have turned cell phones into personal enterprises. They purchase multiple phones and the minutes. In Venezuela one man displayed seven phones on a table on a main street in Caracas. He told a reporter that he makes more money selling minutes than he did as a carpenter.[22] (Using cell phones as a business is not unique to Latin America. This contemporary version of a pay phone has been reported in Asia and Africa. Where there is a population with limited income, landlines are expensive or nonexistent, but because of people's desires to communicate, the cell phone entrepreneur has a ready market.)

Internet usage is as varied as the countries themselves (see Table 11.2). According to Internet World Stats Web site, 2005 data show population penetration varying from highs in Uruguay (34.5 percent) and Chile (25.8 percent) to lows in Nicaragua (1.6 percent). Notwithstanding their growing global importance, Brazil and Mexico still lag in Internet penetration. Brazil's 18,660,650 users represent only 10.3 percent of the population.

TABLE 11.2	INTERNET USAGE		
SOUTH AMERICA	**INTERNET USERS**	**CENTRAL AMERICA**	**INTERNET USERS**
Argentina	5,600,000	Costa Rica	800,000
Belize	30,000	Cuba	120,000
Bolivia	270,000	Guatemala	400,000
Brazil	18,660,650	Haiti	80,000
Chile	4,000,000	Honduras	168,600
Colombia	2,732,200	Nicaragua	90,000
Ecuador	569,700	Panama	120,000
El Salvador	550,000		
French Guiana	3,200	**NORTH AMERICA**	
Guyana	125,000	Mexico	12,250,000
Paraguay	120,000		
Peru	2,850,000		
Suriname	20,000		
Uruguay	1,190,120		
Venezuela	2,310,000		

Source: Internet World Stats, February 2005

Mexico at an 11.8 percent penetration represents significantly less than its NAFTA partners, the United States at 68.8 percent and Canada at 64.2.

The People

When Americans talk about doing business in Latin America, their first observations are often about the warmth and hospitality of the people and their surprise about the flow of activities and flexibility of schedules. For people who are accustomed to precise deadlines and schedules, understanding the Latin American perceptions of time can be challenging. For example, descriptions of the view of time from three Latin American countries are as follows:

- The pace of life is not regulated by the clock as much as by events and people. (Belize)

- The joy of an event or needs of an individual are more important than the demands of time schedule. (Venezuela)
- Time is flexible according to the importance of the appointment. (Paraguay)

While these three comments indicate similar attitudes within the region and contrast with the North American mind-set, it is still important to remember that not all people or countries share this exact viewpoint. The Chilean attitude toward time is closer to that of the U.S. perspective than it is to Mexico's. Brazil falls between the two. No matter what the shade of difference, Americans are expected to be prompt and are likely to have to wait.

Awareness of the differences in ideas about time can reduce the potential for day-to-day frustration in doing business with Latin America. However, another aspect of the culture that must be understood is the differences in the society.

The societies of Latin America are considered more unequal than those of most other regions of the world. The richest earn 48 percent of total income and the poorest just 1.6 percent (compared with developed countries at 29.1 and 2.5 percent).[23] According to a World Bank study, this inequality is deeply rooted and has changed little over time. This poses a serious obstacle to development in the region since income inequality affects access to services such as education and health care.

In Mexico the poor have found a way to express their displeasure with events beyond their control. They go to Mexico City, home to 21 million people, the world's second-largest metropolitan area, the seat of the national government, and march in the streets. In 2003, there were 1,700 demonstrations, including ones where the protesters brought along their cattle. It's estimated that every demonstration costs $4.5 million in lost business in the city.

One federal lawmaker said it amounts to a civil war without guns. The demonstrations bring into conflict businesses' rights to operate, people's rights to get to work, and their quality of life in the city with the right of free speech of the people who voice their grievances.[24]

TABLE 11.3   POPULATION STATISTICS

SOUTH AMERICA

	POPULATION	ANNUAL GROWTH (%)	MEDIAN AGE
Argentina	37,584,554	1.02	29.2
Bolivia	9,073,856	1.56	21.1
Brazil	181,823,645	1.11	27.4
Chile	15,514,014	1.01	29.8
Colombia	45,926,625	1.53	25.8
Ecuador	12,090,804	1.03	23.0
El Salvador	6,470,379	1.78	21.4
French Guiana	186,917	2.25	28.3
Guyana	877,721	0.61	26.2
Paraguay	5,516,399	2.51	21.1
Peru	28,032,047	1.39	24.6
Suriname	460,742	0.31	25.8
Uruguay	3,444,952	0.51	32.2
Venezuela	24,874,273	1.44	25.2

CENTRAL AMERICA

	POPULATION	ANNUAL GROWTH (%)	MEDIAN AGE
Costa Rica	4,301,172	1.52	25.7
Cuba	11,295,969	0.34	34.8
Guatemala	12,328,453	2.61	18.4
Haiti	8,175,610	1.71	18.1
Honduras	6,669,789	2.24	19.0
Nicaragua	5,766,497	1.97	20.2
Panama	3,074,146	1.31	25.9

NORTH AMERICA

	POPULATION	ANNUAL GROWTH (%)	MEDIAN AGE
Mexico	103,872,328	1.18	24.6

Source: World Internet Stats 2005, CIA World Fact Book 2005

Population

What looking at these statistics doesn't reveal is the dramatic growth of the population in the years from 1930 to 1990. During that time Latin America's population quadrupled to 450 million. (See Table 11.3.) Only Africa, growing from 154 to 642 million, exceeded that rate of growth.[25] Also during that time there was migration from the country to cities. Combine the growth in population and longer life span due to generally better health and you can visualize the pressure on infrastructure and governments to provide for their people.

Business Their Way

One key to doing business in this region, according to the head of the Latin American consulting practice at a Los Angeles legal firm is to remember that all the countries have distinct classes in their societies. The very rich, the rich, a fragile middle class, and a large group that is poor. When businesses come together, usually the initial agreements are made at a senior level, drawing from the rich and very rich in Latin societies. At this level cultural differences are few. All parties are well-educated, well-traveled, and experienced businesspeople.

But at the implementation stage when mid-level managers begin to work together, the differences surface. For example, in Mexico the person managing logistics may have only a high school education and little or no travel experience. The U.S. counterpart today may have a degree in logistics management and have traveled or studied abroad. Not only are there differences in culture in terms of values and attitudes toward hierarchy but also there are differences based in life experiences. That's where the challenges begin.

Another aspect of doing business in this region is the importance of personal relationships. Business is done between people as much as between companies. Even lending is sometimes done on the basis that a person is recognized in the community and considered to have good character rather than on financial documentation. The traditional ways of doing business still exist.[26]

Another indication of the general approach to doing business is to look at the Transparency International Corruption Perceptions Index.

Two countries in Latin America rank about 5.0, the dividing point among countries considered to have corruption problems from the ones that don't. The two countries scoring higher than 5.0 are Chile at 7.4, just one point behind the United States, and Uruguay at 6.2. The remainder are below 5.0, with El Salvador at 4.2 and Haiti at 1.5, ranked 145 of 146 countries surveyed.

Now We Know

Latin America isn't a place. Rather it's the designation people frequently apply to countries that are part of North, Central, and South America. They vary in size and geography but share a history as colonies of European nations. The populations are ethnically diverse, and the languages are varied, but some elements of culture are shared. Throughout the region, relationships are the key to doing business while the focus on time is left to the more northerly countries in North America. Although they are now independent nations, freedom from colonial masters didn't generally bring peace and prosperity. Each country struggled to become free and in some cases the struggles continue. Although trade continues to expand, regionally and globally, economic development in the region varies from country to country.

To know Latin America, people must learn about each of the countries, one by one.

I'm Glad I Know

I'm glad I know not to jump into a new country without doing my homework. For me that means developing a business plan and then taking it to the country I'm targeting. No long distance research will tell me if I'm on target or not. The only way to be sure is [to] talk to people in the market. I always contact the attorneys, accountants, brokers, distributors, and freight forwarders. Everyone knows something or someone. You have to go and meet the people in order to see if you're on target.

→→ *An American independent*
apparel agent based in California

CHAPTER 12

The European Union

I Wish I Knew

Before I started doing business in the United States I didn't really understand that all business is transaction based. In Europe it's relationships that matter. You can't just start talking business with people. They will be put off, offended, suspicious, and simply tune you out. You have to get to know each other first. Here it's the reverse. It's business first, or they think you're not serious. It feels odd but you learn.

→→ *French businessman*
working in New York

I Wish They Knew

Coming to Germany don't think of just fast cars and beer. It's not possible to understand a culture or people's behavior without considering the overall system and the historic framework of the environment. I believe that people would learn much faster about another culture if they forgot their preconceived notions and opened to the new experience.

→→ *German businessman*
working in California

Where Is It?

The ads of U.S. airlines offering special fares for travelers headed to Europe frequently highlight London, Paris, and Rome. For the experienced or adventurous, there are also fares to Amsterdam, Barcelona, and Lisbon. For many years and for many people, these 6 cities in 6 countries, the United Kingdom, France, Italy, the Netherlands, Spain, and Portugal, meant Europe. Today Europe can be defined as more than 25 countries stretching from the Atlantic Ocean in the west almost to the Black Sea in the east. In the north it reaches the Arctic Ocean and its southern border is the Mediterranean Sea. According to the atlas, Europe is part of the continent of Eurasia and as such can be seen as a

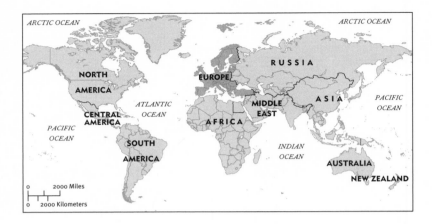

peninsula that reaches all the way east to Central Asia, touching the Caspian Sea. However, most often Europe is considered unique and separate from Asia, separated by history, politics, and culture.

In this chapter our Europe will extend only as far east as the borders of Russia, Belarus, Ukraine, Romania, and Bulgaria. In the west, Europe extends into the Atlantic Ocean to encompass the island nations of the United Kingdom, Ireland, and Iceland.

This part of the world has a long and complex shared history. As one reads about the region it's easy to be caught up in a sense of ongoing conflict. The history of each nation tells of independence and power alternating with periods of war; of expansion and contraction; and of winning and losing colonies, with boundaries enlarged, reduced, and changed again.

Empires grew and dissolved. In the 1800s the Austro-Hungarian Empire included Slovenia, Slovakia, and the Czech Republic. These countries were joined together as Yugoslavia in the 1900s, became independent nations in the twentieth century, and now in the twenty-first century are joined together again as members of the European Union. In the north, Sweden once ruled Norway and Finland. The Netherlands, ruled by Spain in the 1600s, controlled Belgium in the 1800s. Germany ruled Poland, France, Estonia, Denmark, the Czech Republic, and more during the 1900s. The activity on the continent reflects only part of the em-

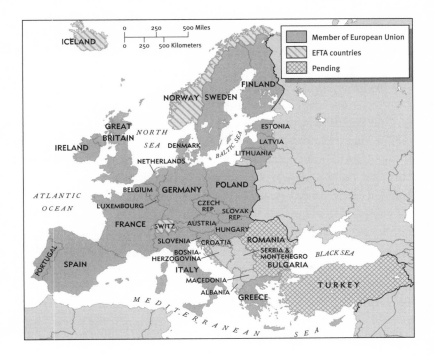

pires of the European nations, which at times stretched east to China and included colonies in the Americas as well as throughout Africa.

This part of the world has been home to the beginnings of civilization. From here came the teachings of the Greeks and Romans, the Italian Renaissance, and countless inventions. Within the EU boundaries, the Protestant Reformation and the industrial revolution emerged. From here came forms of government, legal systems, and people whose ideas shaped the world we inhabit today.

No More Wars

Although many textbooks discuss the founding of the European Union as an arrangement meant to promote trade foremost, the reason for its existence is more than that. Trade was really a tool to reach the goal of creating long-term peace within the region and to change the way people behave toward one another.[1]

Peace in this case required finding a way to ensure that Germany would not become a threat again. Dating back to the 1800s, Germany had been an aggressor nation, the enemy of most European nations in both World War I and World War II. Defeated in 1945, its economy was devastated, as were those of most other European nations. Economic recovery and peace became everyone's long-term goals. One of the first people who voiced the idea that peace could be ensured by joining together was Winston Churchill, prime minister of Great Britain. Less than two years after the end of World War II he said, "We must now build a kind of United States of Europe with the first step [being] a partnership between France and Germany."[2]

Four years later the first step toward the realization of his vision appeared with the creation of the European Coal and Steel Community in 1950. Started by six countries, Germany, France, Luxembourg, Belgium, the Netherlands, and Italy, it was clearly about trade. Coal and steel were the key commodities required to rebuild the economies. When Robert Shuman, then the French foreign minister, explained the importance of the European Economic Community, the name later adopted by members of the ECSC, he stated that one of the reasons was to make any war between France and Germany "not merely unthinkable but [also] materially impossible."[3] The way to ensure this was to connect the countries through institutions and by integrating the economies. Thus the beginning recognized the twin goals of peace and prosperity. (Not stated, but subtly recognized, was a goal to restore European influence around the world that had been lost with the colonies and the wars. This unspoken goal affects policies and attitudes in the European Union today.)

The EU Is?

In slightly more than half a century the six-nation ECSC developed into an institution, the European Union (EU), that more closely resembles Churchill's vision. The institution grew, enlarged from its original six members in several stages. The United Kingdom did not formally join until 1973; Greece in 1981; and Austria, Sweden, and Finland in 1995 for a total of 15 countries. That size was stable until the biggest enlargement, the addition of 10 countries, May 1, 2004. The EU is now composed of 25 countries, with a combined population of 455 million and accounts overall for 28 percent of all world trade.[4] According to the Web site for the European Union, the EU is a family of democratic European countries committed to working together for peace and prosperity.[5]

The member countries vary in many measures, including geography. There are island nations such as the United Kingdom, Cyprus, Greece, and Iceland, as well as landlocked eastern countries such as Hungary, Slovakia, and the Czech Republic. The size of the countries measured by population is dramatically varied, ranging from Germany with more than 82 million people to Malta, less than 1 percent of its size with only 383,600 people.[6]

While they share a commitment to the EU institutions, there is no common government structure even at the national level. There are constitutional monarchies, republics, parliamentary democracies, a decentralized federal state, and a parliamentary state with a constitutional monarchy. One constitutional monarchy, the United Kingdom, doesn't actually have a written constitution. Rather, it relies on laws and traditions to form an unwritten constitution. Some have long histories of self-government and for others, democracy and independence are a recent experience. The EU family is one that is large and diverse.

Connected by Currency

If we consider the creation of the European Coal and Steel Community as a visionary, possibly risky undertaking, then the establishment of a single currency for the EU was downright revolutionary. The ECSC brought together traditional enemies developing common agreements built around trade and economic self-interest. The single currency required that countries commit to acting together, putting aside a measure of national identity, their currency.

The common currency, the euro, even more than open borders, common labeling laws, and environmental standards, marked a long-term commitment of the countries to the EU. Ten years after the 1992 signing of the Treaty of Masstricht that formalized the agreement for a single currency, the first euro notes were issued. Although the phrase "historic event" may be overused, this shift from multiple national currencies to one shared by all 12 countries does seem to qualify. History tells us that it was not easy in 1792 to create a common currency among the former colonies that joined to form the emerging nation of the

United States. Reflect for a moment on the complexities of the shift among highly industrialized nations with advanced, far-reaching economies.

The change was not simply historic in terms of the complexity of the practical aspect but there was also an emotional component to consider. A country's currency is part of its national identity. The French franc, Italian lire, and German mark each had a history and meaning within its respective country. Relinquishing control and creation of the money meant giving up a symbol of national sovereignty in favor of stronger connection to other countries.

Not all the members of the European Union elected to participate in the change, to become part of the "euro zone." The 3 that did not join were Sweden, Denmark, and the United Kingdom. The 12 countries that now use the euro as their currency are Austria, Belgium, Finland, France, Germany, Greece, Ireland, Italy, Luxembourg, the Netherlands, Portugal, and Spain.

For the countries that joined the EU in 2004, participation in the euro is not automatic. There is a minimum two-year waiting period as well as the requirement to meet certain monetary targets. Depending on each nation's economic growth and fiscal management abilities, it's possible that it will be 2010 rather than 2006 before the newest members join the euro zone.

The issue wasn't simply one for historians, multinational companies, and government agencies. It affected the daily lives of every citizen in every country. One day the money was familiar and the next day it was not. People complained that prices were adjusted upward as the national currencies were converted to euros. An indicator of the adjustment period is that two years after the euro became legal tender, cash register receipts still give the total due in the original currency as well as euros.

For some it wasn't the first time currency changed but it is certainly the most dramatic. For an 85-year-old French woman, the euro is her third currency. First there were the "old" francs, replaced in 1960 by "new" francs. After forty years, she still thought of them as new, not the real money that she grew up with. Today she converts prices from euros to new francs, and then to old francs to decide whether the price is fair.

One Community, Many Tongues

In the seventeenth century educated people communicated in Latin; in the middle 1800s German was most useful for a traveler. Two hundred years later, English is the language studied by more than 90 percent of high school students in Europe.[7] But even as the number of English speakers increases throughout the world, it is still only 1 of the 20 official languages of the European Union. The 10 new members in the 2004 enlargement added 9 official languages to the existing selection. In contrast, the United Nations, with 191 members, uses 6 languages.

But in Europe, the officials and legislators have the right to work in their own language. The translation service for the European Union's Parliament must now provide simultaneous translation of all debates into 20 languages creating 380 language combinations. Among the new possibilities are English/Polish, Latvian/Hungarian, and Spanish/Estonian. One problem that now confronts the EU is the lack of experienced translators. Increasingly people rely on relays or bridge languages such as French, German, or English connecting one language group to another.

The use of English within the EU may be spreading in an unexpected way. Many of the documents needed for EU business are presented, studied, and negotiated all in English. This results in the ministries and staff in each country being able to work in English to handle the material presented. English, as a common, shared language, is expanding through its use by both businesses and institutions.

How It Works: Five Institutions, Four Countries, and Four Cities

Although announcements of matters of importance concerning the European Union often emanate from Brussels in Belgium, it isn't the capital of the EU. Rather, Brussels is one of four cities in four countries housing key EU institutions. To tour them all involves visits to Belgium, Germany, France, and Luxembourg. The main institutions are:

European Council The presidents and prime ministers of EU countries plus the president of the European Commission are members of this group. It is the highest-level policy-making body and meets in Brussels.

Council of the European Union This is the main decision-making institution (was the Council of Ministers) and is also located in Brussels. This is the group that must vote and unanimously approve any country seeking membership. Each EU country takes a turn at presiding over the council, with terms limited to six months each year. For example, the president of the council from January to June 2004 was from Ireland and the president from July through December 2004 was from the Netherlands. Their primary responsibility is to chair meetings and to work out compromises to resolve problems among council members.

European Commission Based in Brussels, this is the only body that can initiate legislation. It is also responsible for proposing an annual budget. Further, it must ensure that legislation and treaties that have been enacted are being followed. One representative from each country serves on the commission. The president, often a former prime minister of the country he or she represents, is selected by the Parliament to serve for 5 years. The president assigns commissioners to oversee specific areas. The 2004 president, Jose Manuel Durao Barroso of Portugal, the first to serve after the enlargement to 25 member states, selected 10 of his 24 ministers from the newest EU members.

European Parliament This body represents EU citizens, and the citizens elect members from the member countries. It conducts business in 2 cities, in 2 countries, based in both Strasbourg and Luxembourg. As of June 2004, there are 732 representatives elected for 5-year terms. Parliament approves, amends, or rejects EU legislation and shares authority over the budget. According to Jim Murray, director of the European Consumer's Organization, the European Parliament "affects people's lives more than they realize; it's there every time they go into a shop or do a transaction. It has a hand in rules governing consumer protection."[8]

Court of Justice The court includes one judge from each EU country and is based in Luxembourg. Their job is to ensure the EU law is complied with and that treaties are correctly interpreted and applied. It also reviews legislation to identify conflicts between European law and laws of individual nations.

More than 25,000 employees work throughout these and other EU institutions, including the European Central Bank, located in Frankfort, which manages the euro and monetary policy; the Courts of Auditors, based in Luxembourg; and others too numerous to cover. Thousands of people in multiple places work to make the EU function.

Europe: More Than the EU

Switzerland, Norway, Iceland, and Liechtenstein are European countries that are not members of the EU. They are, however, closely connected to it. Norway, Iceland, and Liechtenstein participate in the European Economic Area that supports close cooperation in matters of goods, services, and capital. In addition, there is freedom of movement for people within the EEA countries. It's useful to remember that Europe has more than the 25 members of the European Union.

Mega Merger: Enlargement 2004

The 2004 addition of 10 countries was the fifth and by far the most ambitious of the EU expansions. The union's size almost doubled from 15 to 25 members, and the population rose to more than 450 million people, an increase of nearly 40 percent from its earlier size of approximately 325 million. But the change is more fundamental than issues that can be counted in physical terms. The countries that made up the pre-May 1, 2004 EU, sometimes referred to as the inner 15, had generally comparable levels of education, experience, and industrial development. The new group brings a significant diversity in its geography, population, and experience with free market democracy. It's difficult to imagine the change for the 8 new member countries that were former member states of the USSR.

In a speech a year before the 2004 enlargement, Ambassador Guenter Burghardt, head of the European Commission Delegation to the United States, said that this change was the political equivalent of expanding an electrical grid, a complex and delicate undertaking. Its purpose is to create the structure for a stable European political order. He went on to state that this was not a United States of Europe but rather a federation of nation-states.

To get an idea of what this means, imagine that the United States joined in a similar union with Mexico and Canada rather than simply agreeing to an open market and to expand trade. One fourth of its people would have a mother tongue other than English. The president may reside in Mexico City, defense could be handled in Washington, D.C., and financial policy be run from Toronto. This presents an almost unimaginable image and yet it is close to the union that 25 European countries have selected.

For the new members, the EU provides access to a market of almost 500 million people and establishes them as free market economies, democratic nations. But it is a change filled with restrictions as well as opportunities. There are thousands of pages of EU regulations to be followed. More will come as countries move to adopt the euro. And one issue of concern is that the regulations reflect compromises to benefit the community as a whole rather than specific to the history and culture of each country. While each country is represented in the Parliament and on the commission, decisions are still made outside each member nation's borders. Will this remind the populations that were part of the former Soviet Republic of their experience when decisions were made in Moscow? Already one survey revealed that 61 percent of the population in Poland, formerly controlled by the Soviet Union, does not trust the EU.[9]

Further, a Los Angeles–based international economist says that the impact of enlargement will be a drag on the economies of the EU members.[10] "It's two to three years too early. The economies of the new countries aren't really ready yet." He believes that the amount of money the EU will have to allot to support the new members will inhibit other activity. For example, by August 2004, Poland had received 240 million euros from EU structural funds, the first of several payments. For the EU, overall enlargement created a larger market and new opportunities but also a larger burden.

Notwithstanding the emerging challenges, it is worth pointing out that the problems and conflicts among these countries are being dealt with by negotiations. The arguments are over quotas, not borders. Poland and Germany are now democratic nations joined together to promote trade for themselves and others.

New to the Union

Poland is the largest of the Central European countries of the EU class of 2004. Its geography has shaped its history. Bordered by two traditionally aggressive countries, Germany and Russia, it was invaded repeatedly. Today it's an independent and influential member of the EU. In recent years it has transformed its economy in preparation for accession to the Union. Today it has the benefits and challenges associated with its new status.

It now competes for business with Western Europe, Asia, and its smaller neighbors such as Slovakia and the Czech Republic, also new EU members. While it offers good geographic proximity to other Western markets, it is considered to have more red tape and a less welcoming government structure than its neighbors.[11] Making the changes that allowed it to join the EU were not a final step but part of a process.

The impact of EU membership isn't felt only at the macro level. For an example of the effects on a single business, consider the story of Zbigniew Sosnowski. A former auto mechanic, he started a bike company in 1989. After 15 years, it is the second-largest bike maker in Europe, employing 900 people. In April 2004 his market expanded to include the United States. However, Mr. Sosnowski now worries that EU labor laws may drive up his costs, making him less competitive.

While Poland struggles to adapt to the responsibilities and regulations that came with its new status, it also is working toward its future. During the negotiations surrounding the proposed EU constitution, Poland was an active participant. Its goal was to establish a voting system to avoid having the EU dominated by the four big countries: Germany, France, Britain, and Italy. The negotiations helped to establish Poland as a country that would, at least on some issues, be willing to speak for the smaller nations.

Will Turkey Be Invited?

The 2004 enlargement is not likely to be the final expansion of the European Union. Four more countries hope to join by 2007. Turkey, Bulgaria, Romania, and Croatia have applied to begin the process. Of the four, the candidacy most in question is Turkey's. It has already waited five years since its first application. In December 2004, the EU agreed to begin the negotiations for membership; however, the process may take as many as ten years before a final decision is reached.

Turkey's physical location makes it an attractive candidate. It rests in the continents of both Asia and Europe. A glance at a map reveals it clearly as a bridge between Europe and Asia, controlling the entrance to the Black Sea. Its borders include Syria, Iraq, Iran, Armenia, Georgia, Bulgaria, and Greece. It touches the Aegean, Black, and Mediterranean seas. The EU is already Turkey's single biggest trading partner. For U.S. companies it can be a door into the EU. According to a Los Angeles consultant representing European companies, Turkey is an important part of the logistics chain to and from Europe. Some of his clients discovered that sometimes there is a financial advantage resulting from moving products into the EU through Turkey than through an EU member state. Clients of this consultant are watching with interest the debate on its membership.

Support for Turkey's membership varies. In March 2004, the British foreign secretary announced, "We (the UK) [are] ready to give any support we can."[12] However, opponents worry that it is too big, too poor, and not European by culture.[13]

Aside from matters of budget, expanding democracy, and protecting human rights, another concern appears to be Turkey's size. Its population of 68,893,918 would place it second only to Germany, the largest current member of the EU. That population would give it significant representation within the EU Parliament, potentially changing the power structure that now exists.

Coming Next: The EU Constitution

After almost three years of work, the first constitution of the European Union is ready to be signed and submitted to the member countries for ratification. The formal signing ceremonies took place in October 2004, which began the two-year ratification period.

During that time the value and impact of the document will be debated at length. Given the differences within the community and a document that some suggest "is so complex that it is completely inaccessible to most EU citizens,"[14] widely differing views are to be expected.

Already, opposing opinions on its value are emerging. For some the closer integration among the members is seen as a benefit. For them it will ensure that the union is not simply a free trade agreement but a community that achieves long-term stability. Others argue that the extended powers of the Parliament, the creation of an elected president, and harmonization of regulations and legal systems will limit flexibility in a time when flexibility is an economic necessity.

One issue of concern is how each country's voice will be considered and how the votes on issues will be counted. A formula of a "qualified majority" was created to attempt to balance the influence of large and small countries. On this one issue alone, the complexity can be confusing. Rather than each country having a specific number of votes, a formula for the qualified majority was created. The formula is that 55 percent of the members of the council, at least 15 of them member states that make up at least 65 percent of the population of the union, are needed to be a majority. An issue that one would wish to be simple—how the votes are counted—isn't. Will the members of the community, the voting public in each country, understand the issues and vote for closer integration or not? Only time will provide an answer. For both sides, clarifying the issues will be critical. Each vote will matter, for it takes all 25 countries voting in favor for the constitution to go into effect. One vote against from a country big or small, and there won't be a written constitution today.

The EU Trades with the World

The EU today is a powerful, global trading bloc. An entity that began slightly more than 50 years ago to facilitate the rebuilding of a region devastated by war now influences trade around the world. One needs only to consider a few statistics to understand its size and importance. For example, the EU and United States together make up 40 percent of world trade.[15] It is the world's largest textile exporter with 15 percent of the market and the second-largest clothing exporter after China.[16] According to Chinese Premier Wen Jiabaoa, visiting shortly after the 2004 enlargement took place, "the enlarged EU will move from China's third-largest trading partner behind Japan and the United States to become its biggest."[17]

The EU's reach extends to all parts of the globe. A partial list of its connections include free trade agreements with Mexico and South Africa and a regional cooperation agreement with the Mercosur countries (Argentina, Brazil, Bolivia, Chile, Paraguay, and Uruguay). It is an active trader with the Economic Community of Western Africa States.

But the EU is more than agreements made by and for the entire group. China has signed a tourism agreement with Ireland, but Chinese travel and tourism will not focus only on Ireland.[18] China recently announced that 27 European countries, including France, Italy, Switzerland, Spain, Belgium, Sweden, and Greece, will be given the status of "approved destinations."[19] This designation will allow tour groups from China to visit these countries more easily, opening a market projected to reach 100 million people. European businesses are already adapting to this new group of travelers. Lufthansa, the German airline, has almost doubled its flights to and from China. Hotels are adding white rice and soup to their breakfast menus and Chinese channels to their TV selections.

In addition to trade that can be quantified as euros and dollars, the EU is an important entity in terms of influence. Collectively and separately, the member states play key roles in World Trade Organization (WTO) matters. In mid 2004 it considered backing Russia's bid to join the organization.[20] Russia is the only major economy that isn't in the WTO. The EU is the largest investor in the Russian market and the 25-member group is Russia's largest trading partner, receiving 51 percent of Russian exports.[21] Although the trading relationship is significant, the relationship has special tensions. Anti-Russian sentiment still exists in the new member states, parts of the former Soviet republic. In addition Russia may lose business in key markets in Eastern and Central Europe to other EU countries. The EU/Russia relationship is a dynamic example of countries simultaneously being friends and foes, united through contemporary economics and historical experiences.

EU Business: Similar and Different

Doing business within the European Union for companies local, regional, and global requires flexibility and curiosity. Managers must adapt to environments that are similar, different, and shifting simultaneously. Products and processes must be global and local for the EU, and the larger European environment are varied markets. However, there are similarities to one another and to the United States.

Nearly 1,000 managers in the United States and Europe responded to a survey prepared by the Human Resource Institute, American Management Association, and the Management Center Europe. Their replies showed significant agreement regarding the key business issues they face and ones they expect to encounter over the next decade. These include leadership, managing change, focus on the customer, technology, skill level of workforce, work ethic, and values.[22] The U.S. respondents include health care costs on their list, and the Europeans include innovation and creativity.

It's valuable to note the commonality in this area, but we must not lose sight of the differences in how business is conducted from place to place. Even as some complain about increased homogenization across the EU, there is no one European way. Although increasingly business regulations emanate from Brussels, individuals in sovereign countries with unique cultures conduct the real work of business.

The EU brings together the more individualistic, linear northern populations with the collectivist, more emotional southerners, including people from Spain and Portugal. The Central Europeans only recently removed from Soviet domination bring their own outlooks and behaviors shaped by that experience. Andre Bergen, head of banking at KBC, a Polish bank, remarked that a generation accustomed to a centrally planned economy still needs time to adjust to a free market. He observed that the Hungarians are "freewheeling" and the Czechs work "by the book," expressing perceived differences as large as those between the Germans and the Italians.[23]

The need to bridge the differences is recognized within the EU. For example, Scotland and Estonia created a program that seeks to build mutual understanding. Crossroads for Ideas promotes exchange between Scots and Estonians to develop mutually beneficial relationships and partnerships, especially among young professionals.[24]

Not everyone opts to participate in a special program. Some workers simply learn by experience. After 12 years of being unemployed, an East German drives 3 miles across the river to Poland to work. He decided that "soon we're all going to be living together" and he could reverse the trend that had been in the opposite direction—in 2003, there were 317,600 Polish citizens working in Germany.[25]

Even countries slated for accession but not yet approved are obtaining business from the EU. Bulgaria and Romania hope to join and new members Hungary and the Czech Republic appear to be preferred as locations for new plants and partnerships over India and Asia. Their cultural and linguistic ties are appealing to countries such as Germany and France. For example, Oracle, the software producer, opened a new center in Bucharest to provide European and global support to customers. The fact that this facility is physically closer than Asia or India makes it attractive to EU companies as a "near-shoring" destination.[26]

No matter which country within the EU you consider, they all have one advantage over Americans when it comes to doing business together. They are able to understand business as a series of relationships rather than a transaction. No matter the differences in cultures, all share an understanding that connections with people are the critical element of all commercial activity.

Time Off?

The average American now works 350 hours a year, 9 or 10 weeks longer than the average European.[27] Although Americans outpace the Europeans overall, there are differences within the communities. Thirty-two percent of the workforce in the United Kingdom put in more than 46 hours per week versus the French,[28] whose law stipulates a 35-hour workweek. An American woman working in London observes that the British seem to have a much better work/life balance than her U.S. compatriots. She commented that at the end of the workday there's time for a drink and some conversation with colleagues, and the workweek doesn't roll over into the weekend. It's delightful, she concluded.

The difference in time worked is not only evident in the weekly hours but also the amount of vacation. Germans have 30 days of vacation per year, while the French have an average of 25 days. That contrasts sharply with the Japanese, who have 18, days and the United States, who have 12. However, the issues of time and work are being discussed and are shifting both in the United States and the European Union. A *Business 2.0* article pointed out the high cost to the extra work time in illness and accidents. The author concludes that the case against an "all-work, no-play mentality is getting harder to ignore."[29] A French product development consultant commented that although her U.S. office staff put in more hours than her French group, they didn't seem to be more productive. "Americans," she said, "are in the office, but they're not really working efficiently."

While the United States considers a shift to a different work/life balance, in Europe there are signs of a move toward more work. In 1999 France made a 35-hour workweek mandatory in hopes of increasing employment. However, by 2004, it appeared to have mainly created complexity and difficulty, especially for small companies, regarding the generation of new jobs. The president of France commented in 2004 that the law should be eliminated because it appeared to be a drag on the economy, and in early 2005 the law was amended to give private sector workers the right to work longer hours by agreement with their employers.

In Germany in 2004 Siemens, the global electrical engineering company, negotiated a contract with a German group of employees to extend workers' hours to 40 from 35 without an increase in pay.[30] The company was able to convince this particular group of workers to agree to the change or risk having their factory closed and their jobs moved to another EU country, one with lower labor rates. No matter where one works, how people try to reach a satisfying work/life balance, it is suggested the longer hours are a reality of life in global economy.

Starbucks and McDonald's Along with IKEA and Zara

Given the size of trade—billions of dollars each year—that flows between the European Union and the United States, it's no surprise that local brands move in both directions. Throughout the book we look for McDonald's in each region. In the EU they are relatively commonplace. There is a McDonald's present in all 25 EU countries. Known for the standardization of its operation and menu, it may be a surprise to learn that they vary within the EU. In Malta, McDonald's offers spring rolls. There is wine in Paris, a pasta bar in Rome, and a Greek Mac on the menu in Finland. While known as an American company, it becomes a participant in each local economy. It purchases goods, buys from local farmers, and employs local staff. In Ireland the chain is the largest employer in the country's restaurant industry.

Another chain that seems ubiquitous in U.S. cities is Starbucks. Its expansion into Europe is more recent and its outlets not as pervasive as McDonald's. Depending on where you are in the EU, Starbucks may be commonplace (London), a newsworthy sign of continued American cultural incursion (arriving in Paris in 2004), or nonexistent (Poland).

But food and other retail influences come West from the East, also. The U.K. fast food chain Pret A Manger has grown in New York and influenced a West Coast chain called Briazz. Trendy handbags from Jamin Puesch, made by hand in France, appear at specialty retailers in Los Angeles. The furniture retailer IKEA brought styles, moderately priced home products, and new ideas from Sweden and changed the furniture shopping habits of American consumers.

While the fashions of Ralph Lauren, Nike, Quicksilver, and the Gap reach across the ocean to Europe, inexpensive but good quality and timely clothing of Spain's Zara and Sweden's H&M have made their way in the United States. Food, furniture, and fashion all are parts of the immense two-way trade between the United States and the European Union.

Where Are the People?

A 1968 book titled *The Population Bomb* predicted overpopulation and worldwide famine. That prediction has not become reality. Today the world is faced with a different risk, that of a declining and aging population. In 2004 it was predicted that world population would peak in 2070, then fall, worldwide. Against the image of increased population leading to food shortages, a peak and decline may seem to be good news. While that is true as far as feeding people is concerned, there are other effects of population trends.

An aging and declining population places demands on government budgets for both pensions and health care. The existing populations are aging. By 2050 the median age in the United States will be 35, while in Europe it will be 52.[31] For example, Germany's public spending on pensions is expected to reach 15.4 percent by 2040, up from 10.3 percent in 2004. Health care costs will rise from 3.8 percent to 8 percent of the GDP in that same period. Because the population is aging with fewer people entering the workforce, not only will outgo increase but also revenues in taxes on income will decline.[32]

This issue is not simply a concern for Germany. It is an issue for all industrialized countries and is obvious when we look at the projected birthrates throughout the European Union. While one international economist worries that all Italians will disappear, there are EU countries with 2004 birthrates even lower than Italy's 0.09 percent. Five countries—the Czech Republic, Estonia, Hungary, Latvia, Lithuania, and Slovenia—actually have negative growth rates. Only Ireland at 1.16 percent and Luxembourg at 1.28 percent are above the 1 percent rate. The remaining 17 countries range from Germany at 0.02 percent to the Netherlands at 0.57 percent.

Does Corruption Exist?

As we continue to refer to the Corruption Perceptions Index as an indicator of the development of free markets and democratic institutions within a country, most of the EU is perceived favorably. From that view, the 2004 report provides additional insight to the differences between the EU countries. Nineteen of the countries rank above the 5.0 level. (In the index, ranks above 5.0 are considered "clean," where corruption is not perceived to be a serious problem.)

Eleven of the group scored higher than the United States. They are Finland, Iceland, Denmark, Sweden, the Netherlands, Norway, Switzerland, Luxembourg, the United Kingdom, Austria, and Germany. Belgium is tied with the United States at 7.5. Those below the 5.0 dividing line are 6 of the 2004 enlargement group: Hungary, Lithuania, Greece, Czech Republic, Latvia, and Poland. Their scores range from 4.8 for Hungary to 3.6 for the Czech Republic. (Turkey, the focus of so much current debate, ranks at number 77 of 145 in the overall listing with a 3.2 score.) The scores below 5.0 are reminders of those systems, methods of conducting business, that free market economies are just developing in some of these countries.

Online Some of the Time

It is Sweden, a European country, not the United States, that ranks number 1 as the country with the highest Internet penetration rate in the world.[33] In Sweden, 76.8 percent of the population use the Internet substantially, exceeding the number two country, Hong Kong at 69.9 percent, and the number three, the United States at 66.8 percent. It is almost 10 percentage points higher than the nearest EU country, the Netherlands. Within the top 22 countries with the highest Internet penetration in the world, EU and EFTA countries hold ten spots, beginning with Sweden in first place and ending with Norway at 49.7 percent holding the twenty-second spot.

Internet usage is another measure of the differences of development within the EU/EFTA countries. As with the Corruption Perception Index, there is a wide variation. Internet penetration ranges from Sweden's level with nearly three quarters of the population online, to a low of 15.3 percent for Greece. Of the 25 EU countries, 7 (Denmark, Finland, Germany, Italy, the Netherlands, Sweden, and the United Kingdom) are above the 50 percent mark. Four of the group (Greece, Hungary, Lithuania, and Poland) have numbers that fall below 25 percent.

France, one of the founding members and traditional leaders of the EU, falls short of 50 percent penetration at 41.5 percent. This places it lower than even Estonia, at 46.2 percent the highest score of the 2004 enlargement group. France's score may reflect attitudes within the population rather than technical ability. Although usage is widespread in the business community, the preference is still for more personal communication. As the head of marketing for a global apparel group recently said, "Just call me. You know, we're not too much into e-mail. It works, but still, a phone call is better."

No matter that today's numbers appear low; changes are forthcoming. For example, in Estonia the citizens can track government expenditures online.[34]

Now We Know

What began as a group of 6 countries coming together to build trade and to establish a foundation for ongoing regional peace is now, barely half a century later, the European Union, a group of 25 countries with a population of over 450 million people. A federation of nation states that span the continents of Europe and Asia, the EU accounts for almost 30 percent of the world trade. EU members are diverse in size, language, and culture yet bound together by the desire to create opportunities for trade, employment, and peace for their people.

I'm Glad I Know

Hands down, I am glad to know about local business customs. Before I go to any country to do business, I always look up information on that country's business culture down to details like how to present your business card. The time it takes to do the research is definitely a good investment. It has shown me how to be the most effective and earned me the respect of my colleagues. They appreciate the fact that I've taken the time to learn about their culture.

↦ *American clothing designer,*
based in California, working in Europe and Asia

CHAPTER 13

Russia *and the* Commonwealth *of* Independent States

I Wish I'd Known

That businesspeople had many of the same concerns I did but that their experience was so limited and different. It never occurred to me that it was still new for them to think of planning, making a profit. It's fascinating to hear the questions they ask [and] also how much they know about. Who would have guessed a first request when arriving in Los Angeles was to see Wal-Mart? They wanted to understand what made it special. Our conversations taught me so much about a part of the world I'd never considered.

> ➤➤ *American marketing executive*
> *based in Los Angeles, after meeting groups*
> *from Russia, Kyrgyzstan, and Ukraine*

I Wish They Knew

You can't rush into doing business here. It doesn't work if you simply ask a few questions, quote a price, and set a delivery schedule and go. Nothing will happen. You have to create trust, a connection. That is done through sharing information, time, [and] a meal or two. Ask lots of questions. Get to know the buyer or supplier. Become an adviser, a person to solve their problem, and slowly educate your contact. Through the question and answer process you gain insights, but more importantly, you build a relationship. You can't push and rush forward. Time and deadlines don't move people. Trust and understanding are the keys.

> ➤➤ *Polish technology executive who lived*
> *and worked in seven countries,*
> *including the United States and Russia*

The Region: Russia and
the Commonwealth of Independent States

With the exception of Russia, the names of the 12 countries that form the Commonwealth of Independent States (CIS) are not well-known in the United States. The countries are Armenia, Azerbaijan, Belarus, Georgia, Kyrgyzstan, Kazakhstan, Moldova, Russian Federation (Russia), Tajikistan, Turkmenistan, Ukraine, and Uzbekistan. For almost 70 years they were united within the Union of Soviet Socialist Republics (USSR), an entity controlled by Russia, the largest country. In 1991 the USSR broke apart, and once again the republics became independent nations. Almost overnight each one was responsible for making its way, seemingly alone, in a complex environment. What are these countries? Where are they located? What's their history?

The Newly Independent States (NIS)

Before forming the CIS, the group of countries that had been part of the USSR was referred to as the Newly Independent States or NIS. Fifteen countries had this designation. Three of these NIS member states—Estonia, Latvia, and Lithuania—decided not to join the CIS. Instead, since they share borders with European countries, they chose to join the European Union. On May 1, 2004, their goal was realized

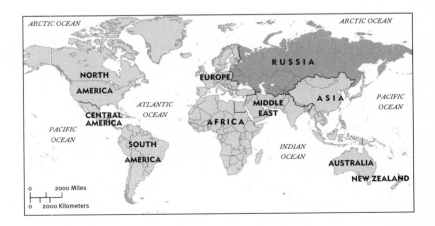

when they all became members of the EU. (See chapter 12). The afore-mentioned 12 republics formed the CIS, continuing their strong links with Russia and one another.

In 2000 Belarus, Kazakhstan, Kyrgyzstan, Russia, and Tajikistan formed an additional connection when they executed a treaty creating the Eurasian Economic Community to facilitate closer ties and the "free movements of goods, service, [and] capital."[1]

Diverse but Still Connected

The CIS countries vary widely in physical size, geography, and location. They span much of Eurasia, the world's largest landmass, stretching across the continents of Europe and Asia. While often referred to as Russia and the Newly Independent States, as if they were one place, some of the countries are located in Europe and others in Asia.[2] For example, Belarus, Ukraine, and Moldova are in Europe, and Kazakhstan, Turkmenistan, Uzbekistan, Tajikistan, and Kyrgyzstan are in Central

Asia. Russia, the largest of the group, spans both continents. As a unit, their bordering countries include Finland, Norway, Poland, Latvia, Lithuania, Estonia, China, Mongolia, Iran, Turkey, and Afghanistan.

The smallest country, Armenia (11,506 square miles), is slightly smaller than Maryland in the United States, which ranks forty-second of the 50 states in size. Turkmenistan is slightly larger than California while Kazakhstan is about the size of Western Europe. But the largest of all is Russia, the largest country in the world, which covers 6,592,849 square miles—twice the size of the United States.[3]

While the overall region is rich in geographic endowments, such as access to oceans, seas, and rivers; minerals; and agricultural areas, the distribution varies dramatically. For example, Belarus, Moldova, Tajikistan, Kyrgyzstan, Armenia, and Uzbekistan are landlocked. This does not mean there is no water *within* their borders, however. They have rivers and lakes within their borders. Kyrgyzstan, for example, has 2,000 lakes, and Armenia has one of the world's largest lakes, Lake Sevan, which covers more than 500 square miles. Unlike their neighbors, they do not have access to any of the 6 seas or 2 oceans that border the region.

In contrast to the six landlocked nations, Russia touches the Black, White, and Caspian seas as well as the Arctic and Pacific oceans. It also has the world's largest freshwater lake and four of the world's longest rivers: Lena, Ob, Yenisey, and Volga.

There are rich agricultural areas, arid deserts, and temperatures that range from hot to cold. Rich deposits of oil and natural gas exist in Armenia, Russia, Turkmenistan, Azerbaijan, and Kazakhstan. However, Moldova, the second smallest of the republics and one of the poorest, must import oil and gas.[4] There are diamonds and gold in Russia, Uzbekistan, and Kyrgyzstan. One of the world's ten largest gold fields is in Kyrgyzstan, and it is mined by a venture between a local company and a Canadian firm.

Belarus is one of the top producers of potatoes in the world, while many of the other countries produce cotton and tobacco as two of their main cash crops. Tajikistan, one of the poorest and the most rural in the group, is home to a denim mill, owned by an Italian company that was built with funding from the World Bank. For all the similarities, the region is so varied that it is impossible to generalize anything about it. To build an understanding of what's there, people must look at individual places, the nations, and even the regions within the region.

A Republic and Not Independent

Chechnya, a small republic located in the Northern Caucasus Mountains in Russia's southwest is likely the only 1 of the 21 current republics widely known outside of Russia. It has been connected to Russia for almost 150 years, dating back to 1859. Strife between the republic and the parent government has existed for much of that time. Approximately 60 years ago, during World War II, almost the entire population of the republic was deported to Siberia and Kazakhstan based on concerns about support for Germany. It was 1957, almost 20 years later, when people were allowed to return to the area and the Chechen-Inqush republic was established.

In 1991 Chechnya, a valuable oil-producing region, did declare its independence, at the same time as the other members of the CIS; however, then president Boris Yeltsin did not allow Chechnya to separate from the Russian Federation. An election in 2002 established Chechnya as a separatist republic but not an independent one.

Although there have been presidential elections and a new constitution has been created, as of 2005, violence attributed to Chechen rebels continues within the region and in other areas. Rebels are allegedly responsible for taking hostages in theaters and schools, for suicide bombing subways, and for setting off bombs that caused two airplanes to crash. While attacks continue within the republic, others have taken place in Moscow and Beslan. A peaceful solution to this conflict is not evident even a decade after their most recent attempt at independence.

Looking Back

Readers may be most familiar with the CIS countries as the Communist foes of the United States during the post-World War II era until the breakup of the USSR. Today, depending on the matters being considered, these nations, including Russia, play the roles of friends and allies, trading partners, and emerging markets that present great opportunities. To understand the opportunities and challenges developing from the new CIS, it is useful to develop a sense of the history of the region as a whole.

The breakup of the USSR in 1991 should not be interpreted as the date these countries became independent. Quite the contrary. Each of these countries had a history and an identity prior to being absorbed into the Soviet Union. The 12 CIS countries' histories cover thousands of years. For example, the first Kyrgyz language can be traced to 1300 B.C., and there was a "distinct Armenian civilization in the sixth century B.C."5

Just as they share comparable challenges in development today, their histories have some similarities. There were periods of growth and development interrupted by intervals of war and occupation. The origins of the peoples can be traced back to nomadic tribes in both Europe and Asia. They share a history filled with stories of conquerors, rulers who came and went: the Greeks, Romans, Persians, Christians, Muslims, Mongols, Portuguese, French, British, Germans, and Poles.

Each group, in turn, brought goods, ideas, religion, language, art, and food. People in the areas fought for their territory and sometimes fought one another. At times there was peace and prosperity. Cities were built only to be lost to other invaders. For hundreds of years the cycle continued. Boundaries were drawn and redrawn. Natural physical limits were ignored, as were the divisions based on tribal history and ethnic groupings. The problems resulting from the divisions haunt these nations today and are evident in the civil wars, ethnic tensions, and exclusions in trade agreements that still exist in the twenty-first century.

More than the ancient history they have that spans more than 1,000 years, what links these countries is the experience of the twentieth century, the years from 1920 to 1991, when they were united as part of the USSR. Each country's experience with Russia playing the role of either invader or guardian was different. However, during the 15-year period from 1920 to 1936, beginning with Armenia and ending with Kazakhstan, they were all absorbed into the USSR. During the ensuing period, the Soviet Union, based in Moscow, controlled each of the other countries. Their economies, legal systems, politics, and even education of the populace were dictated by Russia. Expectations for free nations to participate in the contemporary global economy has proven challenging for all CIS countries.

Religion

Religion was suppressed during the period of control by the USSR, since it was an atheist nation. Since gaining independence, religion has again emerged. Throughout history, Christianity, Islam, and Judaism have been practiced in these countries. Within the 12 CIS nations, the 5 Central Asian countries of Kyrgyzstan, Uzbekistan, Azerbaijan, Tajikistan, and Turkmenistan are Islamic. In Kazakhstan the split between Islam and Russian Orthodox is nearly even. While there are Muslims throughout the other republics, Christianity is the major religion for the majority of countries. In Russia it is the Russian Orthodox faith that is the predominant religion, and throughout the countries the Eastern Orthodox faith is the largest group, with some Jews, Buddhists, and Protestants counted among their populations.

Business Their Way

The legacy of being part of the Soviet system is still obvious in the CIS countries more than a dozen years after their independence. According to the Transparency International Corruption Perception Index (chapter 10), countries in this part of the world have a "legacy of systemic corruption, held over from [the] Soviet era . . . [and an] ingrained practice of 'beating the system.'"[6] The report goes on to state that these countries have "problems that lead to corruption or create an environment that makes it possible. There are weak institutions, low salaries for public servants, limited opportunities in the private sector, and a lack of independent media."[7] In addition, managers who come from state enterprises are being asked to think in an entirely different way. They have been taught to look at facts and assimilate data but are now being asked to be creative, to think freely, and to explore possibilities.[8]

In 2004, a total of 146 countries were included in the Transparency International Corruption Perceptions survey. In the CIS countries' region, Bulgaria in the fifty-fourth spot ranked the highest. However, their rating was only 4.1, still below the 5.0 mark often seen as the division between some corruption and significant corruption in a country. See Table 13.1 for the CIS nations' scores.

TABLE 13.1   CORRUPTION PERCEPTIONS INDEX RANKING

COUNTRY	RANK
Belarus	3.3
Armenia	3.1
Russia	2.8
Moldova	2.4
Kazakhstan	2.3
Uzbekistan	2.3
Ukraine	2.2
Kyrgyzstan	2.2
Georgia	2.0
Tajikistan	2.0
Azerbaijan	1.9

Source: Transparency International Corruption Perceptions Index 2004

The Corruption Perceptions Index results serve as an indicator that the business environment in any given area does not match that of the well-developed industrial nations. This is one set of useful data, but other ways to gauge development exist. For example, CIS member countries have not limited their connections to one another. They are also joining the global trading community. In 1998, Kyrgyzstan became the first to gain admittance to the World Trade Organization (WTO). Moldova and Georgia followed in 2003. Observer status, the first step toward membership, has been granted to Kazakhstan, Belarus, the Russian Federation, and Tajikistan. It is important to highlight that Russia, the largest physical country in the world, considered one of the world's major powers, has only observer status and is not yet a member of the WTO. This can be interpreted as a statement that the legal and financial systems existing in that country do not yet meet world standards for reliability, predictability, and transparency.

Just because Russia is not a WTO member does not mean its connections to other CIS countries are limited. In 2001, Russia, Kazakhstan, Tajikistan, Kyrgyzstan, and Uzbekistan joined with China to create the Shanghai Cooperation Organization (SCO). In addition to expanding trade within the region, the organization's aim is intended to strengthen mutual trust and support peace and stability within the region. It is useful to note that of the five member countries only Uzbekistan does not share a border with China.

Business Is People

As varied as the countries of this region are in terms of religions, languages, climates, and geography, there is a common approach to doing business. The essential element of commerce is the relationship between individuals. You must know someone, be introduced, be patient, and build the connection. "Business isn't done with strangers," said a former U.S. executive. Connections are very important, as evidenced in reports that in parts of Russia people will do business only with people from the region.[9]

Whether the origin of this model stems from early tribal roots or distrust created through years of Soviet domination and restrictions is unclear. In either case, what have evolved are societies where the immediate and extended family is the key cohort. This is the group that provides the structure and guides decision-making processes. Overall, the culture of these nations is collectivist and hierarchical (see chapter 3). The casual American approach of introducing yourself, doing business first, and building relationships later does not fit in this environment.

In addition to an emphasis on relationships over tasks, time is perceived as ongoing and flexible. One businesswoman observed, "They tend to be late people. Not only do they not adhere to strict schedules but they [also] seem to start and end their days later than Westerners." It is also worth noting in the discussion of time that another aspect—long-range planning—is not one of the business skills developed in the traditional organizational environment.

Even when the business discussion sounds familiar, remember the underlying differences. You may hear an entrepreneur from Kyrgyzstan describe shifting his company from a computer hardware seller to a provider of business solutions for his client. You could easily hear the same conversation in California's Silicon Valley. However, during the same discussion his colleague casually mentions that at least 50 percent of all Kyrgyz companies don't pay taxes, and it is just beginning to be considered a problem.

Another representative of the area describes how long it took him to accept the idea that making a profit was acceptable. He described his dismay when, after the breakup of the USSR, as the shift began to a market economy, his wife began selling handmade sweaters and charging a profit. She did not barter for other goods to make an even exchange but actually made money. Although he told the story with pride in her abilities, it is still clear that the transition was painful for him. An entire belief system had to shift.

These comments illustrate the challenges in the economies of the CIS countries: an emerging entrepreneurial spirit and growing understanding of Western business practices set in environments with dramatically different business histories. The move from a controlled state economy to an open market dynamic is ongoing and uneven.

Counting the People

The population and density of these countries are as varied as the sizes of the countries themselves. One way to look at this area is to consider it a potential market of more than 200 million people, with 144 million living in the Russian Federation. The diversity noted in other areas is also reflected in population. While growing in the region overall, population totals are declining in Armenia, Kazakhstan, Belarus, Georgia, and Ukraine. Additionally, the ages vary. The median age in Russia is 37.9, with 70.4 percent of the people falling in the 15 to 64 age bracket (Table 13.2). In contrast, 19.5 is the median age in

TABLE 13.2   MEDIAN AGE BY COUNTRY

COUNTRY	MEDIAN AGE
Azerbaijan	27.3
Armenia	29.7
Belarus	36.9
Georgia	37.0
Kazakhstan	28.3
Kyrgyzstan	23.1
Moldova	32.1
Russia	37.9
Tajikistan	19.5
Uzbekistan	19.5
Ukraine	38.1

Source: CIA World Fact Book 2005

Tajikistan, with 40 percent of the population of 6.6 million under the age of 15.[10]

Ethnic diversity exists in all 12 nations. Russia alone has 120 ethnic groups. Most of the CIS countries have a Russian minority plus groups from immediately neighboring countries. In addition, there are measurable populations of Koreans, Chinese, Greeks, Poles, Tartars, and Germans, depending on the country. The historic tensions among the groups continue today as each country strives to re-create its own identity.

Online and on the Phone

While it is known that business will be done in ways that may be different from the U.S. experience, not everything will be unknown. The Internet and communication by cell phone are two similarities (see Table 13.3). A student in the Ukraine finds and registers for a college in Los Angeles using the Internet. Visitors coming to the United States to learn about American-style marketing bring their laptops (made with parts purchased in the United Arab Emirates and China) so they can stay in touch with home via e-mail. Cells phones are carried on their

TABLE 13.3   CONNECTED BY PHONE AND ONLINE

COUNTRY	CELL PHONE	INTERNET USERS
Azerbaijan	870,000	300,000
Armenia	114,400	200,000
Belarus	1,118,000	1,391,900
Georgia	522,300	150,000
Kazakhstan	1,027,000	250,000
Kyrgyzstan	53,100	152,000
Moldova	338,200	288,000
Russia	17,608,800	6,000,000
Tajikistan	47,600	4,100
Turkmenistan	52,000	8,000
Uzbekistan	320,800	492,000
Ukraine	4,200,000	900,000

Source: CIA World Fact Book 2005 and World Internet Stats 2005

belts just as people do in New York or San Francisco. The penetration isn't as deep, but the indication is there.

What About McDonald's?

It's easy to believe that McDonald's is everywhere, but that's not yet true. Of all the CIS countries, only Russia is home to the Big Mac. There are now 103 McDonald's locations, and the Pushkin Square store in Moscow is the busiest in the world.[11] It isn't just American fast food companies such as McDonald's and Taco Bell that operate in the CIS countries. Luxury brand retailers from France and Italy have also opened stores in Moscow and St. Petersburg, and IKEA from Sweden continues its expansion. Businesses increasingly find opportunities at all price levels and for a wide variety of products in this vast and changing region.

Now We Know

Within the vast area, stretching across the continents of Europe and Asia are multiple countries, diverse in size, geographic makeup, and ethnicity. They are, however, linked by history—especially their history as members of the USSR. For almost 100 years Russia controlled the members of the USSR, until it dissolved in 1991.

Russia and the former USSR members are still connected, but in different ways. Since 1991, the countries that had been dominated by Russia regained their independence and charted new directions. Some countries such as Estonia, Latvia, and Lithuania chose to strengthen their geographical and cultural ties to Europe, and in 2004 became members of the European Union. Others formed the Commonwealth of Independent States maintaining close ties to one another and to Russia. The independence of the individual nations continues to evolve. In 2004 and 2005, elections in Ukraine, Georgia, and Kyrgyzstan showed increased independent political activity. The independent states are increasingly seeking their own voice, separate from the direction of Russia. Similar and diverse, sharing a search for renewed economic and political identity, the CIS countries continue to evolve.

I'm Glad I Know

It's important to remember two things when trying to do business in this part of the world. First, these are proud people who don't easily acknowledge ignorance on any topic. Second, aside from people who live in the major cities, they know little or nothing about the Western approach to business. They've lived with limited contact with Westerners. There wasn't a tradition of independent thinking, entrepreneurship, or exposure to long-term planning processes. They aren't organized, and you see that in their physical environments. It's clean but messy. Contemporary business practices are a mystery and may not seem important. They are very smart and will learn but don't expect to do things the way you would in Paris, Tokyo, or Chicago.

↦ *French businesswoman who lived in Moscow*

CHAPTER 14

The Middle East
and the Indian Subcontinent

I Wish I'd Known

I didn't really understand how long it would take to get things done. Everyone speaks English [and] uses e-mail. It seemed so easy. Your schedule must allow time for interruptions, for conversation, for lots of cups of coffee, [and] for changes. That is essential. Business can certainly be done, schedules met, and quality provided. You just need to allow some time.

→ *American apparel manufacturer*
working in the United Arab Emirates

I Wish They Knew

That this entire part of the world isn't being blown up. That not everyone is violent. That even in the areas most known for fighting, business is being done. Big companies and small, local and global—each country has a business community, and some of us are most concerned with learning and growing our businesses.

→ *Hotel manager from Palestine*
visiting the United States to learn
about operations and marketing

Known by Many Names

Afghanistan, Bahrain, Bangladesh, Egypt, India, Iraq, Iran, Israel, Jordan, Kuwait, Lebanon, Oman, Pakistan, Qatar, Saudi Arabia, Syria, Turkey, United Arab Emirates, and Yemen. Americans know these countries are linked together but may not be clear about their exact locations. Are they the countries included when people talk about the Middle East, the Near East, the Indian subcontinent, Southwest Asia, or the Persian Gulf states? For travelers, the Centers for Disease Control and Prevention assigns Bahrain, Iran, Iraq, Israel, Jordan, Kuwait,

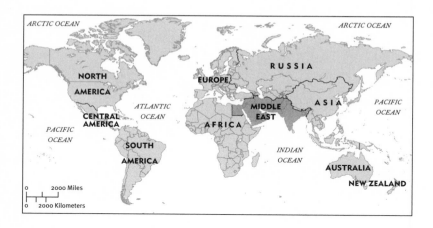

Lebanon, Oman, Qatar, Saudi Arabia, Turkey, United Arab Emirates, Yemen, and Turkey to the Middle East. India, Pakistan, and Bangladesh are considered part of the Indian subcontinent, and Egypt is in North Africa. The online encyclopedia Wikipedia.com lists 19 places under the category of Southwest Asia, including all of the aforementioned countries except India and Pakistan, and adds to that the Gaza Strip and the West Bank, disputed parts of Israel, and further defines specific parts of Egypt and Turkey as falling within this area. Turkey, because of its geography, sometimes counts as Asia, yet it is in negotiations to join the European Union. [1] Different sources divide this region differently. Individual nations can be identified in several ways, complicating attempts to understand these countries that are extremely different yet similar.

To begin, they vary dramatically in size. India is the largest and third most populous country in the world, with an area that is one third the size of the United States. In contrast, Bahrain is made up of 33 islands, only 3 of which are habitable, and covers only 240 square miles. Egypt sits mainly on the continent of Africa, connected to the Asian continent, where the others are located, via a small strip of land. It is that section that makes Egypt a neighbor of Jordan.

The geography is also diverse. The region is home to Africa's longest river, the Nile, which runs into Egypt. The Dead Sea, shared by Jordan

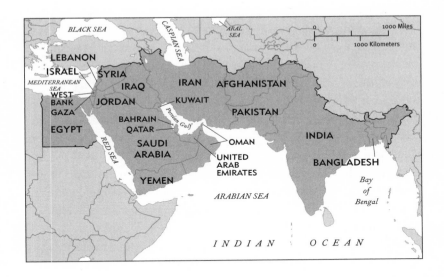

and Israel, is the lowest point on earth. The largest sand desert in the world is shared by Saudi Arabia and Oman, and some of the world's highest mountains are in Pakistan. Among the natural endowments of the area are oil resources that provide much of the world's supply. Best known for their own production are Iran, Iraq, Kuwait, Qatar, Saudi Arabia, and the United Arab Emirates, which are members of the Organization of the Petroleum Exporting Countries (OPEC), the 11-member group that produces 40 percent of the world's oil output. (The other members of OPEC are Algeria, Indonesia, Libya, Nigeria, and Venezuela.) Among the other nations in this group only, Israel, India, and Pakistan are not counted as oil-producing nations.

Our awareness of this area is often shaped by images of war, debates about the costs and benefits of outsourcing, and concern about prices of gasoline for our cars. We seldom reflect on the region's history and its importance in the development of the contemporary world.

Looking Back and Looking at Today

The Middle East could be claimed to be the birthplace of civilization, since history can be traced back thousands of years. Stone Age relics have been found in Israel and Egypt.[2] Kuwait can look back 7,000 years to its beginnings. Libraries are filled with books about the pharaohs of Egypt. Three of the world's major religions—Islam, Christianity, and Judaism—began here. In addition to shared experiences of the region, each of the 19 countries can look back to specific events that and key figures who shaped their development.

One aspect of this region was its place on the Silk Road, the route linking Asia with Europe. The northern and southern routes from China and Central Asia met here. Traders came by both land and sea. They brought not only goods such as silk but also ideas and innovations including musical instruments. Cymbals went to China, and Chinese gongs traveled this route and eventually reached Europe. Material goods, ideas, religion, and culture mingled on the ancient trade routes.

In the twenty-first century, the Silk Road has emerged once more as a route carrying culture and music east and west. The well-known musician Yo-Yo Ma created the Silk Road Project to study the flow of ideas among different cultures along the route in an effort to connect classical traditions of the West with the diverse Middle Eastern and Asian musical cultures. The project produces innovate programs, for example, one that combines new technology with traditional music forms. They organized a collaboration of music and poetry to make a 500,000-line oral poem from Kyrgyzstan accessible to Western audiences. Their work has the potential to keep traditional musical forms and instruments alive through collaboration among musicians from disparate parts of the globe. To reach that goal, the project not only sponsors events and exhibitions but also arranges exchange programs that mentor musicians from the United States, China, India, and Azerbaijan. This modern-day Silk Road continues the process started in ancient times, connecting people and leading to the exchange of ideas and cultures. (For more information, consult the Web site www.silkroadproject.org.)

In addition to being designated as the original Silk Road, some of the Middle Eastern region came to be known as the Fertile Crescent. This area includes parts of what is now known as Israel, the West Bank, Lebanon, Jordan, Syria, Iraq, and Turkey. As implied by the name, an abundance of food was grown here, more than needed to feed its population. The excess was used for trade within the region.

The people of the region lived in groups that expanded from individual families to larger groups or tribes. These tribes established boundaries to conserve and control their scarce resources. The tribal relationships dating back to the early occupants of the area—to the Sumereans, Babylonians, and Assyrians, founders of the first cities as far back as 3000 B.C.—still have importance in the twenty-first century. Families gathered into tribes not only to guard their resources but also to defend themselves. This area was invaded, conquered, and ruled by a variety of foreigners including the Greeks, Romans, Turks, and Persians in ancient times. The Mongols came from the east; the Portuguese, French, and British came from the west; and the Russians came from the north. Each country left its mark.

More than 50 years after their withdrawal, the impact of the British is still apparent in India where English is the language of business and education. India has 18 official languages, but it is the imported language that is spoken throughout the country.[3] While you can recognize the impact of the British rule in the legal and business systems of Great Britain's former colonies, influence is also evidenced in more subtle ways. For example, Pakistan is home to bagpipe bands and hundreds of firms that make bagpipes, kilts, and other traditional Scottish Highland clothing. One family has been in this business for more than 100 years and not only sells in its local market but also has been exporting to Scotland since 1910.[4]

However, it is neither language nor specialty items that you consider when thinking of the British legacy. It is the creation of India, Pakistan, Bangladesh, and Israel that link with the departure of Great Britain in the late 1940s. After years of struggle, India became an independent republic in 1947. In granting independence to the former colony, Great Britain allowed the Muslim prince to take control of the area that is now the Islamic republic of Pakistan. The Muslims feared that the larger population of India, primarily Hindu, would overwhelm them. To complicate matters, Pakistan at that point was two areas, east and west, separated by a portion of India. After a civil war, East Pakistan became the country of Bangladesh in 1971. India and Pakistan as independent nations continued to compete with each other. They fought a war over the area called Kashmir, now controlled in part by each of them and still a subject of ongoing tension. Still considered developing nations, they have the distinction of having developed nuclear weapons, thus making their differences global concerns rather than regional matters. Fortunately, as of 2004 there were signs that these two nuclear powers might be entering a period of cooperation.

When India and Pakistan were emerging as independent entities, Israel came into existence. It was created in 1948 when the United Nations divided the British mandate into Israeli and Arab lands. The area that became Israel, considered the Jewish homeland, was especially important at the end of World War II, taking in survivors from the Nazi era. Unfortunately, its history as an independent state has been filled with fighting and failed attempts at peace. As soon as its independence was established, its neighbors declared war. A settlement was achieved in 1949, but unfortunately it laid the groundwork for further strife. That peace agreement placed the parts of Israel now known as the West Bank and Gaza Strip under the control of Jordan and Egypt, respectively. The West Bank is an area on the west of the Jordan River between Jordan and Israel, and the Gaza Strip is on the Sinai peninsula connected to Egypt.

Wars were fought in 1956, 1967, and 1973. In the 1967 war, Israel took control of both the West Bank and Gaza. (It later signed peace accords with Egypt in 1979 and Jordan in 1994 resolving other issues.) Both areas are occupied primarily by Palestinians, who continue to demand a separate independent state. As of the beginning of the twenty-first century, the violence continues as the Palestinians press for Israel to remove its settlements from Gaza and the West Bank. At the time this chapter is being written, there are plans for Israel to withdraw from Gaza and the northern area of the West Bank. Whether this proceeds and peace finally arrives in this area remains to be seen.

Unfortunately it isn't just India and Pakistan or Israel and its immediate neighbors that have fought or continue to fight. Wars, civil unrest, and violence continue in Afghanistan and Iraq. Bombings occur in Saudi Arabia and Pakistan. Peacekeepers patrol the streets in Lebanon. Fighting continues over resources, territory, religion, and tribal honor. Historical relationships and attitudes reveal themselves in the events that make headlines today.

Government and Business

The forms of government in the area are as varied as the cultures of the nations. India is a well-established democratic republic while Afghanistan has a provisional government. Iraq is in transition. Syria and Yemen are both republics. Iran is a theocratic democracy, while Bahrain and Jordan are constitutional monarchies and the United Arab Emirates is a federation of emirates. Each one has its own government structure, legal system, and business practices.

Several of the countries are Islamic theocracies (Iran, Saudi Arabia, Pakistan, and Afghanistan) where there is no distinction between religious and secular law. It is critical to understand the influence of Islam on the conduct of business. Not only are personal dress and behavior regulated but also the hours and days of work. For example, the workweek is Sunday through Thursday or Saturday to Wednesday, rather than the Western standard of Monday through Friday. As mentioned in a previous chapter, because collection of interest is not allowed, the banking system in Islamic countries had to be adapted to recognize the needs of the businesses and still conform to religious teachings.

Religion

The Middle East is the birthplace of the three monotheistic world religions: Judaism, Christianity, and Islam. All three religions are still represented; however, the majority of the population in this area are Muslims.

While there are Muslims in all these countries not all are Islamic nations. Nor are they all equally strict in how the religion is interpreted into daily life. For example, Muslims are not allowed to consume alcohol or pork. In Saudi Arabia both are illegal. However, Egypt, Jordan (which has been a Muslim country since the seventh century), Lebanon, and Syria are more relaxed in their interpretations and so you will find alcohol and pork there.[5] Additionally, in a traditional Muslim environment, the role of women is extremely restricted. However, there are variations in the dress and participation of women from one society to another. You can find female leaders and businesswomen just as you can find fully veiled women or women who have very little education.

Religion has a more obvious powerful influence in this part of the world than in many others. It often seems that the religious wars between Jew and Muslim and among sects within the Muslim religion fill the headlines without possibility of end. Old relationships, allegiances, and bitter rivalries are alive today.

Business Their Way

To understand the people in the places where you do business, it's necessary to read extensively and talk with people who have experiences to share. In addition, there are studies that can provide insights to the possible similarities or differences and the levels of the systems and infrastructure that are the foundations for contemporary practices.

One of these studies is provided by Transparency International in its annual Corruption Perceptions Index (see chapter 10). The index ranks countries to indicate the level of perception perceived in their activities. The rating scale is from 10 for "clean" to 0 for "totally corrupt." The results for the countries discussed in this chapter, ranked from highest score to lowest, appear on Table 14.1.

The country with the cleanest score in the most recent edition was Finland with a 9.7 score. Bangladesh tied with Haiti at 1.5 for the lowest score of the 146 countries surveyed. (The United States was tied at 7.5 with Belgium and Ireland in the number 17 spot.)

Trade with the World

To obtain an impression of the development level of a country and its participation in the global economy, it is useful to consult the list of WTO member countries. In this region 11 countries that hold that status are Bahrain, Bangladesh, India, Israel, Jordan, Kuwait, Oman, Qatar, Pakistan, Turkey, and United Arab Emirates. Saudi Arabia and Yemen are on observed status. Within the WTO, India is known as one of the leaders of the developing countries. Along with China and Brazil, it has emerged as a strong voice expressing the views of less developed nations, especially in the negotiations concerning issues surrounding agricultural production and distribution.

But trade for these countries is not limited to WTO membership, to activities within that organization, or to formal trade agreements. Iran signed an agreement that will allow Japan to develop a major oil field,

TABLE 14.1   CORRUPTION PERCEPTIONS INDEX RANKING

COUNTRY	RATING
Israel	6.4
Oman	6.1
United Arab Emirates	6.1
Bahrain	5.8
Jordan	5.3
Qatar	5.2
Kuwait	4.6
Saudi Arabia	3.4
Egypt	3.2
Turkey	3.2
Iran	2.9
India	2.8
Lebanon	2.7
Iraq	2.1
Pakistan	2.1
Bangladesh	1.5

Source: Transparency International Corruption Perceptions Index 2004

thus providing a supply of oil to Japan, a country that needs imports to meet almost of all its energy requirements.[6] In addition, Japan's investment will pay for the development of the oil field, which Iran is unable to do.

India continues to work toward a trilateral trade pact with South Africa and Brazil. These three countries are connected indirectly through membership but not yet linked together. Brazil, as a member of Mercosur, is linked to India by its preferential trade agreement with that organization, and South Africa is a member of SACU that is negotiating Mercosur.

Both the European Union and the United States have built trade connections in this region. The EU formed the Euro-Mediterranean partnership, which is a framework for political, economic, and social relations with the region that also includes bilateral agreements with the individual nations. The United States has free trade agreements with Israel, Bahrain, and Jordan and is working toward a broader

Middle East agreement to be in place by 2013. As a step toward that goal it has entered into trade and investment framework agreements with Saudi Arabia, United Arab Emirates, Kuwait, Qatar, Yemen, and Egypt.

Business Is People

It is important to remember the tribal roots that are the foundation of connections in this locale. Each tribe has characteristic speech, dress, and customs. In Iran alone there are 150 tribes, and tribal leaders maintain great influence.[7] Personal relationships and loyalty to family are of the utmost importance. As you may expect, the overall population tends toward high-level anxiety avoidance and strong regard for hierarchy with a collectivist approach to decision-making processes.[8]

The influence of traditional tribes is especially obvious in India, the most populous country. Its tribes are referred to as castes, and there are four traditional castes with thousands of subsets. One is born into a caste based on social, historical, and economic criteria. It is part of people's lineage and cannot change. Discrimination on the basis of caste is outlawed but still significant in politics and business as well as an important factor in social institutions such as marriage.[9]

One American reported that even if a businessperson is educated in the West and lives and works in Europe or the United States, once that person returns home, the decision-making process reverts to the cultural norms of the home country. No contract or agreement could be finalized until it was approved by the tribe's elders. Although these people worked in modern offices, the traditional hierarchy determined who was in control, not the organizational charts in the employee manuals.

Further, it is people's needs and not schedules that control the flow of business. It is said that time is a servant of the people, not people's master. Building relationships through conversation and shared hospitality is essential. To develop business you must spend the time to get to know the people, moving slowly and often indirectly toward the goal.

Counting the People

In contrast to many other parts of the world, the population in all of the Middle East is growing. In all, more than 50 percent of the population is in the 15 to 64 age range except in Gaza, a disputed section of Israel,

TABLE 14.2   POPULATION AND MEDIAN AGE BY COUNTRY

COUNTRY	POPULATION 2005	MEDIAN AGE
Afghanistan	25,791,400	17.5
Bahrain	707,357	29.0
Bangladesh	133,581,700	21.5
Egypt	68,648,500	23.4
India	1,088,056,000	24.4
Iraq	26,095,283	19.2
Iran	68,458,680	23.5
Israel	6,986,639	29.2
Jordan	5,788,340	22.2
Kuwait	2,530,012	25.9
Lebanon	4,461,995	26.9
Oman	2,398,545	19.3
Pakistan	160,166,742	19.4
Qatar	768,464	31.4
Saudi Arabia	21,771,609	21.2
Syria	18,586,743	20.0
Turkey	73,598,181	27.3
United Arab Emirates	3,750,054	27.7
Yemen	16,667,900	16.5

Source: CIA World Fact Book 2005 and World Internet Stats 2005

where the largest segment of its population is under 15 years of age.[10] (See Table 14.2.) The median age is as old as 31.4 in Qatar, and young as 16.5 in Yemen. The Kingdom of Bahrain has the smallest population, approximately the same as the U.S. city of Austin, Texas. The largest in the group is India, the second largest country in the world, ranking between China at number 1 and the United States at number 3.[11]

Online and on the Phone

As you'll note from reading through Table 14.3, Internet and cell phone usage varies as much as the size of these countries. India has 18,481,000 users, the largest number of users considering head count alone. It has only a 1.7 percent penetration of the population, well below the high-

TABLE 14.3   CONNECTED BY PHONE AND ONLINE

COUNTRY	CELL PHONE USERS	INTERNET USERS	INTERNET PENETRATION
Afghanistan	15,000	1,000	0.0
Bahrain	443,100	195,700	27.7
Bangladesh	1,365,000	243,000	0.2
Egypt	5,797,500	2,700,000	3.9
India	26,154,400	18,481,000	1.7
Iraq	20,000	25,000	0.1
Iran	3,376,500	4,800,000	7.0
Israel	6,334,000	2,000,000	28.6
Jordan	1,325,399	457,000	7.9
Kuwait	1,420,00	567,000	22.4
Lebanon	775,100	400,000	9.0
Oman	464,900	180,000	7.5
Pakistan	2,624,800	1,500,000	0.9
Qatar	326,500	126,000	16.4
Saudi Arabia	7,238,200	1,500,000	6.9
Syria	400,000	220,000	1.2
Turkey	27,887,500	5,500,000	7.5
United Arab Emirates	2,972,300	1,110,200	39.6
West Bank	480,000	145,000	3.6
Yemen	411,000	100,000	0.5

Source: CIA World Fact Book 2005 and Internet World Stats 2005

est-ranking United Arab Emirates, at 39.6 percent. (For perspective, remember that Sweden, number 1 in the world, has more than 70 percent penetration, the United States has 66.8 percent, and China has 7.3 percent.) Afghanistan, Bangladesh, Iraq, Pakistan, and Yemen have less than 1 percent of the population online. The Egyptian government, in an effort to increase literacy, is making Internet access available to 20,000 elementary schools.[12]

Is There a McDonald's?

It isn't all war torn. Business goes on. Oil. Tourism. Agriculture. Textiles and apparel manufacturing. Software development. Movies. And, yes, the well-known American brand is there. There are McDonald's restaurants in 13 of the 19 countries. Only Afghanistan, Bangladesh, Iraq, Iran, Jordan, and Yemen do not have one yet. In India, where cows are sacred, the menu has been adapted to be culturally appropriate.

But it isn't the expansion of American retailers such as Starbucks, Kentucky Fried Chicken, or Saks Fifth Avenue to that region that makes headlines today. It is the location of textile production, customer support call centers, and software programming that has emerged primarily in India, Pakistan, and the United Arab Emirates. With a highly educated English-speaking population, India has become a center for technology outsourcing. What was once an issue related to manufacturing jobs has become an issue that touches many industries and many professions. Whether this movement of jobs and services from one country to another is a cost or a benefit is being hotly debated in the United States and other industrialized countries throughout the world.

The word *outsourcing*, when used to mean the loss of jobs in the United States, elicits strong emotions, creating images of shuttered factories, empty computer terminals, and people searching for work. Little attention is given to the counterpart of this trend, which is in-sourcing, the movement of foreign investment and factories into the United States. Foreign-owned assets in the United States, such as factories, distribution centers, and the like, are equal in value to the overseas assets of U.S. firms.[13] While U.S. companies have moved jobs to India, Pakistan, Ghana, and Mexico, companies from India, China, Japan, and Israel have opened factories and offices in the United States. Today it can be difficult to determine from the brand name whether a car is Japanese, American, or German since parts are made and assembled in a variety of locales.

As with all aspects of globalization, this movement of jobs and investments is not unique to the businesses and workforce in the United States. The Trade Consul for Poland discussed the challenge of attracting opportunities to Poland, which now competes with Estonia regarding lower labor costs and lower corporate tax rates. Factory workers in Germany agreed to a contract extending their working hours to avoid losing jobs to workers in Eastern Europe, and Japanese companies do assembly work in China where the cost of labor is significantly less.

Outsourcing for one country is in-sourcing for another. Job losses in one area often create jobs in another. While the negative impact of job loss is clearly seen, what is not always evident are the benefits beyond immediate labor savings to companies that outsource their production and processes. Some of the gain is in creating new markets for their products by providing income to a new group of workers. A recent 12-year study by the McKinsey Global Institute has shown that poverty is reduced by growing the private sector.[14] Not only does the additional income allow people to purchase goods and services but also improved wages and the reduction of poverty are important in other ways. The alleviation of poverty and growth of an educated middle class can contribute to stability. And in this region, stability is something that has been lacking throughout history.

Now We Know

Of all the regions in the world, the Middle East/Indian subcontinent is probably the most difficult to identify. Which countries belong to this region? Which sources are most accurate? Where should Turkey be listed: Asia, Europe, or the Middle East? No matter how you construct a list, it is clear the relationships are ancient, modern, and complex. These nations are participants and even leaders in world trade and at the same time developing countries with all the related challenges. For example, India's importance as a global business center continues to rise and yet its Internet penetration, one indicator of economic development, is less than 2 percent of the population.

Of critical importance to the future of the region is the ongoing political instability. Tensions centering on the relationship between Israel and its neighbors are well documented. Add to this the effects of the conflict in Iraq, the uncomfortable peace between India and Pakistan, and the questions of nuclear capability in Iran. All these factors combine to make this a difficult region to consider for business expansion. Yet, business continues to expand and opportunities appear. What is the risk, and what is the reward? To answer the question, more than book research is required. In this region, as in Asia, relationships are the key to doing business. To build business here, a person needs to plan time to build relationships and to make connections within the business community. The best research may be done in conversations over dinner.

I'm Glad I Know

That when you attend a conference in this area the local attendees will be knowledgeable, engaging people. Well educated and well traveled. However, while the hotels, cars, and apparel are much like [those in] the United States or Europe, attitudes spring from a long tradition of tribe and clan. Time is flexible. You can't proceed in a hurry with a fixed deadline in mind. Flexibility and patience are important. I've learned a great deal and am looking forward to my return visit. I think there's lots of business to be done there.

→→ *American, U.S. Department of Commerce*
adviser to American exporters

CHAPTER 15

Asia

I Wish I'd Known

I wish I'd been prepared for conversations at work that were different from the ones at home. During my first meeting with the vice president of a Korean client company, I was quizzed about my marital status [and] asked whether I had children or not. I was amazed. These questions would be considered offensive if not illegal in the United States. Fortunately, although I was annoyed and uncomfortable, I answered politely.

Later I realized that he was simply trying to learn something about me. There were no female executives at this company. He was used to defining "who a woman is" not by her profession as an executive but by her "profession" as a wife and mother. So, while the questions felt intrusive, I realized that this was due to my "cultural values," and there was no "universal" reason why these questions should be inappropriate. My client was simply getting to know me as part of building our relationship so that we could work together.

↣ *American technology consultant,*
based in California, on assignment in Korea

I Wish They Knew

I wish that people would come here to China, especially to Hong Kong, knowing something of the culture. You can't do business without understanding the culture of the people.

↣ *Chinese woman, an apparel industry consultant,*
based in Hong Kong

How Big?

When people announce that they are working in Asia or traveling there, it's often their shorthand way of saying they're off to Hong Kong or possibly mainland China. The statement is made as if Asia

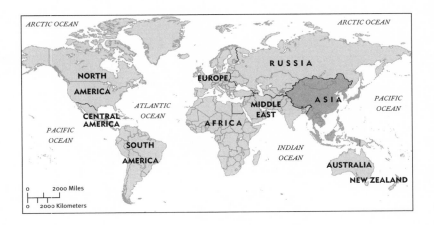

were one specific country, a singular place, like Chile or Australia. But Asia isn't one destination. Rather, Asia is the world's largest continent, covering 17,300,000 miles and home to 49 different countries. It is an area of extremes. Within its boundaries are the globe's 2 most populous nations, China and India, with more than 1 billion people each. Also included are the world's highest point, Mount Everest on the border between Nepal and Tibet, and its lowest point, the Dead Sea in Israel and Jordan. At the most westerly point it includes Turkey, and it extends east beyond China to include Japan.

Not all of the 49 countries that are geographically part of Asia are identified as part of Asia in terms of political or economic linkages. Turkey at the western boundary is being considered for membership in the European Union. India and those on the Arab peninsula are at times counted as part of the Middle East, or they are grouped with Pakistan and Bangladesh and then referred to as the Indian subcontinent. Russia, which rests on both the continents of Europe and Asia, and Belarus, Kazakhstan, Kyrgyzstan, and Tajikistan are part of Central Asia. They formed the Eurasian Economic Community. The name of the organization recognizes their connection to both Europe and Asia.

In this chapter, the focus will be on the part of the continent referred to as Southeast Asia. Even by limiting the geographic scope as such, the area is still large and diverse. There are countries with notable variations

in size, from China, approximately the size of the continental United States, to Singapore, an island nation the size of Chicago (the third-largest city in the United States). Korea covers a peninsula attached to land at the north and is divided into two countries, and Indonesia is made up of more than 13,000 islands.[1] Asia is large and diverse (see Table 15.1).

No matter the number of countries in this area, when considering Asia today the spotlight turns to China. This chapter is no exception. Our focus will be on China, Korea, and Japan. It isn't within the scope of this chapter to provide country-by-country details. Aids to further research will be included in the Resources section. Meanwhile the information included here offers some insight to this dynamic part of the world.

COUNTRY	TABLE 15.1 POPULATION POPULATION	MEDIAN AGE	ANNUAL % BIRTHRATE
Cambodia	14,560,030	19.5	1.8
China	1,282,198,289	31.8	0.57
East Timor	936,053	20	2.11
Hong Kong	6,983,938	39.4	0.65
Indonesia	219,307,147	26.1	1.49
Japan	128,137,485	42.3	0.08
North Korea	25,259,835	31.4	0.98
South Korea	49,929,293	33.7	0.62
Laos	5,612,274	18.6	2.44
Malaysia	26,500,699	23.8	1.83
Mongolia	2,535,013	23.9	1.43
Myanmar (Burma)	53,222,658	25.7	0.47*
Nepal	24,947,198	19.9	2.23
Philippines	84,174,092	22.1	1.88
Singapore	3,547,809	36.2	1.71
Thailand	65,599,545	30.5	0.91
Vietnam	82,851,971	24.9	1.3

*Considers impact of AIDS
Source: CIA World Factbook 2005 and Internet World Stats February 2005

China: Open, Closed, and Open Again

The 5,000-year history of China reveals an advanced civilization that invented silk fabric, written language, and administrative systems, and that created porcelain and the art of using medicinal herbs. It also reveals to us a country that alternated periods of engagement with the outside world and others of isolation.

Founded by native tribes, the Hans, and ruled by a succession of dynasties (a powerful group or family that maintains power over a considerable period of time), it has been known as the Celestial Empire and the Middle Kingdom. No matter its name, the population believed it was the center of the universe. Any foreigner—any person who was not Chinese—was considered to be a barbarian.

Notwithstanding this attitude, China did not always ignore the outside world. The Silk Road stretched from Chinese cities all the way to the Mediterranean. Not only did the Chinese ships operate nearby trading with Korea and Japan but they also ventured to India and beyond. In the fifteenth century a Chinese explorer made 7 voyages from Asia to Africa. His last, in 1433, was an immense maritime expedition with 28,000 people and 300 ships. The trips were not to explore the world but to bring treasures to the emperor. There were horses from Arabia and ivory from Africa. But the return from this journey marked the end of this period of outward travel. Returning sailors were ignored rather than rewarded, and China turned inward.[2]

Less than 100 years after the Chinese ended their voyages of exploration the Portuguese became the first Europeans to arrive. British, Dutch, Spanish, and French explorers and traders, followed them. It took war in the latter part of the 1800s and force to open the Chinese markets. The opening of the country to trade brought more change than the introduction of new goods. Vietnam, Laos, and Cambodia became French colonies. Great Britain took control of Hong Kong and Burma (now known as Myanmar). It was not just the Europeans who took territory that had been part of China's sphere of influence. The Japanese annexed Korea and Manchuria and even held Shanghai for a time.

By the early 1900s, China's conflicts were internal as well as external. Revolution ended the rule of the emperor and marked the creation of the Republic of China. Unfortunately this did not lead to a period of peace and prosperity. Rather, dissent and struggle continued. The Chinese Communist Party fought the nationalists led by Chiang Kai-shek for control of the country. Ultimately the Communists were successful in creating the People's Republic of China in 1949.

Again, the change of government created new struggles and did not lead to wealth and peace. Mao Tse-tung, the leader of the Communist Party, closed China's doors and created policies that led to extraordinary hardship. Both his Great Leap Forward (1958–1961), an unsuccessful program to push economic growth, and the Cultural Revolution (1966–1976) were disastrous for the country. The Cultural Revolution was a time of turmoil and anti-intellectual sentiment. More than 40 million people reportedly starved during that time. There were famines and floods. Schools were closed, music and art censored, and people relocated from cities to the countryside. It was a time of "collective madness and brutality."[3]

It wasn't until the end of the 1970s, when Deng Xiaoping came to power and announced the Open Door Policy, that China moved forward to join the contemporary global economy. In less than 30 years China evolved from an isolated developing nation to one with considerable influence in the world's trading community.

Taiwan: Independent Country or Island Province?

The status of Taiwan, an island off the coast of China, has been the subject of debate for more than 50 years. To some it's an emerging democracy, home of the true seat of the true Chinese government, while to others, including the Chinese authorities based in Beijing, it's a province of China.

Historically it was always part of China, except during the periods when it was ruled by the Dutch or the Japanese. Taiwan's disputed status is a result of the revolution that brought Mao Tse-tung and the Communists to power. The anti-Communist forces led by Chiang Kai-shek fled to Taiwan when it was clear they had lost the civil war. They claimed that they were the legitimate government of China and that Taiwan was the center of Chinese democracy. The Republic of China, as their government was called, was initially recognized by the United States as the official government of China.

It was more than 30 years, from the end of World War II until 1979, before the United States recognized the People's Republic of China (PRC), based in Beijing, as the government of China. This recognition capped 8 years of diplomatic negotiations, including the first visit of the then president of the United States, Richard Nixon, to mainland China. As part of its recognition of the PRC as the legitimate government of China, the United States acknowledged Taiwan's status as a part of China, not a separate country.

Although China agreed that the United States could maintain direct links to Taiwan for trade and cultural activities, the relationships between all three parties are strained by the situation. The United States has pledged to support Taiwan and aid in its defense if necessary even though it recognizes the PRC's view of the relationship. The ambiguity of the attitudes of the parties, the varying levels of tensions, and uncertainty of future actions, create concern throughout the region.

Hong Kong: Special Administrative Region

By contrast, Hong Kong's status is clear. After more than a century and a half as a British crown colony, it is part of China again. It is not simply a province—it occupies the unique status as the Hong Kong Special Administrative Region.

This area on the southern coast of China is about half the size of the state of Rhode Island and one of the world's most densely populated areas. China describes Hong Kong as being part of "one country with two systems." The second system allows Hong Kong residents to travel more freely than those in the mainland and to retain English as an official language. Both of these arrangements support the extensive international business conducted there.

The years of British rule helped to shape the culture of the region. As its connections with the mainland grow, the differences are having an impact. According to a Chinese woman who lives and works for a Hong Kong business development and training organization, it's now necessary to learn the culture of mainland China to take advantage of new business opportunities. "It's different," she said, "and we have to learn to be able to be effective. Their culture isn't the same as ours here."

However, it isn't simply that people in Hong Kong are starting to expand business connections with the mainland. The city is also receiving an influx of mainland Chinese coming to work there. Hong Kong offers new professional opportunities, including a step to a career outside China in the United States or Europe for some.[4]

In addition to being known as a regional center for international finance, home to agents handling product development on the mainland, Hong Kong is known as a shoppers' paradise. According to Mr. Hong Hao, a Chinese business development director for a French company who lives in Shanghai, Hong Kong is a city based on production and consumption. However, he said Shanghai is really the business center of China, and Beijing is the government center. "In Hong Kong," he said, "it's all about looking and buying."

Japan: The Land of the Rising Sun

Another country with thousands of years of history, Japan can trace the lineage of its current emperor back to 600 B.C. Japan, slightly smaller than the state of Montana, is made up of 4 main islands near the coastlines of China, Korea, and Russia. Like the Chinese, the Japanese have had periods when they closed themselves off to foreign influences, including almost 400 years from the 1600s to the late nineteenth century. Their connection to the United States began a little over 150 years ago in 1853. In the ensuing years the relationship between the two countries has been that of both foe and friend.

One historian notes that a distinguishing characteristic of the Japanese is that when in contact with outsiders, they have been willing to learn from them. Initially the influence was from China, including religion and products such as silks and ceramics. The Japanese took the new knowledge and used it for their benefit, which in part is why Japan was the first non-Western country to industrialize.[5]

Through much of its history Japan has been an aggressor nation. Regionally they annexed Korea, Manchuria, and Taiwan. Their efforts to acquire Korea began in 1875, progressed to control of Korea and Taiwan in 1895 after their success in the Sino-Japanese War, and ended with annexation of Korea in 1910. Manchuria came under Japanese control at the end of the Sino-Russian War in 1905. They attacked the United States at Pearl Harbor in December 1941 and that began the United States' active engagement in World War II. Their defeat in World War II ended their expansionist activities. Although economically devastated by the war, they were able to rebuild their country and their economy to become one of the most powerful trading nations. Now the conflicts are about market access and tariffs that are fought with words rather than guns and bombs.

Korea: The Hermit Kingdom

Korea, a country about the size of the state of Indiana, is actually a peninsula attached to the Asian continent in the north, bordering China, and surrounded on east, west, and south by the Yellow Sea and the Sea of Japan. Able to trace its history back to the seventh century Korea has been repeatedly invaded and controlled by outsiders.

Whether it was the Chinese, Japanese, or Mongolians who were the conquerors, each one closed off the country, leading to its label of the Hermit Kingdom.

The most assertive of the invaders were the Japanese, who annexed the country in 1910. Not only did they invade and take control of the country but they also outlawed Korean culture and language. "Schools were required to teach only in Japanese. All Koreans were ordered to take Japanese names, speak only Japanese when dealing with the Japanese, and behave in the Japanese manner. This period is sometimes referred to as the Dark Period."[6] Japan's domination of Korea continued for almost 40 years, until the end of World War II.

Unfortunately, the end of the war and defeat of the Japanese didn't bring freedom and peace to the country. The United States and Russia established a joint trusteeship and designated the United States to disarm Japanese in the south and Russia to disarm Japanese in the north. Rather than withdraw after disarming the troops, however, the Russians established a Communist government. In 1950, the Communist government in the north invaded the south of Korea. Barely five years after the end of World War II, the United States and its former allies, China and Russia, were once again involved in a war. This time the United States and Russia were enemies, and China was Russia's ally. In 1953, after three years of combat with no victor, an armistice was signed, leaving Korea divided into North Korea and South Korea.

Although the Korean War did not officially end and fighting has erupted during the ensuing years, for practical purposes the armistice marked the end of the war. With the end of hostilities came the beginning of development of two different countries, North and South Korea. The differing systems, one Communist and one democratic, have created two dramatically different nations.

North Korea, after half a century, is known as a secretive, unpredictable country that many consider a threat to world peace. Of most concern is the question of its nuclear capability and intentions. In 2002 it expelled United Nations monitors and still refuses to allow them to return. It not only poses a threat to outsiders but is also known for the hardship experienced by its people. The government controls all aspects of life including wages and prices. Poor agricultural processes have resulted in inadequate food supplies to support its population and international aid has been required to help feed its people.

Isolated since the end of the war in 1945, stories began to appear of changes under way. The leaders of North and South Korea met for the first time in 2000. Four years later, there are reports of sales by street vendors indicating some entrepreneurial activity, appearances of imported beer from Singapore, and clothing from China available for purchase. Whether this is the mark of the opening of the economy or not remains to be seen.[7]

Further, recent surveys show a change in some South Koreans' attitudes toward their northern neighbors.[8] Indications are that younger people are looking for more friendly engagement with North Korea. Older, more conservative people see this as "undermining national security."[9] The dynamic between these attitudes and the actions of the two governments will be interesting to observe. Meanwhile the status and actions of North Korea remain important issues for the region and the world.

Complex Connections: The United States with the Philippines and with Vietnam

In early 1898, the United States went to war with Spain to free Cuba. It's unlikely anyone on the planning team expected the war to result in the United States' acquisition of the Philippines, an island nation in the South China Sea. The two countries, the Philippines and the United States, began the war as allies united against Spain, which had ruled the island for more than 300 years. Later that year Spain was defeated, Cuba was freed, and Philippine independence was declared. Unfortunately independence didn't become a reality. As part of the peace treaty (Treaty of Paris), the United States acquired the Philippines along with Guam and Puerto Rico for a total of $20 million.

Almost immediately a War of Independence began, changing allies into enemies. Within two years, by 1902, the war had ended and the Philippines was set on the path to independence supported by the United States. The multistage transition from colony to commonwealth to independent nation proceeded for more than 40 years with 1946 set as the date for full independence. Unfortunately, the Japanese invasion in 1941 brought another 4 years of war to the islands. Finally, in 1945, after World War II the Philippines became an independent nation.

The Vietnam experience is once again a story of allies who became enemies in war. The United States entered Vietnam as it had the Philippines, as a friend. In this case, the original connection was through a 1961 aid treaty attempting to assist South Vietnam in its efforts to combat the Russian- and Chinese-supported Viet Cong from the north.

The country in its early history had been controlled by China, became a French colony in the 1800s, and was occupied by the Japanese in World War II. At the end of the war, the allies disarmed the country in a way that was similar to the program in Korea. In this case, the country was divided between France in the south and the Chinese in the north. Rather than a new peace, the result was war, which ended with France's defeat in 1954. But that still wasn't the conclusion of hostilities. War continued with the Communists in both north and south. The country was seen as having strategic importance in the ongoing Cold War between the United States and Russia. Therefore, support for opposing sides in the Vietnam conflict came from the United States, Russia, and, at times, China, and even other Western countries. After 11 years of involvement (1961–1972), unable to conclusively end or win the war, the United States withdrew. Although peace accords were signed in 1973, fighting continued until North Vietnam achieved victory in 1976 and reunited the country.

The Vietnam War was frustrating and internally divisive for the United States. Many people questioned the U.S. involvement and the purpose of fighting. As casualties mounted and no clear victory appeared possible, public opinion turned against the war and the government. The experience had a deep impact on the nation, splitting families and creating a legacy that continues into the twenty-first century. More than 40 years after the U.S. withdrawal, the Vietnam War and people's experience was still a key campaign issue in the 2004 presidential election.

At the end of the war, the United States terminated connections with Vietnam and created an embargo on all trade. The conclusion of the fighting brought little peace or reconciliation between the parties. So strong was the impact of the war that more than 20 years passed before the trade embargo was lifted and official diplomatic relations between the United States and Vietnam were reestablished.

Trade Global and Regional

It's easy to think of trade with Asia as a contemporary phenomenon bringing ships loaded with containers full of T-shirts and DVD players to ports in the United States, Europe, and Latin America. It is so common that goods made in Asia are purchased in the United States that they are used as part of grammar school geography lessons. A seven-year-old girl asks her grandmother to guess where her shirt was made. Without waiting for a reply she announces that it was made in Vietnam and proceeds to explain where that is. The fact that clothes come from across the world functions as a learning tool.

But to consider Asian trade as solely a contemporary activity, an inexpensive central supply source for the world's consumers, is to miss the real scope of activities that can be considered under the title of trade.

As mentioned earlier in this chapter and in chapter 8, local, regional, and global trade dates back to early civilizations. The history of Asia is filled with stories of the Silk Road, Marco Polo, the Chinese sailing expeditions, and the arrival of the Portuguese, British, and Dutch seeking treasures and goods to trade. This area was not an easy place to establish a trading operation. Although there were periods where each country was willing to connect with foreigners to allow their goods and ideas within its borders, the welcome was seldom ongoing. Doors were opened, closed, and eventually opened again at a later stage.

Today it is unlikely that any country would or could close its doors again. One indicator of the intent of nations to participate in the worldwide economy is World Trade Organization membership (see Table 15.2). One of the major events in recent trade activity was the 2001 admittance of China to that organization. It joined 12 Asian countries that were already members. Cambodia, Vietnam, Laos, and Nepal currently are on observed status and not yet full members. South Korea is a member, but North Korea is neither a member nor a candidate.

China's joining the WTO was a significant event for world trade. It marked a commitment by China to adhere to world standards, to open its markets, and to adapt its institutions, creating new opportunities for

TABLE 15.2 WTO MEMBERSHIP STATUS OF ASIAN NATIONS

COUNTRY	WTO
Cambodia	Yes
China	Yes
East Timor	No
Hong Kong	Yes
Indonesia	Yes
Japan	Yes
North Korea	No
South Korea	Yes
Laos	Observer
Malaysia	Yes
Mongolia	Yes
Myanmar	Yes
Nepal	Yes
Philippines	Yes
Singapore	Yes
Taiwan	Yes
Thailand	Yes
Vietnam	Observer

Source: www.wto.org, September 2005

other nations. However, membership allows China to take advantage of WTO rules, too, extending its reach. As this book is being written, the issue of concern is the removal of quotas in 2005 and 2008. What will be the impact of China's manufacturing capacity? Will China eliminate the textile industries of the United States, Africa, Europe, and Latin America? What will happen to factories in Guatemala and Italy? The agreement to end quotas was made prior to China's WTO membership, prior to its emergence as a key producer of a variety of goods. By mid-2005 the United States, the European Union, and China all have expressed concern about the effect of the increased flow of Chinese-made goods throughout the world. Import restrictions under safeguard provisions, rules to protect local industries have been proposed. Export taxes are in place and enforced. The debate about costs and benefits of quota elimination continues. The only certainty is that trading rules are now changed. The results are not yet known.

China's importance is growing not only in the area of manufacturing but also in policy matters. It joined with other developing countries in the WTO sometimes called the Group of 21.[10] China, South Africa, India, and Brazil are the 4 largest of these expanding economies whose interests do not always coincide with those of the developed nations. It will be important to watch the developments as WTO trade negotiations continue.

However, it isn't only within the activities of the World Trade Organization that the Asian countries are active. They are also creating trade agreements within the region and beyond. Although regional agreements and cooperative groups are proliferating at the beginning of the twenty-first century, they are not new. Almost 40 years ago, in 1967, 5 nations formed the ASEAN group (Association of Southeast Asian Nations). The original group was Indonesia, Malaysia, the Philippines, Singapore, and Thailand. In 1995, they were joined by Brunei, Vietnam, Laos, Myanmar, and Cambodia with Papua New Guinea as an observer. The organization's purpose is to promote economic cooperation and welfare of the people in the region. Its members are increasingly linked to the 3 major economies of the area: China, Japan, and Korea, referred to as ASEAN + 3. In 2004, China signed a free trade pact with the ASEAN nations that will eliminate tariffs on thousands of products by 2015. This new agreement will increase China's political and economic power in the region.[11]

Additionally, consideration is being given to a separate agreement with Japan or creating a Free Trade Agreement (FTA) that would link the ASEAN nations, China, Japan, and South Korea. Because political trust is a necessity for two countries joining together through a free trade agreement, it is noteworthy to see old enemies moving in this direction.

Free trade agreements are being pursued within the region and around the globe. The following is a list of FTAs or investment agreements that were signed or being negotiated in 2004:

- China with Nigeria, South Africa, Chile, Brazil, and New Zealand

- Japan with Korea, Mexico, Thailand, the Philippines, Malaysia, Singapore, Taiwan
- South Korea with Chile, Japan, Singapore
- ASEAN with India

Trade isn't increased solely by agreements related to the reduction of tariffs and elimination quotas. For example, South Korea doesn't limit its activities to merchandise trade. It is an investor, too. In 2001, South Koreans invested more money in China than did Americans.[12]

Beyond merchandise and investment, trade also means that companies take their business expertise outside their home boundaries. American companies going to China and Japanese companies coming to the United States are relatively common. But Chinese companies expanding operations in other places is still news. One example is a story about Chinese construction companies using their locally developed expertise to build a global business. "Chinese companies have carried out projects in around 180 countries," says CHINCA (China International Contractors Association) vice chairman Diao Chunhe.[13] A Chinese company will build a retail project in New York City and others are working on or bidding on projects in Nigeria, Iran, Malaysia, and Algeria.

Trends of the Future: The Brands Are Ours

Although known today for efficiently manufactured products and the availability of cheap labor, Asia's identity is expected to evolve. As the business becomes more competitive locally as well as globally, companies will look for new opportunities as the example of the Chinese construction companies illustrates. In the area of manufacturing, the move may be from manufacturing goods designed by others to creating unique products. In fact, the Chinese government is already encouraging companies to develop and sell their own brands abroad.[14]

The push to create new brands is focused on the future. The concept isn't new to the region. Six of the top 40 brands listed in *Business Week*'s Top 100 Brands (for 2003) are from Japan or South Korea. These include Toyota, Honda, Samsung, and Nintendo. Chinese brand names also are beginning to appear. Haier, China's biggest appliance maker, sells small refrigerators in the United States under its own name.

As if to testify to the rapid movement in this area, Haier branded refrigerators appeared in a 2004 back-to-school advertisement for the mass-market retailer Target.

However, creating a brand is not simply placing a name in an advertisement. Tracing its origins to early farmers who identified their livestock with an indelible mark, a brand is used to distinguish the product of one producer from that of another. Buyers of livestock could make judgments about quality and make selections based on the mark or the brand. In modern times the way a consumer learns about a product, its creator, the promise, and quality is through the mediums of advertising and marketing. According to a recent *McKinsey Quarterly* report, the lack of marketing is the largest obstacle Chinese companies face.[15]

Although challenges exist, Ian Batey, author of the book *Asian Branding* identified 25 categories or products from Asian nations that could become globally recognized strong brands. His suggestions include instant noodles in Indonesia, wood in the Philippines, and beer in Singapore. His point of view is that by creating strong identifiable brand identity, especially for brands or products that already exist, sales will increase and add strength to the economies in the region.[16] However, to achieve this will require a greater emphasis on innovation and creativity rather than the expertise used for efficient manufacturing. There are indications that this process is underway. According to a U.S. embassy official in China, more people are returning to the region having been educated and having obtained business experience in the United States and Europe. They are bringing marketing and development skills to companies they join.

Additionally, some changes are underway in the educational system including the growth of schools from abroad. A French fashion school opened in Shanghai in 2003, starting with just 20 students. Their design instructor is a German woman educated at a prestigious school in London who worked for designers in Paris before creating her own line. Now, as an educator, she says the largest challenge is to get the students to believe in their own ideas. "They expect me to tell them what to design," she said. "They don't expect to create for themselves. It's a slow process, but when they realize they can create something they visualize without my input it's a marvelous moment."[17]

Population and Planning

Almost any conversation about population today includes a reference to China and its 1.3 billion people. Marketers from around the world hope to have even a small percentage of those people as future customers. But to understand a country's or a region's population requires more than a count of individuals. The age of the population and the birth rates all have long-term economic implications.

In both Japan and China, the populations are aging and shrinking. According to recent articles, China, Japan, and South Korea will see their populations move toward old age over the next half century. The aging of the population will bring demands for health care and pensions to be provided for this increasing segment of the population. However, at the same time, statistics indicate that populations are shrinking rather than growing. The result of this trend is that a smaller workforce will be supporting an increasing number of retirees.

Table 15.1 illustrates that only 3 of the 19 countries listed have annual birthrates that meet or exceed the United Nations' standard of 2.1 births per woman as the number needed to maintain population size. Japan at 0.08 is particularly striking. By March 31, 2004, Japan's population rose only 0.11 percent since the government began surveying in 1968.[18] The declining numbers are not unique to Asia but rather are part of a global trend. However, in Asia aspects other than numbers and age will affect the future of the societies and economics.

The Chinese law limiting family size to one child per family was in effect from 1980 to 2003. While not as widely enforced in rural areas as it was in the urban centers, it did have an effect. Not only did it limit population size but it also had unexpected consequences. Many of these children grew up with all the attention and emotional and economic support of their parents and grandparents. This begs the question regarding their future behavior. Will the spoiled, indulged children be compliant workers content to operate within a hierarchical structure? Will they change the workplace and society? This group grew up in a time of economic growth and relative freedom. The horrors of the Cultural Revolution are tales from their parents and grandparents and do not match their life experiences. What changes will that bring about? Will they experience a change in attitudes similar to what occurred in the United States when the people coming into the workforce no longer carried personal memories of the Depression or the rationing associated with World War II?

Related to China's one child policy, improved technology that brought about better medical care and cultural attitudes is the appearance of an unusual ratio between men and women and boys and girls. The worldwide ratio is 105 boys born for every 100 girls.[19] The countries with a higher ratio are mainly in East Asia, and the highest is China at 120, up to an unofficial count of 156 boys to every 100 girls. A recent book by professors in England and the United States called *Bare Branches* suggests that this disparity will have potentially devastating consequences for the countries involved.[20] Their theory is that many of these boys will grow up to be young men without hope for wives or families, and possibly even for jobs. Referring to them as "bare branches" the authors suggest that countries may become externally aggressive to channel the energy of these young men.

There are others who argue that their concerns are unfounded. One writer proposes that these countries will become less aggressive, as people who have only one child will be less willing to put them at risk; therefore, the leadership will avoid armed conflicts.[21] Whichever trends emerge, population size and composition clearly matter for policy makers as well as for marketing professionals.

Foundation Beliefs

Understanding the religious and philosophical foundations of a culture is important everywhere in the world. Throughout history, wars have shaped governments, boundaries of nations, and art and music. Business cultures, too, reflect religion and philosophy. For example, the American approach to life and to business is closely associated with the nation's Protestant heritage. To understand U.S. business practices and attitudes people focus on what is called the Protestant work ethic, the idea that hard work is seen as an important element of leading a good life.

In Asia, many of the world's major religions are represented and have influenced people's behaviors. The dominant religion in the Philippines is Catholicism while Islam plays the primary role in Indonesia. However, throughout the largest part of the region the most influential philosophy and religions have been Confucianism, Buddhism, and Taoism. In Japan, Shinto holds an important place along with the other three. It is Japan's oldest surviving religion and is practiced primarily in that nation.[22]

Confucianism is often referred to as a religion although it is not one; it is a philosophy originally taught by the Chinese scholar Confucius. Dating back to about 500 B.C., his teachings shape the daily lives of people throughout Asia. Confucianism defines rules for the interaction among people, their roles and obligations to one another. Harmony is gained through appropriate relationships among people.

The concept of harmony is a critical element of Taoism, also. However, in this religion harmony is not just among individuals, rather it is with all elements of the universe. For adherents of the faith it is important to achieve a balance in life and with nature.

Buddhism is the only one of the three belief systems to include the idea of an afterlife and that living in an appropriate way today is to aid the search for a better life later. It teaches that life is filled with suffering and that there is a continual cycle of life, death, and rebirth. Through leading the life of a good Buddhist, you can escape the cycle and reach Nirvana. Elements of the good life include not saying things that will hurt others and respecting life in all its forms.

One of the main elements of the Shinto religion is the respect of ancestors and worship of *kami* or spiritual forces in all aspects of nature. There is an emphasis on rituals that relate to day-to-day activities. For example, ceremonies might include a request for blessings for the birth of a child or opening of a new building. But Shinto was important historically in ordering social values such as courage, politeness, and reserve.[23]

In some cases the elements of the varied religions are interwoven or elements of each practiced by individuals. Singularly or in combination, their influence is evident throughout Asia.

Relationships Rule

While business cultures vary throughout Asia, one aspect is consistent no matter where you go. Relationships, personal connections among the parties, are necessary. Unless people are properly introduced, until they know something about one another, business cannot commence.

While connections and introductions are important and valuable in other places, in this region they are critical. People do business with people they know.

However, what is meant by a relationship, and how is one established and maintained? The major economies represented by China, Japan, and South Korea have philosophies that are both similar and different. These three philosophies, *Guanxi*, *Wa*, and *Inhwa*, respectively, shape the conduct of business in these three countries and provide an indication of what to expect in the region overall.

While Western cultures also have a variety of styles of business relationships, none is an exact parallel to these three. For an American businessperson whose relationships are often transaction-based, the emphasis on harmonious relationships and personal connections may be puzzling. Some of the key elements of each of these three philosophies are described below.

Guanxi

People considering the Chinese market quickly learn the word *Guanxi*, often described as an idea of favors being exchanged to do business. But this simple view doesn't capture the full sense of the connection. *Guanxi* is not simply an agreement to help one another but a commitment among individuals to offer assistance when needed. *Guanxi* relates to the Confucian concept of family as the important unit and the relationship, and obligations of one member to another as elements of the emotional connection.

Although *Guanxi* relationships are not only within a family, the respect expected is similar. The obligation side of the equation is that the assistance must be repaid, although not necessarily immediately. There will be a balance, a maintenance of the connection, and a harmony over the time of the exchanges. If not, the arrangement can be terminated. This is one aspect that distinguishes the Chinese approach—that there is the possibility of ending the relationship. In business behavior, it allows movement from one company to another rather than the lifetime employment more common in Japan. This flexibility is evident in mainland China and Hong Kong today. Managers, especially ones with technology and Western management skills, are in high demand. They move quickly from one company to another. Their *Guanxi* relationships may stay intact when they move. This is possible because another characteristic is that the relationship is between individuals. The obligation is of one party to the other rather than the Japanese view where the group is the key figure.

Wa

The culture of Japan is based on the group and a person's affiliation; group membership is of critical significance. The Japanese philosophy, *Wa*, places the emphasis on harmony within a group. Group loyalty, the submerging of personal goals to those of the group, is of utmost importance. It is important to build consensus, maintain harmony, and know that over time the individual will benefit. The ongoing harmony is especially important since membership in a group is long-term, hence, the traditional idea of lifetime employment with one company. Although that is no longer the only option available, it still represents the tendency.

Along with the importance of the group is the consideration of respecting the hierarchy. Hierarchy is still part of everyday life in Japan, according to Sheldon M. Garon, professor of history at Princeton University. American society may celebrate initiative and reward upstarts but most Japanese still define themselves by their affiliations and their rankings in these groups.[24]

Inhwa

The Korean philosophy is different from and again similar to both the Chinese and Japanese. As with the Japanese, there is an emphasis on harmony but between individuals. The Confucian understanding of the roles of parties within a family or an organization is important in Korea as in China.

Inhwa in Korea begins with the idea of harmony with an emphasis on relationships between unequals such as boss and subordinate. Along with harmony exist the concepts of loyalty, mutual obligation, and responsibility. This reflects the strong Confucian ideal of hierarchy in which each person's role is defined and must be adhered to. The older takes care of the younger, and the younger must be loyal to the older person.

Since this form of relationship, like the Chinese *Guanxi*, is between individuals, the Koreans, too, are more individualistic. The emphasis on maintaining harmony leads to a reluctance to directly provide negative information. According to one writer, bad news will likely be delivered at the end of the day, if at all, to avoid making an entire day unpleasant.[25]

Business Their Way

A Los Angeles-based attorney with more than 20 years' experience in Asia says there are two words that hold the key to doing business in all the countries in that region. The words are *patience* and *friendships*. Patience is required because of the difference in the perception of time, the contrast between the American short-term focus and the Asian long-term view. He warns American clients not to go with a plan to "get the deal done and get on the plane." Further, he says if you want to show you're serious, allow some extra time and let people know there isn't a rush.

There is a distinction between building a business relationship and a personal friendship. Most relationships connect through the various levels of the hierarchy and remain somewhat formal. A friendship between two people who are on a similar level can be more relaxed and also helpful to both parties in developing their business activities. The friendships allow for exchange of information and insights into issues that affect negotiations that may not be possible in a formal setting. In one case a negotiator learned that the key issue was job retention although the negotiating team discussed only production and pricing.

In these hierarchical societies where decisions are made by consensus within the group, communication is subtle and the issues may not be obvious. Having working relationships horizontally as well as vertically can provide valuable knowledge.

Although chapter 2 deals with basic differences in communication styles, it's still worthwhile to look at the topic again in this section. Most Americans practice an active/direct/linear style of communicating. This approach can be visualized as a straight line, almost an arrow from start to finish. We state what we want to achieve and why. For example, "We want to create a joint venture with your company because (fill in the blank)." Action comes first, and reasons follow.

An American woman who worked for several technology companies in Asia says for her the image of the communication pattern is a zigzag line moving up a ladder from side to side and from bottom to top. At multiple points are stops allowing discussion and consensus building. Reasons for action are presented and discussed before the goal is stated, since the actual goal may change as discussions proceed. This pattern of starting, stopping for discussion, and moving ahead again is by nature a slower process than the arrow moving from one point to another. This image again provides a reminder that patience is a necessity in this environment.

Notwithstanding an overall emphasis on patience, subtle communication, and harmony, individual styles and experiences may vary. Questions from Chinese and Korean colleagues can be surprisingly direct. Topics may come up that surprise Americans. Remember that individual style, facility with a language, and the tones of voice all shape our conversations. Within every general pattern, there are exceptions. Awareness of differences as well as similarities allows people to adapt as needed.

Understanding the communication styles and knowledge of essential issues are necessities when negotiating contracts. But it is vital to realize that the Asian view of a contract and its meaning differs from the American interpretation. For an American, a contract is a final achievement at the end of a process. It captures the decisions of the parties and their agreements and lays the foundation for the work ahead. It provides a document to guide anyone who reads it through the work to be shared, such as the allocation of costs and profits and methods for resolving disputes. In contrast, a contract in Asia is seen to capture the intent of the parties but is not an absolute fixed agreement. It is assumed that as circumstances change the contract may change, too. When the parties share such different views, is it any surprise that books are full of stories detailing misunderstandings and difficulties? Strong relationships between the parties are the key to resolving the differences.

Corruption Perceptions Index

Business in Asia differs from that in the United States because it is relationship-based rather than transaction-based. It also differs because of the patterns and perceptions about the processes. The Corruption Perceptions Index (see chapter 10) for 2004 underscores the differences in the region.

Four countries in Asia are ranked in the top 25 or "cleanest" countries scoring higher than 5.0 on a 10 scale. Singapore is number 5 at 9.3, Hong Kong is number 16 at 8.0, and Japan is number 24 at 6.9. The first two are ahead of the United States, which is number 17 at 7.5. (Taiwan, an important part of the region although not recognized as an independent country, is number 34 at 5.6.) Malaysia at 5.0 is just at the dividing line. All other Asian nations fall below that level, with Bangladesh at 1.5 at number 145. Of the 145 countries surveyed, South Korea ranks number 47 at 4.5 and China with a 3.4 score is number 71, tied with Syria and Saudi Arabia.[26]

While this data can be used to show that businesspeople, risk assessment professionals, and academics consider dishonesty as severe in many countries of the world, it also has broader implications. These survey results also indicate that business processes, rule of law, and institutions may still be in the developmental stages. Businesses wishing to operate in this region may find some challenges. Additionally, some countries need support from the world community to help create ways to do business, run their governments, and be able to avoid the corruption.

Online All the Time

The Internet World Stats Web site reports Internet users, as of February 2005, for all the Asian countries except North Korea, a country that generally does not reveal statistics. In the report China ranks first with 94,000,000 users, approximately 19 times as many as Hong Kong. However, simply considering the user count provides only a partial picture of the Internet usage within a country. Perhaps more meaningful is the percentage penetration in the population. In that case Hong Kong, with 69.9 percent penetration, far exceeds the rest of China, which has only 7.3 percent.

Only 5 places in Asia (Japan, Hong Kong, South Korea, Singapore, and Taiwan) exceed a 50 percent penetration rate. Compare these statistics to worldwide figures: 21 countries reach or exceed 50 percent. Only Sweden at 74.3 percent exceeds 70 percent. (The United States is number 3 in the world, just behind Hong Kong, at 66.8 percent.)[27]

In addition to being known for its rapid growth in Internet usage, quintupling in four years, China is also known for its government monitoring. The government not only checks online activity but has also arrested and jailed people for messages or postings that were considered subversive.[28]

Burgers, Coffee, and Board Shorts

American fast food arrived in China more than a decade before the country officially stepped into the global trading community with its WTO membership. Kentucky Fried Chicken opened its first unit there in 1987, predating the arrival of McDonald's by 3 years. Today the two groups have almost 1,000 units spread throughout the country.

Marking how common the sight of the golden arches is, a Harvard professor made the following observations: "So common are they that McDonald's (in Hong Kong) made a transition from a trendy exotic outpost of American culture to a purveyor of ordinary food for ordinary people."[29]

Another representative of American culture is Starbucks, the Seattle-based purveyor of coffee. A recent entry to the traditional tea-drinking Asian market, the chain now operates in 14 countries in the Asia Pacific region. Visitors to Japan, Taiwan, Beijing, and Hong Kong can return home with T-shirts and coffee mugs bearing the Starbucks name along with the city. Now travelers can collect Starbucks branded merchandise at home and far away.

If one considers Starbucks' attempt to convince tea drinkers to select coffee as their preferred beverage a significant undertaking, Quicksilver's challenge is immense. For Quicksilver, the California surf-ware company must introduce surfing, skateboarding, and snowboarding to be able to sell their sports-related clothing. In 2004, Quicksilver opened its first store in mainland China, in Shanghai, located between an Adidas store and a Starbucks. According to Quicksilver's chief executive, Robert B. McKnight Jr., the work to develop the market will be "worth the effort because there are more teenagers in China than people in the United States."[30]

Now We Know

Simply looking at a map won't tell you much about Asia. First, countries that are located on the continent of Asia aren't always considered part of Asia. Turkey is sometimes counted as an Asian country and yet it has applied for membership in the European Union. It is part of Asia and at the same time, not Asia. Even after one decides if a country is part of Asia, it's necessary to remember that it isn't one homogenous area. Rather, each of the countries has a unique history, distinct culture, and complex relationships with its neighbors. Today's trading partners may be yesterday's foes. Korea, Japan, and China, powerful leaders in the twenty-first century, were once enemies rather than allies.

To effectively conduct business, it's critical to understand the historic relationships and specific cultures of each nation. Most of all, one must be aware that throughout Asia personal relationships are the key to all commercial activity. Investing in office space, advertising, and legal advice isn't enough. To create a successful operation you need to invest time and personal energy to build individual connections with people, one by one.

I'm Glad I Know

It took me several years to grasp all the subtle ways that communication styles differ. It isn't only the words but also the sounds of the conversation that can lead to misunderstandings. For example, the spoken Chinese language can sound very aggressive. It's much easier now that I know that people aren't really yelling at me; it just sounds that way. Trying to communicate in a new language, a new way can be challenging, even frustrating. But it's worth the effort to understand more than the words. It's important to learn the sounds, the patterns of presenting information. Knowing that people aren't yelling, just talking, allows you to reach across the barriers and find the ways to connect.

→→ *American woman*
working at a U.S. embassy in China

CHAPTER 16

Australia *and* New Zealand

I Wish I'd Known

You need to shout for a round. As odd as that statement may seem, it's an important element of building good relationships when you're doing business in Australia. When people get together they automatically take turns paying for the drinks. They call it "shouting for a round." If you don't volunteer to take your turn, it's considered extremely rude and unfriendly.

→→ *American transferred to Australia*
with a technology company

I Wish They Knew

How in this day and age can people still not understand that New Zealand and Australia are not the same place? That we have always been two different places with different histories, different governments, and different ways of doing business? It's annoying and insulting to have to keep explaining.

→→ *Australian businessman*
recently arrived in Los Angeles

Fact or Fiction?

For some people the name Oceania brings to mind early science fiction stories that described lost cities and monsters beneath the sea. More factually, Oceania is a region of the world in the Southern Hemisphere. It is home to more than 25,000 islands. Some are too small for habitation, and others are well populated and bear familiar names. The largest landmass in this area is Australia, which has the distinction of being both the smallest continent and the largest island in the world. Other places in the area connected to the global economy are New Zealand, New Guinea, Fiji, the Solomon Islands, and island groups included in Micronesia, Melanesia, and Polynesia.

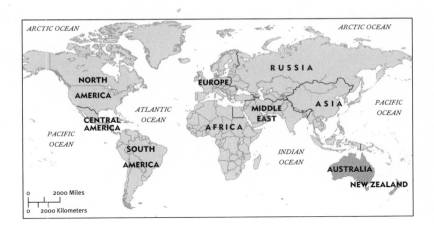

In this chapter we will limit our discussion to the two major countries of this region: Australia and New Zealand. Although they are each independent, democratic nations, people often refer to them as if they shared a common boundary, much like Canada and the United States. They are actually separated by the Tasman Sea; it takes four hours to fly from one to the other, and you'll need a passport to travel between them.

A Continent and Many Islands

Australia and New Zealand are located relatively close to each other but a significant distance away from major industrialized countries in Western Europe and North America. Australia is 11,790 miles from Paris and a 12- to 14-hour flight from Los Angeles or San Francisco. Closer to Asia with a flight between Sydney and Tokyo slightly more than 9 hours, they still maintain cultures that are Western.

The country of Australia is really two islands, Australia and Tasmania. In total, it is slightly larger than the continental United States; it is the sixth largest and least densely populated country in the world.[1]

New Zealand is made up of islands with the majority of the population living in the north and south islands. Their combined area is approximately the size of the state of Colorado. In addition, Stewart

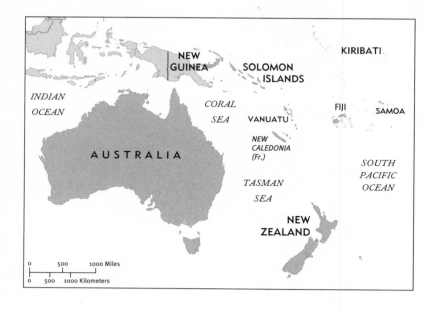

Island and several smaller ones are included as part of the nation. The 1642 Dutch explorer Abel Tasman named New Zealand, but there is no record of exploration until England's Captain James Cook's first visit in 1769. In 1770, Captain Cook claimed both Australia and New Zealand for the British. Today both countries are part of the British Commonwealth. New Zealanders show a greater allegiance to Great Britain than Australians. New Zealand is a dominion of Great Britain, a status held since 1907, and is a constitutional monarchy. Australia, while also a member of the British Commonwealth, has been an independent country since 1986. While it is a democratic federal state, it does recognize the British monarch as the head of state.

The People

As much as Australians and New Zealanders proclaim their individuality, the casual observer is first aware of the similarities between the two. The head of state for both is Her Majesty Queen Elizabeth II of England. The populations are predominantly Caucasian and English speaking. Australia is the largest English-speaking country in the southern hemisphere.[2] Their flags both incorporate Great Britain's Union flag.

Original Inhabitants, Convicts, Jailers, and Free People

The majority of the Europeans to settle and develop these countries came from the United Kingdom. But look beyond the place of origin and you discover the different backgrounds of these two countries and the early settlers. Both countries were populated before the Europeans arrived. The Maori traveled from Polynesia to New Zealand around A.D. 800. The Aborigines populated Australia for some 38,000 years before the European influx.[3] An early point of distinction between the two sets of settlers was in their attitudes toward the native populations. The New Zealanders treated the Maori as equal citizens, while the British immigrants to Australia who maintained a white Australian policy, forbade landownership to Aborigines.[4]

Beyond the differences in how each treated the original inhabitants, the settlers were also different. Although the place of origin for both was mainly the British Isles, most people who came to New Zealand did so by choice. They were a middle-class and working population looking for a new start. Alternatively, most of the people who arrived in Australia were transported there by force and under guard.

For the British, Australia was not only a new colony that might provide tea or spices but also a land to be used as a penal colony to take pressure off the overflowing prisons and poor houses in England. The fact that it turned out to be rich in copper and gold was simply a bonus.

Convictism

Convictism, the transporting of convicts, in this case moving them from Great Britain to Australia, shaped the development of a country. The Europeans who founded and developed Australia were mainly sailors, convicts, and jailers. Between 1787, when the first prisoners sailed to Botany Bay, and 1868, when transport ended, over 160,000 people made the trip. The convicts were said to be indistinguishable from ordinary British and Irish working-class men and women. Of the total almost 80 percent were men and mainly British, Irish, and Scottish.[5]

Historical research reveals that many of the people were serving relatively short sentences of seven years or less. This is seen as an indication that they were not the worst of the overflowing prison population. Records indicate they were treated well in the sense of being given adequate food and clothing. It was important to maintain their health and sense of well-being since they were there to build the new country and not simply to serve out their sentences.

They became architects, schoolteachers, maids; they founded newspapers; they built roads, churches, and public buildings; and they explored the territory. People worked at the trades they knew so they could create a society similar to the one they left. One report indicates that local governors preferred educated convicts and that being a convicted forger almost guaranteed a small public service post.[6] While not the entire island was a work camp, it was in fact a penal colony with all the harshness that implies. Yet for many this was not prison in a traditional sense. They were better off than they would have been had they remained in Britain, so they elected to stay in the new country after they gained their freedom. The founding of the country by convicts and their jailers is still an important legacy in modern-day Australia.

The People Today

Table 16.1 provides a glimpse of the size of one country compared with the other. The population of Australia is almost six times as large as that of New Zealand.

People of Australia and New Zealand wish not only to be recognized as different from each other but also to be distinguished from Americans, Canadians, and Britons. One New Zealander points out that they each have distinct informal names for their countries and themselves. New Zealanders sometimes call their country *Aotearoa*, the Maori name

COUNTRY	TABLE 16.1 POPULATION	POPULATION MEDIAN AGE	AGE 15–64	ANNUAL GROWTH
New Zealand	4,059,900	33.1	66.5%	1.09%
Australia	20,275,700	36	67.1	.93%

Source: CIA World Factbook 2005 and Internet World Stats 2005

TABLE 16.2   CULTURAL DIFFERENTIATION

COUNTRY	POWER DISTANCE	INDIVIDUALISM
Australia	36	90
Canada	39	80
Great Britain	35	89
New Zealand	22	79
United States	40	91

Source: Hoefstede

for New Zealand. They refer to themselves as Kiwis for a bird that is found only there. Australians sometimes call their homeland Oz and refer to themselves as Aussies. Although they share ties to a common point of origin these are clearly different places with particular cultures.

By looking at two dimensions of Geert Hofstede's model of cultural differentiation we can gain some insight to New Zealand and Australia and the three countries associated with them: Great Britain, Canada, and the United States.[7]

Power distance measures the degree of acceptable inequality within a society. The lower the score, the more egalitarian the society is considered to be (see Table 16.2). New Zealand is known for its belief that humanistic progress is as important as materialistic progress.[8] Further, it is proud of having a civilized culture focused on ecology and social welfare.[9] Based on that prevailing attitude, it isn't a surprise that it has the lowest power distance score of the aforementioned five countries.

Although the scores for power distance and individualism for the United States and Australia are very close, Phillip Knightley, author of a book on Australian history, sees distinct differences between Americans and Australians. According to Knightley, "Americans developed a culture of rugged individualism, scorn for the weak, while the Australians have an ethos of mutual help and social obligation, belief in mateship."[10] *Mateship* is defined by the *Australian National Dictionary* as "the bond between equal partners or close friends; comradeship." This closeness and mutual reliance may arise from the conditions the early settlers encountered. Imagine the situation of convicts who are trying to survive on a large continent that is mostly uninhabitable. That environment required people to cooperate so they could survive.

In contrast, the United States has only small areas that are not suitable for habitation. American pioneers banded together to cross the country, joining the wagon trains shown in Western movies; however, once they reached their destinations, they split up again. If an individual wasn't satisfied or successful in one area, it was possible to go to another frontier and survive alone or with companions.

On the subject of equality, New Zealand and Australia were among the first countries to give women the right to vote. New Zealand was first in 1893, and Australia followed in 1902, 18 years before the United States gave women the right to vote.

First Nations

The history of the relations of the European settlers with their first nation, or native population, the Maoris reveals New Zealand's egalitarian emphasis. While relations were not idyllic, they did grant citizenship to the Maoris. Today they represent approximately 15 percent of the population and have representation in the government reflecting that size. A Los Angeles–based organizational consultant who recently visited New Zealand said that she noticed the respect accorded the Maori culture by the New Zealanders. She said it was evident when reading the paper and listening to conversations and stories that they were an integral part of business and society.

However, Australia's treatment of their first nation population was decidedly different. Aborigines had occupied the land for thousands of years before the Europeans arrived. However, the immigrant Australians did not begin to recognize the rights of the Aborigines until the 1990s, with the signing of the Mabo Peace Treaty. In fact, it was not until 1973, more than 200 years after Captain Cook claimed the land for the British, that they eliminated the requirement that you had to be white to be an Australian.[11]

Recent government reports state that the "Aborigines are the most socially and economically deprived group in Australia." They may be able to change that situation by achieving direct representation within the government.

Business Their Way

A New Zealander who has worked in the Western United States says that Americans who work in both the United States and New Zealand will find business processes and appearances very familiar. But under the familiar surface are differences that can surprise American visitors. These differences can be as simple as titles or styles of dress. But the subtleties exist and must be noted. There is simultaneous admiration of and resistance to doing things the "American way." In New Zealand, people are proud of their "Kiwi ingenuity" and want to discover their own solutions to questions.[12]

This enterprising spirit is revealed in a recent report by the Global Entrepreneurship Monitor (GEM). The report compiles the results of surveys that examine innovation and growth among existing businesses in 40 countries. According to a 2003 report, Chile, Korea, New Zealand, Uganda, and Venezuela were the top 5 countries for entrepreneurship in the world.[13] The report points out that New Zealand is more entrepreneurial than the United States and significantly more so than Australia.

The observations of a New Zealander returning to his home city of Hamilton after working in Australia for three years reflect the findings. His comment was that "business start-ups have become sexy again, and the numerous incubator setups are impressive."[14]

In noting the differences between Australia and New Zealand, the report pointed out some issues in the cultures. On the positive side are the "have a go spirit," early adopter mentality, and global outlook. Unfortunately these attributes are offset by a persistent negative perception of entrepreneurship, aversion to risk, resistance to change, and possibly most important an inability to see an unsuccessful attempt as a method of learning rather than as a failure.[15] The final point, the inability to see a potential positive outcome from initial failure, is the opposite of the American attitude where failure is considered a step toward success. This outlook has been the foundation of the American entrepreneurial attitude. There's always something to learn and something new to try.

However, not all business in either country is conducted by entrepreneurial, start-up enterprises. Australia has become a place for regional headquarters of multinational companies to do work in Asia.

Although New Zealand may be considered more welcoming of entrepreneurs, professionals from there often go to Australia to work because its larger economy, five times the size of New Zealand's, provides more opportunities. People from both places are accustomed to travel for pleasure and for business. An Australian working in California said, "Oh, everyone travels as soon as they get out of college. They usually go to Europe but sometimes to the United States. No matter where [in the world], they go, and occasionally they stay and work."

A second report sheds light on the business culture in both nations. In Transparency International's 2004 Corruption Perceptions Index, New Zealand, with a score of 9.6 out of a possible 10.0 is number 2 in the world, following Finland at 9.7. Australia comes in at number 9 with a score of 8.8, ranking above the United Kingdom at 8.6 and the United States at 7.5.

The concept of equality as a core value in the cultures of both Australia and New Zealand shows clearly in their approaches to business. Their approaches flow from their commitment to a fair and reasonable social system. They intensely dislike officiousness, authority, and people giving orders. Especially in Australia, this attitude may trace back to the founders. The prisoners who came had to take orders; it's possible that their descendants carried forward a distaste for authority and orders. Further, it is considered important not to be "a tall poppy" in the very egalitarian culture of Australia, although current indications are that this admonition is less important in terms of showing individual success than it is in terms of not trying to pull rank or being seen as a braggart.[16] "We are equal as mates," seems to be the message.

Trade

Today trade provides a dynamic connection between the two countries. The official link is the Australia/New Zealand Closer Economic Relations (CER) trade agreement signed in 1983. Begun with only trading in goods, it expanded to include services. According to one estimate, the CER increased their two-way trade by 500 percent.[17] Today both countries rank number 1 for each other, with the European Union falling into second place for each of the two. The other main partners include the United States, Japan, and China.

Great Britain was once the main trading partner for both Australia and New Zealand, but that changed when Britain joined the European Union. However, Australia has one product that is a leading export into Britain: wine. In 2004, Australia became the number 1 wine exporter to the United Kingdom, taking the spot traditionally held by France. Australia is ranked in the top 4 of wine-exporting countries after France, the United States, and Italy.

Although Australia and New Zealand have such strong two-way trade, they continue to examine ways to ease their differences in conducting business and thus create closer economic ties. At a recent meeting of the Australia/New Zealand Forum, a group of academics, government representatives, and businesspeople, one item discussed was the possibility of a joint immigration zone. Creation of that zone would allow people to travel between the two countries without needing passports. Many issues remain to be resolved before this could happen, but it is interesting to learn that it is being considered.

As you can see from the list of trading partners, the two countries are not isolated in their activities. As members of the WTO, both are now seperately and collectively adding to their existing trade agreements. One area that is getting increased attention is the deepening of connections in Asia.

The ten-country ASEAN group and the Australia/New Zealand CER created an agreement calling for economic partnership. Its goal is to double trade and investment between these groups by 2010. The members of ASEAN are Brunei Darussalam, Myanmar, Cambodia, Indonesia, Laos, Malaysia, the Philippines, Singapore, Thailand, and Vietnam. By the end of 2004, both Australia and New Zealand had trade agreements with Singapore. Thailand and Australia signed their agreement in July 2004, and New Zealand and Thailand have started negotiations to create their own agreement.

Strengthening and deepening trade and economic relations with China is a major priority for the Australian government.[18] China and Australia already conduct significant two-way trade, and Australia is one of the few countries in the world officially recognized by China as a designated tourist destination.[19] The two countries have begun work on a free trade agreement feasibility study due for completion at the end

TABLE 16.3   INTERNET USAGE

COUNTRY	% PENETRATION	INTERNET USAGE
Australia	65.9%	13,359,821
New Zealand	52.2%	2,110,000

Source: Internet World Stats 2005

of October 2005. New Zealand plans to start working on a free trade agreement with China in 2005.

Even with the growing interest in Asia, Australia and New Zealand still maintain important relationships with countries in the West. Australia now has a free trade agreement with the United States. The United States is the destination for 11 percent of Australia's exports and accounts for 18 percent of its imports.

While New Zealand is not officially seeking a free trade agreement with the United States, according to the CEO of the United States/New Zealand Council, a U.S.-based group of business and political leaders, some people believe an agreement should be created. Ellen Gordon, the CEO of the group, stated that it is in the national interest of New Zealand to have a free trade agreement with the United States, as the United States is its second-largest trading partner after Australia. However, there may be political impediments to establishing such an agreement. New Zealand has declared itself a nuclear-free zone and will not allow ships with nuclear weapons to dock in its ports. Because the United States will not reveal which of its ships carry nuclear weapons, no United States ships are allowed into ports there.

New Zealand is also pursuing ties with Latin America. It is working on a trilateral agreement that includes both Singapore and Chile, due to be concluded by 2005. The Chilean leader of the negotiations said the deal was "about much more than trade.[20] It is about science and technology and innovation," he said, adding that the deal would boost all three economies and complement their other global trading arrangements. According to the GEM 2003 report, two of the most entrepreneurial countries in the world are New Zealand and Chile. An agreement creating closer ties could create an exciting and vigorous trading environment.

The Home of Middle Earth

New Zealand is known for sheep, wool, and the America's Cup. It's an exporter of agricultural products, including the kiwi fruit that it introduced to the United States. But most recently one product has taken attention away from all other exports and activities. That industry is the movies, specifically the *Lord of the Rings* trilogy. Suddenly New Zealand became Middle Earth.

In 2001, the prime minister announced that up to $9 million would be spent on projects aimed at capitalizing on the release of the trilogy and the 2001 America's Cup yacht race. Response was so great that the government appointed a minister for *Lord of the Rings* to determine which projects would have the greatest benefit for New Zealand.

The promotional activities were not only to create interest in New Zealand as a tourist destination but also to remind people that the film was made there "using local skill and creativity and attitude."[21] Fascination with the films and their making continues. Tales are told that the producers were required to mark and map every rock and bench in the national park where the film was shot to return everything to its original state. People watch the films and want to see the location.

While New Zealand is using a movie to promote itself as a tourist destination, Australia has launched an advertising campaign to change its image. No longer does the country want to be known for the outback, beer, and "shrimp on the barbie." In 2004, it began a campaign to re-brand the country from an unsophisticated part of the world with intriguing wildlife and friendly people. Now the goal is to convey that Australia has "authenticity" with a focus on the character of the people who represent Australia.[22]

Now We Know

Australia and New Zealand aren't one country with two names, but two separate countries with similar but distinct histories, economies, and cultures. People from Australia and New Zealand share a historic link with both Canada and the United States and all trace their founders to the United Kingdom. Although similarities in the cultures still exist today, each one is also different, shaped by experiences and geography.

Although trading ties both nations to Europe and the United States, new relationships are developing with Singapore, Thailand, and China. These two countries have sophisticated economies and are active participants in global trade.

I'm Glad I Know

I'm glad I took the time to find out what cricket was and who the big soccer teams were. Plus, I learned them for each of the big cities because there is amazing competition here. Sports are everywhere and fill the conversation, but it's certainly not about the NBA or the Yankees.

↠ *American working for*
a U.S. technology company branch in Australia

CHAPTER 17

Africa

I Wish I'd Known
It took a long time to understand that there is U.S. time and African time. All my planning would have been easier if I'd known that time is more flexible in Africa. "On time" has an entirely different meaning than it does in Los Angeles.

➤➤ *Los Angeles businessman promoting business*
between California and African companies

I Wish They Knew
It would help if people realized that each country on the continent is different. There is not one Africa. Neither is there a group that can be labeled the African people. I wish people would take the time to learn something before they decide Africa is their target market.

➤➤ *African businessman visiting California*

Home of Humanity

Africa, the world's second-largest continent, is so large that the United States, China, India, and New Zealand could fit within its coastline. The Sahara Desert, which covers most of the northern half of the continent, is as large as the continental United States.

But size is only one of the notable aspects of this continent. According to some historians, "the ancestors of all humanity evolved in Africa."[1] There is evidence that 3 million years ago people walked the land. Furthermore, approximately 100,000 years ago, groups of modern humans left Africa and "progressively colonized the rest of the world."[2] They traveled to Asia, Europe, South America, and even Australia and New Zealand. In this way Africa can be considered home to the humanity of the world.

The story of those first travelers is captured in the histories of their descendants and the lands they helped to create. In this chapter we

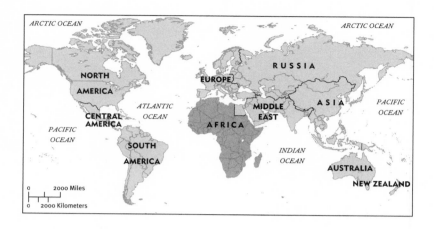

focus on Africa. The people who remained in Africa developed the civilized art of living peaceably in small societies. Theirs was a tribal existence without formal states. The creation of states and countries only came about after the arrival of the Europeans and the Arabs. They came, they colonized, and eventually departed, leaving behind a continent that was immeasurably different.

Africa: One Place or Two?

If you look at a political map of this vast continent you see lines dividing the area into 54 countries, large and small. The largest is Sudan at almost 970,000 square miles. The smallest is the Seychelles, a fraction of the size of Sudan, measuring only 175 square miles. But it isn't the disparity in size that raises the question of whether Africa is one place or two. The query reflects the differences in cultures as well as the location of the countries within the continent.

Geographically, the Sahara Desert is the dividing line. Is the area on the northern border that shares a coastline on the Mediterranean considered Africa? Was its culture shaped by the Arabs and the introduction of Islam? Is the area at or below the Sahara Desert line considered Africa? Was its culture shaped by a strong European influence?

The most northerly countries—Algeria, Morocco, Tunisia, Egypt (which has a land connection to the Arabian peninsula), and Libya—

are sometimes considered to be more Arab than African. The BBC recently hosted a discussion asking for listeners' replies to the question.[3] Although the answers were split, several respondents argued that if you're on the continent, you belong to the continent, adding that Africans are Africans no matter if you are from the north or south, if you have a light or dark complexion, or what your religion and culture are. This question certainly begins to highlight the complexity people face when learning about the countries that are part of the African continent. The following is a list of the African nations.

Algeria	Angola
Benin	Botswana
Burkina Faso	Burundi

Cabinda (Angola)	Cameroon
Cape Verde	Central African Republic
Chad	Comoros
Côte d'Ivoire	Democratic Republic of the Congo
Djibouti	Ethiopia
Egypt	Equatorial Guinea
Eritrea	Gabon
Gambia	Ghana
Guinea Bissau	Kenya
Lesotho	Liberia
Libya	Madagascar
Malawi	Mali
Mauritania	Mauritius
Morocco	Mozambique
Namibia	Niger
Nigeria	Réunion (Fr)
Rwanda	Sao Tome and Principe
Senegal	Seychelles
Sierra Leone	Somalia
South Africa	Sudan
Tanzania	Togo
Tunisia	Uganda
Western Sahara	Zambia
Zimbabwe	

Looking Back

The history of the African continent began with the movements of dinosaurs close to 95 million years ago. Anthropologists are still discovering the stories of this ancient history. However, it is easier to trace the history of relatively more recent times.

Discovery of a mariner's handbook, an early business traveler's guide dating from the first century A.D., tells us that people came to Africa to trade, and if they came for that reason, there was something of value to be obtained.[4] In this case, it was most likely the Romans who came to the northern part of the continent for grain. Obviously the land was occupied and farmed. Throughout the vast area, a multitude of tribes developed their own cultures, figured out ways of coping with difficult environments, survived, and multiplied. They had no organized states but rather occupied and moved within unmarked boundaries.

The outlines of most of the nations that exist today evolved as colonists arrived and claimed specific territories. The first to come were the Romans and Greeks, followed by the Arabs, Turks, and Europeans. Although some Europeans arrived as early as the 1500s, they were most active during the 1800s. In the mid-1800s, when the Latin American countries were gaining their freedom, the colonial powers were asserting their influence in this area. For more than 100 years into the mid-1900s the Europeans established colonies, controlled trade, and generally ruled the continent.

For example, the Dutch, followed by the British, took over South Africa. The Germans colonized an area that is now Tanzania. The Italians were in Ethiopia, the Belgians were in the Congo, and the French were in Tunisia, Morocco, and Algeria. This list is only an indication of the colonial activity on the African continent. To grasp the full extent of Europe's involvement and the legacy of the colonial nations, we have to examine the history of each country.

The change from dependent colonies to independent states didn't arrive simultaneously or quickly. After Egypt gained its independence from Great Britain in 1922 it took another 34 years for Morocco and Algeria to become sovereign states. Ghana followed in 1957 and thus began a decadelong period when colonies changed their status to independent nations. Somalia and Gabon gained independence in 1960, Nigeria in 1961, Uganda in 1962, Kenya in 1963, and Lesotho in 1966. Interestingly, this period of upheaval in Africa was also a period of great social change in the United States. This isn't a complete list nor did the 1960s end the move toward independence. Eritrea didn't gain its independence from Ethiopia until 1993.

The boundaries of these new countries generally reflected the outlines of the colonial territories. They were created for reasons that served the Europeans without regard to tribal history in terms of territories or relationships. In some cases the disregard for prior circumstances created a legacy that led to problems still present today. For example, Rwanda is home to two tribes, the Hutus and Tutsis, who have a history of hostility. The result has been civil war, violence, and death.

Even before the country gained its independence from Belgium, the fighting started. In this country, slightly smaller than the state of Maryland, war was almost continuous for more than 40 years, including the April 1994 genocide when the total lives lost exceeded 800,000.

The tribal fighting is not limited to Rwanda. Burundi, the Democratic Republic of the Congo (formerly Zaire), and Sudan have suffered from ongoing hostilities that pitted tribes against one another. In Sudan, the 21-year civil war, including genocide in the Darfur region, ended in 2004 because a peace agreement negotiated by the United Nations was signed in December of that year. Sudan, which is much larger than Rwanda and almost one quarter the size of the United States, actually had two wars going on at the same time, one being the tribal conflict in the Darfur region, where people trace their origins back to the thirteenth century. The other war was between the north and south, based on religious differences. The disputes spilled over to the neighboring countries of Burundi and the Democratic Republic of the Congo. Tribal loyalties and refugees from the conflicts carried their allegiances to new locations. The result has been death, destruction, and famine in the region.

Not all countries have had the same experience. South Africa, which struggled through the apartheid system, endeavors to honor its various tribes. A protocol officer involved in the inaugural ceremonies for Nelson Mandela, the first elected black president, discusses South Africa's efforts to properly honor the chiefs of the local tribes, while at the same time satisfying the protocol required for the visiting heads of state. This challenge included properly seating 1,000 guests for lunch!

Each country has its own story to tell and to understand the dynamics in any nation, people must look back and learn about the history of the tribes that were the original inhabitants.

Diversity of the People

The people are as varied as the geography. There are descendants of the original tribes, the Arabs, the Turks, and the Europeans. There are people from China and India. For example, in Tanzania there are 130 ethnic groups. In Uganda, more than 90 percent of the population is of African descent, and in Tunisia a similar percentage is of Arab ancestry. Not only are the 950 million people on the continent different because of ethnic origins and allegiances but also because of starkly different levels of education and wealth and poverty.

This diversity is evidenced in attitudes that shape people's approaches to business. There is no one African way. Studies of cultural orientation reveal some of the differences. South Africa with its Northern European (British and Dutch) influence is closer to the United States regarding attitudes toward areas of time and emphasis on the individual than are Egypt or Nigeria.[5] Countries in Eastern Africa (Ethiopia, Kenya, Tanzania, and Zambia) and Western Africa (Ghana and Sierra Leone) tend to be closer to Nigeria.[6] Their view of time is more flexible, and they are generally more collectivist in terms of respect for tradition and hierarchy. Although the studies are for only a limited number of countries, they do underscore that similarities and differences exist.

In addition, Americans working in Africa report that it is vital to understand the importance of the group, family, or tribe. All these countries are based on tribal societies that are family and relationship oriented. An international trade consultant cautions that family takes precedence in many dealings. In his experience with African clients, he found this to be especially true in the decision-making process. He commented that even for clients who are educated in the United States or Europe, decision-making processes were not an individual, independent activity. Nor was it simply a matter of reaching consensus within the management group. A decision cannot be finalized until the tribal leader gives approval. Only after a tribal leader's agreement can a transaction move forward.

Unlike Latin America, where Roman Catholics are in the majority in almost every country, such consistency of religious affiliation doesn't exist in Africa. Some of the countries are Muslim (Algeria, Morocco, and Tunisia) and others are mainly Christian. There are Hindus, Jews, and Ethiopian Orthodox. Moreover, it is important to note that indigenous, traditional religions are still popular and that many African independent churches combine Christian and traditional African beliefs.

Democracy Is Freedom to Speak

After years of coups, dictators, wars, and turmoil, some countries have elected governments and are considered democracies. In 2002, the

Afrobarometer conducted a survey in 12 sub-Saharan countries to explore people's ideas about democracy. This survey, which was conducted by a consortium of African and American social scientists, revealed there is overall support for democracy with 69 percent of the respondents preferring it to other forms of government. However, this degree of preference varies from country to country. The highest was 85 percent in Botswana and the lowest 40 percent in Lesotho. Of most interest may be the definitions of the meaning of democracy. For most of the survey group (40 percent) it was interpreted as civil liberties, especially freedom of speech. Only 9 percent of the people associate democracy with voting and elections. Unfortunately, only 58 percent said they were satisfied with democracy in their country.[7]

Counting the People

As of early 2005 the estimated total population for Africa was 900,465,411.[8] Given the diversity of the sizes of the countries, it is expected that population sizes will vary. The largest country by that measure is Nigeria with 154,468,571 people, although it is not the largest country on the continent. Sudan, physically the largest country and about one quarter the size of the United States, has only 35,035,677 people.

TABLE 17.1   POPULATION OF THE TEN LARGEST AFRICAN COUNTRIES

COUNTRY	POPULATION	% GROWTH RATE	MEDIAN AGE
Algeria	32,557,738	1.28	23.8
Democratic Republic of the Congo	57,261,205	2.99	15.8
Egypt	69,954,717	1.83	23.4
Ethiopia	70,600,043	1.89	17.4
Kenya	33,393,408	1.14	18.6
Morocco	31,003,311	1.61	23.3
Nigeria	154,468,571	2.45	18.1
South Africa	48,051,581	-0.25	24.7
Sudan	35,035,677	2.64	17.9
Tanzania	37,103,500	1.95	17.6

Source: CIA World Fact Book 2005 and Internet World Stats 2005

However, another issue beyond density and gross size of population is important to consider when looking at Africa: the HIV/AIDS epidemic. The statistics in Table 17.1 consider the impact of HIV/AIDS. South Africa has the highest HIV/AIDS rate and thus the lowest projected growth rate. However, the majority of the rates are near or above the 1.9 percent annual rate that means populations will double in 36 years if the rates remain steady.[9] While research suggests that these rates will be less, it is predicted that by 2100, Africa will have captured the greatest share of the increase in world population growth.

AIDS: More Than a Health Care Issue

HIV/AIDS is not a problem restricted to Africa. It is a worldwide epidemic. However, the numbers of those infected and dying in Africa and the implications for the continent are of grave concern. HIV/AIDS is the leading cause of death in sub-Saharan Africa. In 2002, 2.4 million adults and children died. This number is not an aberration but part of an ongoing crisis. The problem did not just surface in 2002. Between 1999 and 2000, more people died of AIDS in Africa than in all the wars on the continent. By one estimate, 6,000 Africans die from AIDS each day. Each day, an additional 11,000 are infected.[10]

It's easy to see the problem as only a matter of health care. If that were the only issue, then people could concentrate on obtaining medicine and finding ways to distribute it to those in need. But the effects of the epidemic are multifaceted and will have long-term consequences for the continent and its countries. One key issue is that increased poverty levels can be attributed at least in part to the effects of HIV/AIDS.

To obtain a picture of the process, consider the following scenarios dealing with people who have the disease. Those who are ill can't work or work less, thus being less able to purchase or grow what they need. Spending declines, and those who depend on consumers have fewer customers. Food production is reduced because people can't work on the farms. Limited savings are used up. The family unit can't care for itself. To offset lost income, children must work rather than attend school. When their parents die they are orphans raised, if they are lucky, by other members of the family.

Not only are there fewer children in schools but also some of the people who die are schoolteachers. So even children who are able to attend school suffer from a reduced quality of education. Diminished education as an outcome of either scenario does not bode well for populations that must compete in today's connected world.

Alan Whiteside of the University of Natal in South Africa described the disease as a "hidden tax" and said bluntly, "Africa is not and cannot be competitive unless this issue is firmly addressed."[11]

Emerging Trade

African trade is both ancient and modern. It is local, regional, and global. Traders were active before the Europeans first came to the continent. What is now Zimbabwe traded with Asia. Cape Town was on the trade route from Europe to Asia. Today the United States, the European Union, China, and India are active on the continent, and the majority of the African countries are members of the World Trade Organization.

Although there is currently increased interest in the continent and new business activity, Africa's activities represent only approximately 2 percent of world trade.[12] The world's second-largest continent, the richest in natural resources still lags behind most of the world, economically. To increase their level of trade, Africa faces challenges beyond negotiating the initial trading relationships.

In addition to the effort required to develop new policies and infrastructure to expand trade, revising its image is a critical issue for Africa. Headlines about African nations frequently feature death, destruction, war, and famine. A recent article in the *Economist* reported that in one week, coup plots had been uncovered in two countries, government forces killed demonstrators in another, and dissidents were being tortured in a third.[13] Reading reports like this makes it easy for people to think that all of Africa is in chaos. While these events pertain more to sub-Saharan Africa than to the whole continent, such distinctions aren't often made. People don't think of individual cities or even parts of countries. The image of turbulence and danger touches all the cities and all the countries, thereby reducing interest in opening new markets. How can you plan to do business where you can't believe your people and products will be safe? Thus, a negative perception, a tarnished image, becomes a nontariff barrier limiting opportunities for trade expansion and economic development.

The problems aren't image. Violence does exist, and to the extent that it is widespread in a country or region, it limits economic activity for the local community not just newcomers. Individuals and companies can attend only to short-term survival rather than investment and planning. In addition to the problem of violence, Africa is plagued by corruption that continues to grow. According to Transparency International's 2004 Corruption Perceptions Index, only 2 of the 34 African countries surveyed ranked at or above 5.0 on the rating scale. The score of 5.0 is considered the dividing point between "clean" and "totally corrupt." Botswana's score was 6.0 and Tunisia's 5.0. The remainder of the countries scored from 4.6 for South Africa to 1.6 for Nigeria, placing it in spot number 144 of 146 countries surveyed. This may be a side effect of continued violence, poverty, and lack of organized governmental and legal processes and procedures in some countries.

In addition to limiting the opening of new businesses, the reputation for violence and corruption translates to a lack of foreign investment, money that can help an economy grow. Rather than experience large capital inflows, Africa has experienced the reverse, the flight of capital. In 1999, more than 50 percent of Africa's wealthy had moved their money outside the continent as compared with 17 percent in Latin America and 3 percent in Asia.[14] Changing those statistics requires the creation of a more predictable, stable business environment where the rule of law is effective, property rights are recognized, and violence as a solution to problems is eliminated.

Notwithstanding the problems, there is still trade going on regionally and globally. Regional organizations have formed to support and expand trade. These groups include the African Union, the Southern African Development Community, Economic and Monetary Community of Central Africa, the African Forum, and the New Partnership for Africa's Development (NEPAD).

Although recent emphasis has been on developing preferential agreements within the continent, the 2004 World Economic Forum's African Competitiveness Report suggests this approach will not be successful. The study's authors state that agreements with developed countries have "greater promise at the present time."[15] Africa is moving in that direction with negotiations under way for trade deals with the United States and SACU (the South African Customs Union of South

Africa, Botswana, Lesotho, Namibia, and Swaziland.) Already in place is the AGOA, the African Growth and Opportunities Act. This agreement is best known for its textiles provisions but covers many product categories, including energy and chocolate. Not only will retailers acquire garments from AGOA countries but they can also purchase candy made with cocoa from Ghana.

The European Union and South Africa have a trade agreement that dates back to 1999. In addition to working to expand trade through tariff reduction, the EU has worked to eliminate nontariff barriers. For example, advisers worked with flower growers in Kenya informing them of what pesticides to avoid so that their products could enter the EU market. Additionally, the EU is expanding trade in the northern part of the continent. Algeria participates in a Euro-Mediterranean Accord and on June 1, 2004, an agreement with Egypt came into effect. Challenges and opportunities abound for trade in Africa. It will take time to see the results of both the regional and multinational linkages now being developed.

AGOA

AGOA is the African Growth and Opportunity Act, an agreement between the United States and 37 sub-Saharan countries. Signed in 2000, it requires countries to qualify to be included, and the group changes from time to time. The agreement eliminated U.S. import barriers on virtually all of sub-Saharan Africa's exports to the United States. The improvements in trade balances have been slow to develop.

Some of the largest imports into the United States came from Nigeria, South Africa, and Gabon—the major energy exporters.[16] However, best known are increases in the textile and apparel sector. The United States imports of textile and apparel have more than doubled in 2002.[17] Other sectors, such as South Africa's automobile sector or Uganda's technology sector, are just beginning to benefit.

One reason for the increase in textile imports to the United States was a change in the original AGOA rules. When the agreement began, all fabric used in garments made in Africa for export to the United States had to originate in the United States or an African country. Now the rule has been changed to allow acceptance of third party textiles. This rule or exemption about point of origin permits textiles to be imported into Africa, generally from Asia, cut and sewn in Africa, and sent to the United States without export restrictions.

The importance of this rule is difficult to overstate. For example, Lesotho is one of the countries that has benefited from AGOA. Factories have located there, and jobs have been created. However, current economic growth would not be sustainable if the exemption from the point of origin rule is eliminated.[18] Fortunately, it was extended in 2004, but the issue will appear again in three years. Some countries are already preparing for changes in the agreement. Mauritius, another beneficiary of textile growth, is becoming a diversified economy with a focus on finance and tourism. A Los Angeles consultant to the AGOA negotiating team says Mauritius plans to become a regional banking center. Its banking sector investment is more than $1 billion, and it is extending its commerce with India as well as South Africa.[19]

African Designs, Dutch Creators

Textiles aren't only exported from Africa; they're imported, too. Since 1864, Vlisco, a Dutch company, has been the number one supplier of textiles to Africa. Operating under the brand name Real Dutch Wax, it produces textiles solely for the African market. It has subsidiaries in Côte d'Ivoire, Ghana, and Benin, but its most expensive lines are still made in Holland. Known for bright colors and good-quality cotton the textiles are often used for trading. The prices for its goods are "more stable than many African currencies."[20] Its exclusive designs are not reprints of historic African images but rather a "European imagination of African tastes."

Business Their Way

Reports about business in Africa range from discouraging to hopeful. People call Africa the "worst economic tragedy of the twentieth century" and add that most sub-Saharan African countries are more impoverished now than when they became independent.[21]

No matter how poor most countries may be, it doesn't mean that business is not being developed as we note in the Trade and AGOA sections in this chapter. In addition, some countries are creating businesses within their borders. The 2003 Global Entrepreneurship Monitor's report includes favorable reports about two African countries: Uganda and South Africa. Uganda ranked as one of the top five entrepreneurial countries worldwide along with Chile, New Zealand, Thailand, and Venezuela. South Africa is defined in the group as "Medium Entrepreneurial Activity," in a group that includes Germany, Israel, and Switzerland.

Which report is the real Africa? The answer once again has to be there is no "one Africa." There are similarities and vast differences among the African nations. One area of similarity, referred to repeatedly by American businesspeople is that the interpretation of time all over Africa does not match the U.S. concept. A protocol officer from Los Angeles described a visit she arranged with a group of professionals from several African nations. Their day was scheduled to begin at 9:00 A.M. When they hadn't arrived by 9:20 she called the group leader. She inquired whether there was a problem and if they were lost. She was assured all was well and that they were coming. When she asked for an estimate of their new arrival time (hoping to hear no more than another 15 minutes), she was astonished to hear that 11:00 A.M. was the plan. Needless to say, they weren't able to meet with all the people on the original agenda.

This story was repeated in many forms until finally one consultant who works with nonprofit organizations doing trade development said he figured out that there is a concept of African time. He's observed that the people who visit are polite and interested in the appointments that are scheduled. They simply have a different sense of priorities and the flow of time. Their expectation is that others are equally flexible, and they are shocked to learn otherwise.

Time plays a part in establishing business relationships. As is true in Latin and Asian cultures, people want to know about you before doing business. Therefore, it's necessary to allow time for nonbusiness conversation. The focus is on building long-term relationships rather than moving through quick transactions. Overall, expect a higher level of formality than you might adopt with American colleagues.

One type of behavior that limits business expansion was already mentioned in the section in this chapter on trade. That problem is corruption. It isn't only the global trade community that perceives widespread corruption. The Afrobarometer conducted a survey in April 2002 regarding African attitudes. The survey was conducted in

12 African countries with 1,200 respondents in each country and more than 21,000 interviews. The results were that the majority viewed corruption as pervasive and 52 percent of the population thinks that public officials are corrupt—not an environment that favors business development.

But before we lose hope, remember that not all African countries are identical. Lesotho prosecuted 18 foreign companies accused of paying bribes to local officials to secure contracts on a multimillion-dollar project to export water to South Africa. Lesotho is a mountainous country resting entirely within the borders of South Africa. In explaining the action, the minister for justice, human rights, and constitutional affairs stated, "We want it to be an example to Southern Africa and the rest of the world."[22] The local chief executive was convicted of accepting the bribes and sentenced to 18 years of imprisonment for taking bribes connected with this case.

South Africa: From Outcast to Star

Today South Africa is known as the business gateway to Africa. Its regional links alone provide access to more than 140 million people.[23] But as recently as 1990 it was an outcast among the nations of the world. During the 1970s and 1980s its goods were boycotted and its policy of apartheid—institutionalized racial segregation—widely condemned.

South Africa, like the other countries of the continent, was populated for thousands of years before outsiders, in this case the Dutch, arrived in 1652. They established outposts to provide provisions for ships traveling the trade routes. In a sense the beginnings of South Africa's European connections were based on trade. These original colonists were joined by French and German settlers who became known as the Boers (farmers).[24] The arrival of the British in 1814 prompted the Boers to move from the coastal areas to the interior of the country. This migration, called the Great Trek resulted in wars with the native population and the beginning of white control of much of the land. The ensuing years were a period of turmoil. Gold and diamonds were discovered, and the British extended their territory. Between 1899 and 1902 the Boers fought the British and lost. In 1910 the Union of South Africa came into existence as a British Colony.

Apartheid, the policy of segregation based on racial groups, began in 1948. The system of government and internal policies built around that policy lasted for almost 50 years, continuing even after South Africa became an independent nation in 1961. During that period the African National Congress (ANC), a political party organized in 1921 and banned in 1960, fought with words and with arms, alone and with other groups, against the inequities of the system. The best known ANC leader is Nelson Mandela. Mandela was jailed along with others who fought the government. For Mandela the 27-year period of incarceration didn't lead to silence or diminish his efforts to eliminate apartheid.

It wasn't until 1989 with the election of Frederik Willem de Klerk that Mandela's dream began to be realized. He was freed from jail, the ANC was granted legal status, and within two years most apartheid laws were abolished. While the result, a South Africa with a new constitution and equality for all the races, is sometimes called Mandela's Miracle, the credit really goes to many people. The two people most often associated with the dramatic change are de Klerk and Mandela, who shared the Nobel Peace Prize in 1993.

The ten-year anniversary of the first free election and inauguration of Nelson Mandela as the first black president of South Africa was in 2004. The decade of freedom brought many changes, many of them positive. South Africa is growing as a political and economic leader in the region and the entire continent. It has a developed infrastructure to support business that includes a stock exchange ranked as one of the top ten in the world.[25] Although a large portion of its own population is extremely poor, it is the regional supplier of food for relief efforts.

However, there are still significant challenges. There is still insufficient housing and employment for its 47 million people. More people in this country than any other in the world are living with HIV/AIDS. The nation's level of income inequality is among the highest in the world. Nearly 60 percent of black South Africans live in poverty compared with only 3 percent of whites.[26]

Even countries that view South Africa as an attractive market recognize the complex realities of the business in the environment. A writer discussing South Africa as one of Canada's "hottest export markets" points out that the country has two distinct economies.[27] First is the formal economy with a population that is advanced and educated. Second is the large, less educated population creating a separate segment in which the economy is still developing. The first decade of freedom has brought about many changes, but the work is not yet complete.

World Cup: A Game and a Symbol

The World Cup of soccer takes place every four years. It ranks with the Olympics as the largest sports event in the world. Soccer, or football as it is known in most places, is truly a world sport followed and played by people of all races and colors.

In 2010 the World Cup will make history for its choice of venue as well as for the country that wins the games. This will be the first time the competition will be held in Africa. In fact, the country that will be the host, South Africa, was banned from participation for more than 30 years, from 1964 to 1992, because of its apartheid policy. The timing of South Africa's selection coincides with its celebration of the first 10 years as a democracy.

For South Africa, being awarded the World Cup is important as it symbolizes its acceptance in the world community. This decision acknowledges the dramatic changes and progress that have occurred. Additionally, it hopes to benefit on an economic basis. The World Cup is projected to create more than 150,000 jobs. That is immensely important to a country with unemployment calculated at more than 30 percent.[28] The events surrounding the World Cup could add several billion dollars to the economy.[29] For a country struggling to house and educate its population, that's a significant benefit.

Food and Drink

South Africa is the only sub-Saharan country and only the second country on the continent to be home to McDonald's. The first McDonald's in Africa opened in Egypt in 1990 and the first McDonald's in South Africa opened in 1995. In 2004, there are 90 restaurants employing 6,000 people. According to the McDonald's South Africa Web site, 97 percent of the food served is locally produced.

Wine is old and new in South Africa. Vines and wine production go back to the arrival of the Dutch settlers in the 1700s. Although it has a 300-year history, the wine business was tightly controlled by the government bureaucracy until the end of apartheid. The country's isolation limited information sharing and innovation. However, 10 years later changes are abundant. According to the *New York Times* wine writer Frank Prial, the country is now beginning to make "world-class wines."[30]

Uganda: War and Progress

Uganda, a country slightly smaller than Oregon, is located in Eastern Africa bordering Kenya on the west and the Democratic Republic of the Congo on the east. Some recent reports about this nation illustrate the disparate realities that exist in Africa today. According to the 2003 GEM report, Uganda ranks as one of the five most entrepreneurial countries of those surveyed. The others in this top group include New Zealand and Chile.

But that ranking shows only one small glimpse of this African nation. February and March 2004 articles reported the arrival of a bookmobile that provided books to primary schools in the country, where none were available before.[31] This is a step toward educating the population. Less encouraging was a report titled "No respite; a massacre in Uganda."[32] That article told of another horror in an 18-year guerilla civil war.

In the same period, Uganda agreed to participate in the East African Community, creating a common market with Kenya and Tanzania. According to the Uganda Web site of the Export Promotion Board, this agreement was created in response to the global trend, where trade negotiations are increasingly being carried out under regional blocs. The formation of a customs union in East Africa is not a matter of choice, but a necessity.[33]

In addition, an online search reveals the Women of Uganda Network (WOUGNET), a Nongovernmental Organization (NGO) established in 2000 to develop the use of information technology to address problems of sustainable development.[34] The reports of events in and involving Uganda provide a glimpse of the coexistence of destruction and progress throughout Africa.

Online All the Time

With 6 percent of the world's population, Africa has less than 2 percent of its population using the Internet. As the size of countries varies, so does Internet usage in both the overall numbers and by penetration.

TABLE 17.2   ONLINE ALL THE TIME

COUNTRY	INTERNET USAGE	POPULATION PENETRATION
Algeria	500,000	1.5
Democratic Republic of the Congo	50,000	0.1
Egypt	2,700,000	3.9
Ethiopia	75,000	0.1
Kenya	400,000	1.2
Morocco	800,000	2.6
Nigeria	750,000	0.5
South Africa	3,523,000	7.3
Sudan	300,000	0.9
Tanzania	250,000	0.7

Source: Internet World Stats 2005

The largest numbers of users are in South Africa with 3,523,000. Table 17.2 lists figures for the 10 countries with the largest populations.

It isn't just the number of users or the penetration of the population that can be intriguing. The increase between 2000 and 2005 for some countries in this group is startling. According to Internet World Stats' Web site, both Algeria and Sudan have increased by 900 percent; however, as impressive as that figure is, the largest gain was in the Democratic Republic of the Congo. There the increase from 500 to 50,000 users translates to a 9,900 percent gain. Although the percentages are high, the base numbers remain very small. Nevertheless the indications are clear, technology is spreading in Africa just as it is in the remainder of the world.

Now We Know
All of Africa isn't alike by any measure. It's a large continent, large enough to hold the United States, China, India, and New Zealand between its coastlines. Within its boundaries are 54 independent countries

both large and small, with diverse populations, resources, and stages of economic development. Each country's history is specific, many shaped by their experiences as colonies of European powers. In some instances independence arrived less than 20 years ago.

Many factors have limited overall growth in the continent, but one current factor is its image as a region filled with violence and corruption and a population overwhelmed by an ongoing AIDS epidemic. While there is truth to these issues, they are not the same in every place. To understand Africa as a whole, people must first learn about the individual countries. Some places are poor and stagnant, while others have economies that are growing. Trade and business exist. Some is local, some regional, and some global. To take advantage of opportunities requires researching the possibilities country by country.

I'm Glad I Know
When I travel to Africa I now expect it to be different. I know I can't change the way I would act at home, and I can't do things the African way. You have to adapt and follow the lead of the people who know how things are done in this area. It's hard going from being the leader to the follower, but if you do, you learn what you need to know.

↣ *New York–based American project coordinator*
for an AGOA supporting organization

CHAPTER 18

Getting *to* Know You

I Wish I'd Known

Simply, I wish I'd known more of the culture before I started working in a company from the U.K. Some sort of brief education would have made it far easier. What [is considered a] compliment to a British person [who is] native to Great Britain? What [is considered insulting] because of conflicts in culture? It's helpful to know a few things about the culture of the people you work with.

➜➤ *Los Angeles–based video game designer*
working for a U.K. company

I Wish They Knew

A survey conducted in 130 countries revealed several common points of advice for Americans abroad. Among the top were 3 that touch on conversation and personal exchange. They are that they wish Americans would "listen instead of talking all the time, turn down the volume, and try learning a few words or two in our language."

➜➤ *Excerpt from congressional testimony*
of chairman of business for Diplomatic Action, a business group
working to enhance the image of Americans worldwide

Meeting and Greeting

It's people, both individually and in groups, who accomplish the tasks that shape our world. No matter their interests, professions, or home, their connections to one another have similar beginnings. Whether in person or online, the starting point is in the form of a formal introduction followed by conversations that often extend beyond specific business matters. As with other aspects of professional behavior, each culture has an appropriate way of conducting the initial encounter. We call this meeting and greeting. Previous chapters have explored the reasons and influences of behavior. In this chapter we'll look at observable activities.

So familiar are we with this initial process that we seldom give it much thought. However, meeting someone is actually a multistep activity. We begin with the announcement of names (Hi, I'm George Smith.) and proceed to a physical action (a handshake or a bow). Finally, we conclude with the exchange of cards providing detailed information about ourselves in writing. Each part of this procedure varies by culture and tradition. It is in these variations that the opportunities for surprise, strong connections, and moments of discomfort exist. The following section highlights some of the variations people may encounter.

What's Your Name?

Our names have special meaning to each of us. They tell the world who we are. For most of us, our names were gifts given by our parents. Whether they are names we would have selected, they are ours, and we want them to be pronounced, spelled, and used in the way we believe is correct. This is simple when everyone is familiar with the pattern of names, such as their order (given name followed by family name).

However, these patterns vary widely. Sam Smith may be Mr. Smith in one place and Mr. Sam in another. In most Western countries your given name is followed by your family name, generally your father's name. We can usually assume that for Sam Smith "Sam" is his given name and Smith is the family name. Mr. Smith may also have a middle name that may be another family name. However, in other places the name order may be reversed. Additionally, people's names may include their father's, mother's, grandparent's, or even a name given to all the family members of one generation. In contrast, there may be only a given name combined with an initial and no surname. To avoid calling Mr. Smith "Mr. Sam," do your research before addressing him. (See the Resources section for places to look.)

In Japan and China, the given name follows the family name, thus reversing the Western order. A person with the given name "Ichiro" and the family name "Suzuki" is thus called "Suzuki Ichiro" rather than "Ichiro Suzuki." It takes some practice to remember that he is Mr. Suzuki rather than Mr. Ichiro.

In China, as in Korea, a generational name may also be included. This name, given to all people in the family born in a certain generation, is placed between the family name and the given name. Thus Lu Teng Hui has the family name Lu, the generational name Teng, and the given name Hui.

To add to potential confusion, in an attempt to simplify the process, some Asian professionals elect to arrange their names in the Western order, first name followed by family name. Some people even take Western given names. While Chinese, Korean, or Japanese names such as Ruan Xiao or Yao Pei or Guowei may prove difficult to remember, names such as Frank, Stacy, or Sam ease introductions and the names are easier to recall.

On a recent trip from Shanghai to Los Angeles, a Los Angeles–based importer, Larry, was seated next to a Chinese college student who was visiting the United States for the first time. During the flight, they discussed the issue of names, complications, and misunderstandings. Somewhere between Shanghai and Los Angeles, Larry had the privilege of selecting an American name for the visitor. The person who left his home with the given name of Qiang arrived at his destination as Matthew. He received a new name for a new place.

In Latin and Central America and Mexico, people generally use two surnames, both their father's and their mother's. A father's name directly follows the given name; the mother's name is last. This can lead to some awkward moments if you aren't careful. You may automatically pick the last name listed on a business card and assume it is the family name—the one to be used formally. A gentleman named Carlos Perez Martinez would be Mr. Perez, not Mr. Martinez. When women marry, they add their husband's surname to their name and generally are addressed as such. For example, if Señorita Ana Maria Mendoza Gonzales marries Carlos Perez Martinez, she would be Señora Ana Maria Mendoza Gonzales de Perez. She would be introduced as Señora Perez.

In South Africa names may reflect British ancestry with the use of multiple initials for the first name coupled with the family name. Other names reflect Dutch and French Huguenot heritage. These are the names of the Afrikaners, also known as Boers (farmers), whose family names begin with van, de, or van de, all of which mean "of." In other instances, names indicate a family's tribe by the selection of a person's given name.[1] In Iceland and Ethiopia, both men and woman follow their given names with their father's given names. Russian names may include a patronymic, a name derived from the father's first name. For example, in the name Svyatoslav Alesevich Bryl, Svyatoslav is the first name, Alesevich identifies this person as the son of Ales, and Bryl is the surname. For women, names almost always end in "a," whether it is a given name such as Olga or the family name; for example, Tsvetkov becomes Tsvetkova.[2]

In Saudi Arabia names are generally organized in the same order as the Western style, with given name listed first and family name last. However, the middle name may be a patronymic beginning with "bin," used to mean "son of" (it can also mean "from"). For example, in the name King Fahd bin Abdul-Aziz al-Saud, Fahd is the given name, bin Abdul-Aziz is the patronymic, and al-Saud is the family name.[3]

While the variations in the order of names can be confusing, the problem can be intensified because of variations in spellings and translations. Moving from the vastly different alphabets of the Arabic, Chinese, Korean, Japanese, and Cyrillic languages adds to the confusion when names are translated into a Latin alphabet. No matter how names are arranged or spelled, they represent a person, a unique individual to be addressed with care and respect, so be sure to check and be sensitive and careful.

Formality Is Essential

Knowing the order of a person's name isn't sufficient to ensure a satisfactory introduction. Titles must be used and formality honored. The general form of an in-person introduction is similar everywhere. You state the first and last name as well as a person's title. The pattern requires that the oldest or most important person be named first. (The protocol derives from the days when people were presented or announced to a monarch.) The formal process is more complex than a simple "George, I'd like you to meet Sam." A formal introduction would go as such: "George, may I present Sam Sylvester, the CFO of our biggest client. Mr. Sylvester, Mr. [George] Greenway is the president and founder of our Super Company." A good and useful introduction includes information about each person that will help him or her to start a conversation.

People from around the globe repeatedly mention that the casual American leap to first names is one of the most startling behaviors they encounter. A German businessman working for a French company in California says that he worked with colleagues for years and never used their first names. He went on to say, "In Germany, first name address is reserved for close friends. It is not uncommon that colleagues who work with [one another] for decades still address [one another] as Mr. or Ms. and the last name." No matter where you go outside of the United States, the move from formal to informal is not automatic. You are invited to use a person's first name and should wait for that invitation.

Will We Be Friends?

Just as the formal in-person introduction, the handshake can be traced to the times of kings, queens, and knights. At that time, a handshake allowed the parties to check for hidden weapons. In addition, the firmness of the touch was an indicator of the strength of the bond between the parties. A strong handshake was a sign of willingness to join in battle. In contrast, a soft or limp handshake was a sign of a lack of commitment between the parties.

In a business setting, we still find meaning in the type of handshake we receive. In some subtle, almost unrecognizable way, we expect the gesture to indicate the potential in a business relationship. The communication is given, received, and interpreted through our cultural expectations.

How does someone from Malaysia who is accustomed to a 10- to 12-second handshake interpret the brief 3- to 4-second handshake of an American? If you expect a strong Norwegian grasp, what happens if you receive the gentle touch appropriate in Singapore? What does it mean if the greeting is extended using one hand or if both hands clasp yours? Is eye contact direct or are eyes averted? Are we beginning our relationship committed to the shared enterprise, or do I need to find another partner? Unless we know what's appropriate in an environment, it's difficult to recognize and interpret the signals.

Although the duration or style of a handshake may vary from place to place, the common element is the physical action that demonstrates the connection between the parties. This contrasts strongly with the traditional Asian greeting of a bow. With a bow there is no physical contact, no shared touch. The two parties stand some distance from each other. Rather than a direct gaze, the head is averted, thus showing respect and submission. An extensive protocol exists to determine the depth of the bow required depending on the relationship between the parties. This also creates a more complex greeting ritual than the Western handshake, which is standardized regardless of rank and gender. In current business settings that involve Westerners, the Asian greeting is often modified, combining both a handshake and a slight bow of the head.

While women shake hands with men and other women in many places, it is important to remember that this is not universally appropriate. In Muslim countries and in India, where many people are Hindus, men and women do not touch in public. In this case, a smile and nod are sufficient for greetings and introductions. If women feel that a handshake is acceptable, they will extend their hand to initiate the contact.

A kiss may also be part of a greeting. Colleagues may wish to express some additional warmth. It can be surprising and unusual to receive a kiss on the hand during a formal European greeting or a kiss that extends to both cheeks. Accept the gesture and try to avoid bumping noses.

The Card Exchange

The small document that contains a person's name, title, and contact information has different meanings in different places. It can either be understood as a way to facilitate future contact or as a representation of the person handing it out. In the first case it's called a business card, and in the second it is called a name card. The difference is subtle and important. For most Americans, a card is considered a business card. It is a piece of paper that contains information and that completes an introduction by providing contact details. It must be easy to read, clean, neat, and clear. Its purpose is to confirm the spoken exchange that takes place in the introduction and to provide the details necessary to extend the connection.

In many other parts of the world, especially Asia, the same piece of paper is known as a name card, with emphasis placed on the person. A name card gives more than a person's name. It indicates the company a person works for and the person's place within the company. In collectivist cultures, where hierarchy and a person's place in the structure are important, the card provides significant information. Knowing the title and rank of a person is important so you know how to proceed in business activities.

As with the other elements of the introduction process, the treatment of the card must be careful and formal. No matter how confusing things may be, avoid writing reminders on the cards. Consider that a name card represents the person who gives it to you, and so writing on someone's card at a meeting in Beijing, as you may do in Chicago, is akin to writing on the person. (The image that comes to mind is a cartoon with words written on someone's forehead.)

Always look carefully at a card that is presented to you and at the person giving it to you. Present and receive cards using both hands, as if you were handling a precious object. In a meeting, place the cards in the order that the people are sitting in front of you on the table. This can be a useful tool that will help you remember the names and titles of the attendees.

Be thoughtful about where you place the card when you put it away. A shipping manager in Los Angeles describes a deal in Korea that was lost not due to the price or service but because of the manner in which a business card was handled. After the usual greetings and exchange of cards, the American sales manager placed the Korean manager's business card in his wallet, returned the wallet to his back pocket, and sat down. The meeting went on, but the deal was lost in the instant that the American sat on the Korean's business card. Remember, it's a name card; it's about a person, not about business.

When traveling to a destination where the alphabet differs, it's useful to have your card translated into the local language on the reverse side of your standard card. This is useful to facilitate introductions, shows respect for the people you meet, and establishes you as knowledgeable and courteous.

Now We Talk

Once the steps of the introduction are safely navigated, you must select appropriate conversational topics. Whether at home or across the globe, picking subjects to discuss with new acquaintances can be challenging. If a business discussion isn't appropriate, is the type of car you drive or where you live the right beginning? Do you follow the admonition of an Englishman's mother to talk roads, traffic, and weather to avoid saying anything offensive?

Even if the people gathered are business colleagues, in a social context neither business nor family are likely to be the first topics selected. When the emphasis is on building a relationship, people prefer not to talk business. That's done at work. In the United States, a familiar conversational opening in such situations is to ask what people do or where they work. Outside the United States that query may be considered inappropriate or even rude. Social time is to get to know people individually and to learn their interests and ideas, what books they read, and where they travel. Business is not the only topic where it's best to let someone else initiate the conversation. Family, religion, and money all fall into that category.

However, conversation in a business setting can become confusingly personal. In Asia and Latin America, for example, it's important for people to know one another, to develop the trust that is the foundation of business activities. Accordingly, questions may range far past the business under consideration and include marital status and opinions about family, politics, and religion. Americans can find it startling and uncomfortable. It's useful to realize that the goal of conversations is to better understand each person to build a relationship and to find shared interests and viewpoints.

To the surprise of many, politics may be part of daily conversation wherever people from around the globe find themselves. A man from Los Angeles working for a British company said, "For an American it's fairly rare to spend a lunchtime conversation discussing the latest current events or what's happening in politics. But lunchtime conversations with my British colleagues can consist of, 'What's better for Great Britain, having the monarchy or doing away with it?' Now, as an American, I'm saying to myself, 'What?! The monarchy has relevance?' But my colleagues find the topic as compelling as Americans find Sunday's football game scores."

To build effective connections it's important to avoid the cliché that Americans know nothing of current events beyond their own neighborhood. A common theme runs throughout conversations with people in different places with varied backgrounds: "Americans don't know what we're doing, what's important to us, or what our place is." Knowing even a little can have an immense impact. Today to find out about almost any part of the globe requires only an Internet search. You want the news from Estonia, Kenya, or New Zealand? No problem. Prefer to check the *Asia Times* or the *Bulgarian News*? The Internet can help with that search, too.

According to an international business consultant, it is actually simple to learn what's happening around the world. About a month before a trip or a meeting with a client from another country, she sets up a news alert on the Google Web site. Whether it's from Chile, South Africa, France, or Kyrgyzstan, the news arrives daily. By simply watching the headlines and reading select articles over several weeks, it's possible to see what's happening in that area. In a very easy way you can appear knowledgeable, build a repertoire of topics for conversation, and have a better understanding of the issues your client or contact is confronting.

But it isn't just news, politics, and business that people expect to discuss. What you've read, where you've traveled, and interests beyond the obvious are to be shared. A manager from Los Angeles discusses experiencing a shift in a professional relationship from cool and formal to relaxed and friendly after just five minutes of dinner conversation. What brought about the shift? A five-minute discussion about what wine to drink with dinner. Suddenly there was a shared interest. "It was remarkable," she said. "We went from somewhat stiff conversation to laughter. Now, five years later we're working on a new project and have dinner together whenever we're in the same city."

A Topic That Travels

Wherever you are, there's a team that matters. It's difficult to overstate the value of sports as a conversational tool. It can be as safe as weather and traffic while helping to establish you as knowledgeable about local events. People have been known to talk for hours about whether Manchester United is the team to beat, or whether there will be another Yao Ming, or whether soccer will ever be really popular in the United States.

Americans are known for their interest in their national sports but—unfortunately—they are also known for their narrow focus, even hubris, in naming the competitions. One comment from a Business for Diplomatic Action (BDA) survey was: "If we had an athletic competition called the World Series, [you'd think] it would occur to us to invite other nations." What isn't well-known is that more than 25 percent of the players in two of the U.S. major league sports, baseball and basketball, were born outside the United States.[4]

Knowing something about the sports that are part of another nation's culture provides more than just a conversational tool. Understanding the games enables you to translate informal business language. Just as U.S. speech is filled with sports references, so too are the languages of many other places. For us there are home runs, slam dunks, and touchdowns. In South Africa business situations are compared with soccer, cricket, or rugby.[5]

While the games are different, some of the words are similar. The image of a bat and ball varies according to location. Are you in India where a bat and ball are part of the game of cricket, or are you from the baseball countries of the United States, Canada, or Japan? Know the game and initiate the conversation; catch the opportunities as they appear.

Not Just the Subjects: Words Count, Too

Even when all parties agree on the topics to be discussed, chances for misunderstandings exist. According to an Australian who has worked in New Zealand and the United States, English as a shared language of commerce can still be confusing. He says that English appears to be similar except for different accents. The confusion and occasional amusement often come from colloquial differences and local slang. There will even be different vocabulary terms, such as the use of the word *fortnight* to mean 14 days. "When I told someone in San Diego I was arriving in a fortnight," says the Australian, he was always asked, "now when exactly will you be here?"

These misunderstandings among people who speak English are not unusual when some of the people use American English and others use British English. Words, spellings, and pronunciations vary. Problems arise because the expectation is that the language is the same, and people assume words have the same meaning. It isn't always so. For example, "to table" an item at a meeting in the United Kingdom is to consider it immediately. In the United States it's to set it aside for discussion at a later time. The same word in this example has opposite meanings. There are so many examples that books have been written to translate English into English. The *British English A to Zed* of 2001 has nearly 5,000 British words and expressions translated into their American equivalents.

Conversations vary in still other manners. What is polite in the form of exchange in one place may be rude in another. For example, in Chile it's acceptable to interrupt while someone is speaking. In France, people seem to speak simultaneously. In the United States, either of these behaviors is considered rude, as polite dialogue requires that people take turns speaking.

Intellectual arguments please and engage the French. They debate and correct one another as a matter of course. In Asia, the Middle East, or Africa—cultures where it's important to preserve appearance, to save face, and to maintain harmony—that approach would be unacceptable. Watch, listen, and pay attention to learn the appropriate patterns.

No English at All?

Although English is now known as the language of business around the globe, there are still times and places where interpreters are required. In some instances the parties to a discussion or negotiation may speak English or another common language but only at a casual conversational level. To conduct business, a fluency is necessary; thus, an interpreter is required. Further, the time for translation allows each party to work in their own language, sometimes a matter of pride, and to reflect upon the discussion while the translation goes on.

Using an interpreter effectively is a special skill developed with practice. People who use them frequently recommend the following:

- Select your own interpreter. Do not let the other party make the choice.
- Meet with the selected interpreter and explain your business, the transaction, and your goals. Help them to understand your perspective to help them explain everything accurately.

- Do not look at the interpreter when you are speaking. Always look at the person you wish to address—your colleague or client. Speak to them just as you would if they understood your language.
- When they reply, look at them as if you understood their words. By your physical actions, where you look, establish that the conversation is between the two parties, not with the interpreters.

Furthermore, assume that everyone involved speaks English well, even if they don't reveal that immediately. A formal presentation of government officials in Dalian, China, was done entirely through interpreters. The American's remarks were made in English, then translated into Chinese. The responses in Chinese were then translated into English. Only after the conclusion of the official portion of the meeting did the senior member of the Chinese delegation switch to English. His English was excellent, in part because he had attended graduate school in North Carolina.

The Body Speaks

Communication is more than words. Our gestures, where we look, the volume of our voices, and the movement of our bodies extend our messages. The following are a few examples and cautions:

- Direct eye contact can be considered disrespectful or challenging in Africa and Asia, although it's respectful in the United States and Europe.
- Using the left hand to present items, to eat, or to shake hands is considered rude in the Middle East and India.
- In Arab countries, avoid sitting with the soles of your shoes showing or your ankle resting on your knee. Sit with your legs crossed at the ankle.
- Avoid all public displays of affection such as hugging or kissing.
- People of the same sex holding hands as they walk and talk indicates friendship and goodwill.

Gestures that mean something is fine in one place can be extremely volatile and rude in another. (Check the Resources section for sug-

"And now I'd like a volunteer to help demonstrate the power of nonverbal communication."

gested guides on this topic.) Although there are many cultures where conversation is animated, where people touch their colleagues, and where they gesture broadly, refrain from following along until you're certain of the meanings. Be prepared to be surprised. Although China is known as a place where people are reserved and formal, individuals may be demonstrative and touch you during a conversation. In South Africa people like to be physical while talking. Differences abound from place to place and person to person.

Another issue that is part of communication is the volume of our voices when we speak. Americans and Italians are known for the sounds of their conversations. Their words reach those who are participants in their conversation and those in the surrounding areas. Americans are accustomed to relatively big spaces, and so they communicate with big voices. It is valuable to learn to turn down the volume, to adjust to smaller spaces and quieter patterns. The differences in sound were obvious on a train ride through France. In one car rode two Americans and their French guide. Everyone who rode with them knew quickly that they were from California, traveling for business, and taking a one-day holiday. Their words reached from one end of the car to the other. The French guide approached two women who had been sitting across the aisle and posed a question in French. After replying and watching him return to his seat, the two women broke into giggles. What the guide hadn't realized was that they, too, were Americans who had been speaking in English. Since he couldn't hear their words, he had assumed they were French, because they were using the French level of volume: quiet and private.

Now We Know

In our own environments, meeting people and beginning a business relationship is a fairly simple process. We know the pattern and rules of introductions. But if you travel a great distance or welcome someone from across the globe, the simple act of saying hello is fraught with questions. Do I really know which is the person's first and last name? What is the appropriate length of time for a handshake, and is one actually acceptable? Once we've navigated the introduction, what can we talk about?

The only way to answer these questions and others regarding basic customs connected with meeting, greeting, and building connections is to do some research. Included in the Resources section are some recommendations of books and Web sites that can help. Talk to people who are already doing business in the country that you are to visit. A little checking will help you avoid making mistakes and ensure that you create an excellent first impression.

I'm Glad I Know

I try to research something about sports and how to find out about sports wherever I go. Whether I'm interested or not, I try to know what championships are about to happen or are just ending. I've been able to start lively conversations by asking whether Lance Armstrong should try for another win in the Tour de France or the chance for Brazil doing well in soccer at some specific time. The topic is generally neutral, and it always surprises people that a woman knows anything about sports. Somehow it breaks the ice in a way nothing else can do.

→→ *American woman, college department chair*
who travels annually to Europe

CHAPTER 19

Practical Matters

I Wish I'd Known

I wish I'd checked for holidays before I planned my trip. A Sunday in Paris wasn't a sweet adventure because it was Bastille Day, the national holiday celebrating the end of the monarchy. The city was a collection of cordoned-off streets, policemen asking for IDs, [and] closed shops and restaurants. Instead of a day in the museum refreshing my spirit, I ended up frustrated, working in my room.

→ *Fashion designer living in California*

I Wish They Knew

I sometimes think it's easier to work in Asia because the people there realize there are different time zones. It's hard to get Americans to recognize that and understand how to work with people in different places. Because they don't travel, they don't know your place, or your time schedule, and it makes working together more difficult.

→ *French woman, founder of a retail chain in Paris,*
with experience in North America, Europe, and Asia

Making Plans

Previous chapters looked at time as a concept that was part of people's attitudes and beliefs. Questions included topics such as whether multiple activities can be handled simultaneously or must be done in sequence. In this chapter we move our attention to more concrete pragmatic issues. What day and time is the meeting? When should I go, and what shall I wear when I arrive? The answers vary, but the questions provide a planning outline regardless of the destination.

When I Arrive, Will You Be There?

When arranging a schedule it's easy to overlook two practical questions: Is there a holiday? And if there is, what's its impact on the work schedule? Many holidays are specific to a country or the predominant religion of the region. Imagine that you are coming to San Francisco from Estonia. Would you think that the third Thursday of November (Thanksgiving) is a holiday and that many offices, stores, and restaurants would be closed? If you arrive in India on January 26, April 14, August 15, or October 2, you may be surprised. Each date is a holiday. They are the birthday of the founder of the constitution, Independence Day, the day the constitution took effect, and the birthday of Mahatma Gandhi, respectively. Each one is an important date for India but unknown to many American professionals.

Further complicating the matter is that some holiday dates are set using the lunar calendar and thus change from year to year. Two well-known examples are Ramadan, the Islamic month of fasting, and the Chinese New Year. The lunar calendar is 13 months and totals 354 days. Accordingly, holidays that fall on specific dates on the lunar calendar will change every year on the Western solar calendar. Ramadan is the ninth month of the lunar calendar. In 2005, Ramadan will begin on October 5, and in 2004 it began on October 16.[1] Chinese New Year began on January 22 in 2004 but began on February 9 in 2005.

The precise day of a holiday isn't the only variable to consider. Query the pattern of time off. Is there a bank holiday on Thursday, and do people add Friday to make a long weekend? Is the procedure similar to that in Venezuela, where it is recommended not to make appointments two to three days in advance of the holiday? Planning a trip to Hong Kong early in the year? Allow time after Chinese New Year for work to return to normal. A professional in the apparel business advises that it's easiest to get appointments about three weeks after the holiday. It's difficult to do so earlier than that, she says, because people are trying to get caught up and aren't ready to start on new projects.

In addition to specific holidays, vacations pose additional challenges. Imagine your surprise if when you answered the phone one June morning all you heard was a man's voice shouting, "What's wrong with you people? Don't you understand anything? August is vacation time, not work time. What's wrong with you people?" The caller is an Italian man in the design business working between Florence, New York, and Los Angeles. His frustrated outburst is a result of a conversation with a client who created a production schedule that included a significant amount of work in August. His passionate statement reflects the traditional European attitude: August is a time for vacations and not business.

From mid-July to early September, business activities are almost nonexistent in Europe. People go on vacation—not the current U.S. style of vacation where people check voice mail and e-mail. A French businesswoman was amused when an American acquaintance complained that her e-mail sent mid-August hadn't been answered. The French woman explained that people are on vacation, as if that explained everything.

But the pattern is changing for some people in some places. Vacations may be divided up through the year and taken in blocks of a week or two rather than in blocks of four. In Italy an architect says, "We close for only two weeks. The owner gets sick if he's gone any longer." However, he concedes that for most of the time from mid-July to mid-September, the staff works shorter hours and the pace is more relaxed.

Although August is a traditional and popular month for vacations even in the United States, it isn't the rule everywhere. For example, in Chile and Bolivia because of the reversal of the seasons in the southern hemisphere, vacations are more likely between January and March than in August. But don't assume it's true throughout all of Latin and Central America. August is a popular vacation period in Guatemala.[2] Before you plan, ask some questions.

Can You Confirm the Day, Date, and Time?

Even after the questions of holidays and vacations are settled, you still have to verify business hours and days of the workweek. In most Western or Anglophone nations the workweek is Monday through Friday. Service industries have schedules that vary, and many Americans include some work time on Saturday or Sunday, if only to check their e-mail. If your business takes you to the Middle East, the workweek may be from Saturday through Wednesday, from Saturday through Thursday, from Sunday through Thursday, or from Monday through Friday.

There isn't a simple formula to determine starting and ending times for a business day in the United States or around the world. Mornings may start at 7:00 A.M. or at 9:30 A.M. Lunch in the United States can be a snack in the car between meetings, but in Mexico City it can be two hours in a restaurant. The break in the day may start at noon or at 1:30 P.M., and the time to head home can be 5:00 P.M. or 8:00 P.M. Every place has its own special pace and schedule.

Even after you discover the best dates and times to arrange a call or visit, other differences regarding dates and times can create confusion. For example, there is more than one way to write a date. The U.S. convention is to write month/day/year. The date of August 10, 2004 thus can be shortened to 8/10/04. However, in other places the order is day/month/year. Using that model, the date 8/10/04 becomes October 8, 2004 or 8 October 2004.

A San Francisco woman credits confusion about dates for the fact that she now celebrates her birthday twice a year. Her actual date of birth is April 11, written 4/11. For her European friends this form meant November 4 was her birthday. Not wanting to embarrass anyone when the error was originally made, she never corrected them. She now receives cards and gifts in April and November. While this is an excellent experience for birthdays, it's more problematic for professional appointments. What date shall I be there? Know the model before booking the flight.

Time can also be expressed in two ways. Americans work in 12-hour increments from midnight to noon and back again, using A.M. or P.M. to indicate whether the time is morning or evening. But how do people manage with a 24-hour count that ends at midnight (24 hours) and begins at 1:00 A.M.? When told a meeting is at 16 hours or 1600, how do you know when to show up? (A simple calculation solves the problem. Subtract 12, and there you are: 16 hours becomes 4:00 P.M. Anything after 12 noon is automatically afternoon or evening. So the dinner at 20 hours is at 8:00 P.M. It's quick and easy.

Time is more than meetings and dinners. In today's world it's constant calls between Dallas and Paris and Seattle and Beijing. Conference calls bring together people on three continents who are days and many hours apart. And if distance and basic problems with time zones aren't enough, the entire matter becomes more complicated in the summer when some places observe daylight savings times and others do not. A Southern California executive coach tells of monthly conference calls bringing together people in California, Chile, South Africa, and Colorado. The hardest part of their collaboration was establishing a time to talk.

Looking Good

Daily papers and monthly magazines focus on clothing and providing advice on the latest styles and hottest fashions. It seems that no matter what language people speak or wherever people travel, there are discussions of what to wear. In light of this, it's easy to forget there is a purpose to clothing: to protect the wearer from the elements and to provide warmth and decency. As we know, definitions of decency vary widely wherever you are.

In addition to fulfilling the basic requirements, clothing throughout history has been used to reveal status in society. From the richly embroidered robes of kings and queens to the status labels of shoes and handbags today, people use garments to make statements about themselves. Clothes are uniforms that show rank, even as badges and emblems are added to jackets, statements are screened onto shirts, and initials are used as jewelry. Wearers proclaim their individuality and their beliefs with their clothes.

Clothes have been used to visually define position within the corporate hierarchy. The designations of white-collar and blue-collar jobs used a shirt to identify status. Wearing a white (starched) collar meant the worker had a position at a desk. He could wear the starched collar because he wasn't required to do manual labor. The blue collar, generally a soft collar, was indicative of manual labor. Moreover, the color blue was the color worn by servants, the only people who wore blue in the sixteenth century.[3]

Thanks to technology, today's garments can do more than keep us warm, make statements about our professions, or announce our beliefs. There are fabrics that incorporate thermoregulators to keep the body warm or cold, fabrics that include microscopic whiskers that can repel spills, as well as textiles that can change color. These fabrics are not just samples used for marketing. The U.S. government sent socks made of materials that could apply moisturizers to the troops in Iraq.[4]

One of the latest developments in clothing takes the concept of personal security in a new direction. The Take No-Contact jacket is a waterproof nylon parka. In addition to keeping the wearer dry, it can emit 80,000 volts of electricity at the wearer's flick of a switch.[5] But most people do not select coats that serve as weapons to defend themselves.

Rather, they are more concerned about what to pack and how to look appropriate wherever they are.

What's most appropriate for business is a look that is contemporary, conservative, polished, and neat. The conservative aspect applies to skirt lengths, necklines, and the amount of jewelry or decoration worn. While most people want to express a personal style at times, it may be best to remain conservative. A Texas entrepreneur traveled to Chile for a job interview. He wore cowboy boots, an elaborate belt buckle, a turquoise bracelet, and gold chains. Although his product and price were excellent, he lost his bid to a Belgian who was wearing a blue suit. The buyer felt the Texan was more interested in show and making money to buy jewelry than in providing great quality. While this may be unfair and inaccurate, perception counts.[6]

In addition, do not attempt to dress in the local style of the country you are visiting. Remember that clothing can indicate status in addition to personality. There is a risk that the message from the clothing would not be appropriate. Guides to proper dress in various regions can be found in guidebooks and online sources such as the newsletter Journey-woman (www.journeywoman.com). Information in this newsletter about business attire in various locations is provided by businesswomen who are contributors.

To create a look that balances a contemporary feel with one that is conservative, keep in mind the cut and colors. Solid colors and pieces that you can layer and adapt to get multiple looks provide the most choices. Frequent travelers start their selections with standard colors such as black, blue, or gray—colors that are dark and don't easily show wear and tear. To eliminate wrinkles, hang the item in a steamy bathroom. Finish drying things by using your hair dryer. Your wardrobe should be professional but still, keeping with the latest trends. That fashion element can be introduced by adding a tie or shirt in a fashionable color. Is pink the thing for spring, or is white the new black this year? Shirts, scarves, sweaters, and ties can change your look, even when you wear the same suit or skirt throughout a trip. Remember to think about accessories. What shoes are you wearing? What jewelry? While less is best in terms of decoration, a good pair of shoes and a good watch work to create a look that is professional and personal. See more clothing suggestions in chapter 21.

Focus on what's appropriate for the season and weather plus the physical aspects of the trip. Will it be hot and humid or wet and cold? Will you be riding a subway or walking through a city? Especially for women, these factors influence the choice of shoes to bring. No matter how stylish high stilettos may be, flat shoes are a better choice for walking. For women, especially those traveling to Asia, another matter to consider is the type of toilet to expect. Not all places have Western-style bathrooms. In Asia, the squat toilets are common in old and new buildings. A new office building outside Shanghai has lovely marble bathrooms with new ceramic toilets that require users to squat. Utilizing a squat toilet while wearing a narrow skirt and stilettos would be a physical feat of startling proportions.

Recall that one of the basic purposes of dress is decency. While decency is defined differently from place to place, one easy way to think about this is in terms of preparing for travel. Follow advice from an image consultant who counseled clients that less skin showing signified greater authority. This was a viewpoint demonstrated within U.S. corporations in earlier times when the more senior people generally wore long-sleeved shirts. Only beginners showed up in short-sleeved shirts, even in summer. In a time when styles are often casual and revealing by traditional standards, it's a useful guide. Stay covered, and look professional.

For travel to the Middle East, Asia, or any Muslim country, it is especially important for women to be thoughtful in their dress. Skirts should fall below the knee, shoulders should be covered, and a covering for the head should be kept at hand. In some places, a blouse that is open enough to reveal even just a collarbone can be unsettling. Some may rebel at the idea of giving up their personal style. However, conservative dress in these areas is extremely important. It demonstrates respect for the customs of the host country, and that is a critical element required to build constructive relationships.

Gifts to Give

Giving and receiving gifts are integral parts of doing business. They are given to express hope that a new endeavor and relationship will go well and to celebrate the success achieved. Gifts can express appreciation for hospitality and assistance provided.

"He says he's shocked and humiliated to be given a gift as utterly useless as a squeaky rubber hedgehog. The deal is off."

Unfortunately, the warm sentiments represented by offerings can be diminished through errors in selection and presentation. Giving gifts, like everything else, is shaped by tradition, culture, and personal attitudes and comes with rules and prohibitions. In the United States we are most familiar with regulations that limit the value of a gift that can be received within a corporate environment. Is it $50, $25, or absolutely nothing? Step outside the U.S. business culture, and the issues are more complex and subtle.

Ensuring that a gift fulfills the goal of deepening the connection between the parties requires some research to avoid common errors. If you know the recipient personally, it may be easier because you can select something based on the recipient's personal interests. If not, some of the following information may prove helpful.

It can be surprising how many ways there are to make mistakes when a person's intent is so positive. In addition to the choice of gift, errors can be made on how a gift is wrapped, the number of items given, and the color of the gift or gift wrapping are open to interpretation.

For example, knives, no matter how special, can be interpreted as a sign of ending (rather than extending) a relationship. Wrapping a gift in red paper in China signifies good luck. In Japan or Africa, this would be an error since red is associated with blood in Japan and death in Africa.

Reminders of death, funerals, and mourning are frequently mentioned when discussing gifts. An American executive bought gifts at Tiffany's to bring to China. The store is famous for its blue boxes with white ribbons. In China, white is associated with mourning, as black is in the United States. To present a gift with white ribbons would therefore be an error and detract from the gift, embarrassing all involved. Fortunately for the executive, his assistant noted the problem and changed all the ribbons from white to red.

Although it is generally not advised to take wine to people in a country known for wine (France, Australia, Chile, Bulgaria, or South Africa, among others) a wine connoisseur may appreciate a special bottle from your wine-producing area (all 50 states in the United States now make wine). It's worth the effort to take a limited edition California wine to a collector in Paris if you know it is available only in California. The gift then recognizes the recipient's interests. Does your partner collect stamps or birdhouses? Are there children in the family who love Mickey Mouse?

But if you don't know the person well enough to personalize the offering, some suggestions and cautions follow:

- Aside from knives, the only gift that should always be avoided is a bouquet of red roses. No matter your location, red roses symbolize romantic love. Given that interpretation, taking red roses to your new business partner's wife would not be wise.
- When considering alcoholic beverages, determine not only whether it's a wine-producing country but also the religious laws of the area. While liquor may make a good present in Japan, in the Middle East it would be inappropriate. Islam prohibits alcohol consumption so it would be seen as extremely insensitive to give an alcoholic gift to someone in a Muslim country.
- When invited to a home for dinner, flowers are a good choice, but be careful about the details beyond the issue of red roses. For example, depending on where you are, a specific type of flower

may be connected to funerals or mourning. This is true for chrysanthemums in France, Italy, or Germany or calla lilies in Germany and the Czech Republic. In Ireland avoid red or white flowers, and in Germany, don't select red carnations. Marigolds and yellow flowers may also create a stir, especially in Chile where yellow roses signify contempt. As if color and type weren't complicated enough, you need to ask how many (odd number or even?) and whether they should be wrapped.

- The number of any items, not just flowers, can be of significance, too. For example, the number 13 is considered by some in the United States to be an unlucky number. Avoid the number 4 in China. In Cantonese it sounds like the word for death.

- Presentation of the gift can be as important as its selection. Gifts should be given with a bit of ceremony. Hand the package to the recipient using both hands. If you try this, you can get the feel of the presentation, the aspect of a special or precious item being given. Be sure to look at the person and express appreciation or good wishes.

- When doing the research about dates for holidays also check to see if gift giving is part of the celebration. If so, you'll be prepared and maybe there's a special item associated with the holiday making the issue of selection easy to handle.

- As much as wrapping gifts is important, it's probably wise to wrap the gift once you reach your destination. Given the current airport security procedures in the United States, it is recommended that gifts not be wrapped so they can be easily inspected. Pack the wrapping materials. Plan something simple, and assemble the presentation when you arrive.

- Depending on where you are, your gift may be opened immediately or set aside. A gift presented in Chile may be opened immediately, and you should do the same when receiving one. In Asia or the Middle East, however, where maintaining harmony and saving face are critically important, gifts are opened after the giver departs. This avoids any potential for embarrassment of the parties involved.

- Know the appropriate time in the business development for gift giving. In Asia it is common at the beginning of a relationship, while in Europe or Latin America gifts are exchanged later.

Also be cautious about admiring the possessions of your hosts, or you may end up with an unexpected gift. In Latin America as in the Middle East, custom requires that if visitors admire something, the owner must give it to them. But a recent dinner in Los Angeles demonstrated that this custom is not limited to visitors in other countries. During this dinner with a group of Iraqi visitors, a member of the host committee complimented one of the Iraqi guests on her shoes. Immediately the visitor insisted the woman try on her shoes. Only because they didn't fit was she able to avoid accepting them as a gift.

In Europe or Asia, a lunch, dinner, or formal banquet may be the most appropriate gift. If hosting a meal in appreciation for one given for you, be sure it is at the same level of food and service. This is an area where local assistance can be invaluable in selecting a restaurant and a menu.

Two good gifts that travel well are good quality pens and books. If the recipient is comfortable in English, a book on a topic of shared interest, be it business, politics, or sports, can make a thoughtful gift.

Make Yourself Known

One of the easiest ways to differentiate yourself is to send a thank-you note for a gift, dinner, or extended kindness. People remember the thanks they receive and the ones that never arrive. Slip a few thank-you cards into your luggage when you travel. Surprise people with your prompt thoughtfulness by mailing a note to them before you leave. This also saves you from having to remember the task when you return home.

If you keep the note simple and are prompt, you'll be remembered for having extraordinarily good manners. A few lines written by hand, a phone call, or even a brief e-mail (if it's the only way you'll ever be able to express the sentiment) are all appropriate. Books are filled with formal suggestions, and it is good to follow them. But above all, a personal expression and acknowledgment shortly after a gift is received or an event takes place is strongly advisable.

Now We Know

Planning for a trip isn't just a matter of deciding when to be at the airport and what shoes to take. Planning begins with selecting the destination and determining when to check the business hours, annual holidays, and vacations, not just the seasons and weather. Before you pack, think about the culture and style of the country and the businesses you will be visiting as well as the local climate. Appropriate dress is defined in many ways.

To ensure that you are seen as a thoughtful professional who knows all the details, including knowing the importance of gift giving, verify that your present is appropriate for the destination. Do the yellow flowers or travel clock carry negative or insulting meanings? Be practical, plan ahead, and benefit from your travels.

I'm Glad I Know

I know that it isn't expected, but my opinion is that a gift is as essential as a handshake when greeting someone in Asia. It's best if it's a small gift, representing your country, state, or business. It not only starts everyone off on a good note but it [also] shows you respect their culture, and they will respect yours.

↠ *American female production manager*
for a California apparel company

CHAPTER 20

Dining

I Wish I'd Known

I wish I'd done some research before I traveled to know more about what was considered polite as far as food is concerned. Eating together is so important for business. I should have checked to learn more about special regional foods and what the pace of meals was likely to be. I would have been more at ease.

↠ *American sales executive who lived*
in Ethiopia and travels to Europe and Asia

I Wish They Knew

The importance of the business lunch cannot be emphasized enough. In Spain taking time to talk at the end of the meal, a little chat after the food, is expected. The point of the meal is being together and just talking, not rushing.

↠ *Trade commissioner from Spain*
working in the United States

Dinner Isn't About Food

Although we seldom think about it, a shared meal is an emotional, intimate activity with special meaning. It bonds the participants to one another. In some cultures, people do not feel that they can talk in a friendly way unless they've eaten together. An 1879 book of English manners said that to be invited to dinner was a "greater mark of esteem than to be included in any other gathering."[1] The power of a shared meal cannot be overstated even when it's a quick lunch.

The act of sharing food may resonate so strongly because it calls to mind a time when food was scarce. For centuries, the only food that was available was what people hunted, grew, or foraged for. There were no quick runs to Marks & Spencer or KFC to pick up a take-out meal. Food was hard to acquire, so to share it was giving a gift that represented great effort. Today when we share our meals, we offer another scarce commodity and that is our time. In addition to the food offered, we take the time to be together and to share ourselves.

No matter where you are or what the meal, it is an offering of friendship and so important that to refuse it is to refuse the friendship.[2] Given the importance of sharing food, it is hardly surprising that traditions about the conduct of a meal have evolved. Meals have acquired a set of rules, protocols that guide the participants through the ritual of eating together. Some of the rules come into play in only the most formal situations, and others apply to a quick snack at McDonald's. In this chapter we'll focus on some key areas of the dining experience and offer some tips that can be useful no matter where meals occur.

The Legacy of Kings and Queens

The European courts not only gave us traditions of handshakes and forms of introduction but also shaped our approach to creating the rules, or the etiquette of dining. *Etiquette* comes from the French word meaning "ticket" or "label." At the court of King Louis XIV of France etiquettes or signs were posted telling people to stay off the king's grass, among other instructions. Evidently it was an effective way to communicate rules of behavior at the court. Abiding by these strict rules was one way to gain favor with the king in the very competitive court environment. The courts and some of the rules are long vanished, but the word *etiquette* continues to be used to mean "the rules of proper behavior."

Proper behavior is important today, just as it was in the seventeenth century. Following the rules of contemporary etiquette and knowing the nuances of polite conduct can be a personal competitive advantage. To understand today's rules it's not necessary to learn the elaborate rituals and restrictions of diplomatic circles. All you need to know are the basic rules and to keep in mind that the purpose of the rules is to make people more comfortable.

The protocols or rules that provide structure to an event, a dinner, or a meeting allow people to feel at ease. In addition, having knowledge of the format and procedures is comforting to most people. They can understand their role and that of others.

To feel comfortable and to help others be at ease, it's important to understand the rules of the place. What is appropriate and polite differs

"It's customary to allow one's hosts to break the ice, Mr. Dalton."

from one location to another. In each country and region there are traditions and rules about sharing a meal. Before having an important meal in a new environment, check on the local customs. As useful as it is to consult a book or Web site, it's always good to speak with someone who has been there or who lives there. Check in advance, avoid surprises, and enjoy the meals.

Connected Roles: Guest and Host

Whether you most often attend business meals as a guest or as the host, it's important to understand both roles. The words *guest* and *host* come from the same Indo-European word *ghostis* or *stranger*.[3] Although the word *stranger* describes an individual, it really speaks to the idea of a relationship. The status of stranger comes into existence only in comparison with another person. Taking this view of the root gives us the understanding that these roles—guest and host—are always connected. No matter the culture or the differences in what constitutes appropriate behavior, the guest/host relationship is exceptional. One cannot exist without the other.

Each of the roles comes with its own privileges and responsibilities.

The host selects the guests, time, place, and menu. He or she is in charge. The guests are given the gift of a meal. In turn, guests are expected to help the host create an enjoyable, positive atmosphere.

Here is an overview of some of the host's and guest's responsibilities. The host has the following responsibilities:

- selects guests with the idea of creating a pleasant environment
- creates the seating plan and clearly communicates it to the guests
- indicates when the meal begins and ends
- in a restaurant, arranges to pay before the meal begins to avoid any discussion
- if guests can select their meals, makes recommendations to indicate price range and number of courses so that the guests are at ease
- keeps the conversation going and involves everyone
- indicates when business may be discussed, if at all

When entertaining outside a restaurant, it is important to be sensitive to eating patterns in another way. A Korean woman discusses her early experiences in Los Angeles as a guest in an American home. When she was asked if she wanted something to eat, she said "no" although she was hungry, expecting that the question would be posed again. The host did ask one more time, but she again said "no." At that point the host felt it would be rude to push his guest and didn't ask again. The Korean woman, whose training taught her to accept food only after it was offered three times, spent a very hungry evening!

The guest has the following responsibilities:

- wait to start eating until the host gives the signal
- talk with other guests, especially those seated to the right and left at a table
- if ordering in a restaurant, select mid-priced items
- remember to thank the host when leaving and send a written thank you
- if at someone's home, bring a gift (not necessary in a restaurant)

Not only is talking with people at dinner or another activity the responsibility of a guest but it is also the essential element of most business gatherings. You attend not for the food but to be with the host and the other guests.

The choice of conversational partners at dinner can be more important than just indicating politeness. A story from a recent trade mission to China illustrates that point. At a banquet that was part of the visit, one of the European participants spoke only with another colleague in his group. While their conversation was stimulating, his choice was not wise. He missed the opportunity to build connections with the Chinese officials seated at his table. These were the people he hoped to meet when he took the trip.

Possibly more significant is the damage to the relationship with the person who planned the trip, invited the potential clients, and arranged the seating. "Never again will I do this for him," she said. "I can't rely on him to behave in a polite and serious way. It was insulting to the people who came to meet him." Although he later blamed the language barrier, it was noted he didn't try. If he had, he would have discovered that everyone at the table spoke enough English to share a conversation at dinner.

About the Money

It's possible to avoid the awkward conversations and the uncertain reaching for wallets that often occur at the end of a meal. Who should pay can be simple to decide.

If there's clearly a host, it's easy. The host pays for the meal. When the host is a woman and the guests are men, it is wise to sometimes arrange the payment before the meal to avoid a discussion when the check is presented. This can be accomplished by talking to the server or the captain before guests arrive.

In some situations, no one person is the host. The person who issued the invitation, especially if the guests are there to provide information or other assistance, takes on the role of host and pays for the meal.

If it's a casual meal and people agree to share the expense, avoid pulling out calculators and worrying about pennies. Unless someone in the group ordered and drank a fine wine without sharing, adding major cost to the meal, split the total equally among the people at the table. Avoid putting out five credit cards for five people, especially if the meal is outside the United States. This common practice is not common elsewhere. No matter your location, in your hometown or across the world, be sure you carry enough of the local currency to pay for dinner, in cash, just in case you can't use credit cards. Telling your colleagues you'll send a check if they'll cover you won't seal a deal.

One experienced international lender commented that a large part of international business is shared meals. "Some of them have value, and others don't. You'll pay for a lot of meals that don't bring any business. You can't worry about it. Take the chance, have that lunch, and see what happens."

Do We, or Don't We?

When the question is "Do we leave a tip?" the answer, if you're in Egypt, may be, "Yes, we do." In Australia, the reply may be, "No, we don't." The answers vary from country to country and knowing whether a tip is to be left requires a bit of research.

The origins of tipping are not entirely clear. Some stories indicate that tips were given so servers could buy themselves a drink, to ensure they wouldn't consume drinks that the customer ordered. Another version explains the origins of tipping to payments given to peasants to guarantee the king safe passage as he traveled. No matter the origins, today a tip is given to express thanks for good service. No tip is required for bad service.

However, tipping is customary in many places for a variety of services. Tips are provided to cabdrivers in London, but seldom in Hong Kong. The staff in hotels, airports, and restaurants are the most frequent recipients of tips. While 15 to 20 percent of the total bill may be the general rule in most restaurants, it is important to know that in some places, such as France, it is automatically added into the bill, unlike the United States where the bill presented is for the meal only, with some exceptions. Also, in France it is customary to add a little, in cash left on the table, to the tip included in the bill. The amount varies from a euro to an additional 5 percent of the bill, depending on the place and the service.

Most travelers expect to tip people who assist them with their baggage at the airport or hotel, taxi drivers, waiters, and the room service staff. They don't always remember or expect to tip for two other services. First, there is the tip for the person who cleans the room. This is usually left in the room at the end of a stay; however, if the visit is extended, a tip at the midpoint is suggested. The second often surprises travelers: It is the tip expected by a restroom attendant. Be prepared with some small change to leave behind.

To identify the tipping etiquette at your destination simply consult one of the Web sites, such as the BBC's International Tipping Etiquette or The Original Tipping Page, for detailed information.

Where Should I Be?

As you'll recall, one of the host's responsibilities is to organize the seating arrangements for the guests. Planning who sits where is not simply a matter of avoiding putting two extremely shy people next to each other. You need to consider the relationship between the parties and the purpose of the gathering. Are there hierarchical rules to be observed, or is the concern creating good conversation? When it comes to formal diplomatic or corporate functions, order is even more challenging. "Hierarchical seating arrangements make up one of the most intricate aspects of protocol."[4] To avoid last minute confusion and awkwardness, check reference guides and write down the seating plan in advance, when it's quiet and calm.

No matter how aware we are of the importance of seating, jet lag and the more common casual approach can create complications. A female executive discusses her first business trip to Japan, announcing with a laugh that the first important thing she did was wrong. Invited to a dinner in a private room at a restaurant, she and her team were the first to arrive. Tired from the trip and still jet lagged, she immediately sat down, selecting a chair in the middle at one side of the table. Suddenly she noticed her team and the representatives of the host company engaged in somewhat agitated conversation.

When pressed, they explained that she had taken the place of the most senior member of the host group. She offered to move, a solution that wasn't acceptable as she was the highest-ranking guest and had selected her place. She stayed in place; the host arrived and took another seat. Having been briefed before he walked in, he didn't appear upset or offended. She said it was probably because she represented the customer in the transaction that no problems were created. But it taught her an important lesson: to check before going. It's the seemingly small decisions, like where to sit, that can create tensions in a relationship.

Tools for Eating

The earliest tools for eating are our hands. They are the instruments used to prepare our meals and to move food to our mouths. While hands are still the basic devices in parts of the globe, many people use utensils.

During early history the use of knives expanded from being solely a weapon used to hunt food to a tool that enabled efficient sharing of a meal. Originally only men were allowed to possess knives, and they cut portions of meat for women. Later, spoons made from bits of wood expanded the choice of utensils.

The last of today's common eating tools to come into existence was the fork, a useful but originally controversial device. Forks probably evolved from spears and skewers used to roast and hold meat in place. Earliest reports of a fork being used come from Venice in the eleventh century. Although the stories about the first person observed using one vary, one theme is common throughout. Using a fork was considered scandalous and heretical, a rejection of nature.[5] The first fork on record in the United States was in 1630. About that same time King Louis XIV refused to use one as he considered eating with a fork to be unmanly.

It took almost 200 years, into the 1800s, for the fork to become a common and popular eating instrument. Now it's possible to identify multiple types of forks depending on the intended use. There are forks for salad, dessert, oysters, fish, and meat. There are small ones for seafood cocktails and large ones for serving a meal. When lined up for a formal meal, the variety can appear overwhelming and puzzling. Although we seldom see an elaborate arrangement, it's easy to determine which one to use at what time. The utensils are organized so that the ones farthest away from the plate are the ones to be used first, hence following the motto that you eat from the "outside in."

Other items associated with meals also evolved over time. Plates, which now come in a variety of shapes, sizes, and colors, were first listed in the inventory of King Charles V of France in the late 1300s. Napkins were at first large and shared by many. As utensils became more popular, the napkin shrank in size and moved to individual usage.

For people who use knives, forks, and spoons to eat their food, there are two styles of handling the utensils. One is known as the American style and the other continental or European. At one time, everyone ate American style until European royalty decided they didn't want to be like the "common folk" and created the continental style of eating.

The American style requires moving the fork from hand to hand, depending on whether you are cutting the food or delivering it to your mouth. Continental or European style leaves the fork in the left hand and the knife in the right whenever they are in use. Which is more mannerly, and easier to manage? That's the subject of endless debate.

Your style of eating, once learned, is difficult to change. Stories tell of American spies uncovered by the Germans during World War II because they automatically moved their fork and knife from hand to hand. How one uses utensils, whether they stay in one hand or move back and forth, does not dictate good manners.

However, where you place your hands when not actively eating is another consideration. Once again, what is acceptable depends on where you are. You may keep your hands in your lap when not using utensils in the United States and Ireland, but in Switzerland or France it's necessary to keep at least your wrists (never your elbows) on the table.

The hands, the original eating tools, are still the preferred device in countries such as Morocco and Ethiopia. It requires skill and practice to eat neatly with fingers and to use bread to guide the food from the plate to your mouth. In Ethiopia, it is a mark of accomplishment to end the meal with a clean shirt. The most important of the protocols when eating with your hands is to use only the right hand even if you are by nature a left-handed person. The left hand is associated with personal hygiene, and to use it to eat or to offer food to another is extremely insulting.

In addition to hands and Western flatware a third type of utensil are chopsticks. Dating from 1750 B.C. they predate all other eating tools.[6] In

Japanese the word for *chopstick* means "bridge," and in Chinese it means "fast fellow," recognizing that their use allowed the eater to move food quickly from the plate to the mouth. Today the exact shape and material used to make chopsticks varies from country to country. They can be made of wood, metal, or porcelain and have flat ends or points. However, to a Westerner accustomed to a knife and fork, they can be extremely challenging.

Before a trip to Asia it's useful to develop your chopstick management skills. One way to gain some ease is to put a rubber band around a pair of chopsticks about midway between top and bottom. Then try picking up some rice. Once you master that part, remove the rubber band and try again.

In addition to chopsticks, porcelain spoons are used for soup. They can also serve as a resting place for morsels too large to consume in one bite. Toothpicks may be part of a proper table setting but there will not be any knives. Historically, knives were not included because they are weapons. As a sign of trust, they were set aside.[7] Here again is an example of the belief of the significance of a shared meal as a time for friendship and goodwill.

Some of the Basics

While the rules surrounding meals depend on the location in the world, type of cuisine, and formality of the meal, there are a few basic protocols to keep in mind.

- Food can't fly. Even at a buffet don't move food directly from the serving tray to your mouth, not even a small appetizer. Food must always go from the serving dish to a personal plate before being consumed.
- Napkins stay on your lap unless you leave the table. If it's in the middle of the meal, it rests on your chair. At the end of the meal, put your napkin to the left of the plate, neatly folded.
- Cut your meat into a few small pieces, eat them, and repeat the process. (Only children have their meat cut up into little pieces all at once.)
- Chew with your mouth closed, and do not talk with your mouth full.

- Slurping, belching, and sucking your lips are rude in some places and in others express appreciation for the fine food.
- Once used, forks, knives, and spoons never touch the table. They must rest on a plate once they've touched any food.
- Never eat food from your knife or butter your bread with your fork.
- Bread plates, if they're used, are located to the left of the plate to be used for the main course. Your glass or glasses will be on the right.
- Never apply lipstick or comb your hair at the table.
- When using chopsticks
   – do not rest them standing straight up in your rice. That's a symbol of incense used at funerals.
   – always put them on a chopstick rest or beside your plate. Do not put them on your plate after they've been used.
   – do not gesture with them as you're speaking.
- Never fill your own glass during a Chinese banquet. Fill your neighbor's glass thus signaling that you would like yours filled.
- When eating with your fingers never lick them or put them in your mouth.
- Don't bring up the subject of business unless your host does. If you are the host, either avoid the subject entirely or start the discussion near the end of the meal. The French expression "never before the cheese," which is served at the end of a dinner, captures this idea. Dinner is not about food nor about business but about people.

What Time Is Dinner and Where?

Of all the variations in the protocols surrounding shared meals, the differences in the timing of meals may be the most startling. If your normal time for dinner in Atlanta is 6:00 P.M., then an 11:00 P.M. dinner in Barcelona can be quite a shock. Meals shape the rhythm of our days, and a change in pace can be disturbing. Times of meals vary around the world. A senior banker for a global bank now works in Los Angeles after a recent posting to Mexico. Originally from Argentina, he is still trying to adjust to mealtimes in the United States. He commented to a colleague that eating lunch at noon feels almost like having lunch at breakfast time.

Knowing in advance that dinner is at 6:30 P.M., a frequent time for a banquet in China, or 9:00 P.M. for dinner in London helps you plan. Trying to adjust to new hours can create unexpected results. A business development consultant and her client traveled to Mexico City for meetings with a new partner. Knowing that dinner wouldn't begin until 10:00 they decided to eat prior to their 7:00 P.M. meeting. Having a small snack would allow them to avoid severe hunger pangs in the middle of their meeting. To their surprise, their hosts arranged dinner at 8:30, the minute the restaurant was open. Suddenly the Americans were confronted with a dinner menu hours earlier than expected. Politeness demanded that they order and eat. The kindness of their hosts meant that they ate before they were hungry in an almost empty restaurant.

The length of time it takes to eat dinner can be surprising as well. When you are used to meals that run no more than an hour, it can be uncomfortable to sit through a three-hour dinner. If you're accustomed to servers who clear away plates before everyone is finished eating, to encourage you to leave the table, the idea that a table in a restaurant is yours for as long as you wish can be surprising. It's helpful to remember that in most places meals are for sharing time and conversation with people. Restaurant patterns reflect that intent.

Americans are not the only ones who find changes in meal schedules surprising. Recent designation of European countries as approved travel destinations is creating an increase in Chinese citizens who are traveling to Europe. There they find a very different eating experience from their normal routines. One of the differences that troubles visitors is the time it takes for a meal to be served. The food doesn't all appear minutes after the meal is selected. Rather, individual courses arrive over a period of time. According to tour organizers, it's difficult to get the travelers to understand that three courses are served throughout the course of three hours.[8]

No matter where you travel, meals with business associates will most often take place in restaurants. The casual U.S. invitation for dinner at home is extremely unusual. Not only are most residences small by U.S. standards but people are also very private. A European businessman explains, "One's home is considered to be almost a sacred place, reserved for friends and family. Invitations to dinner with your colleague or supervisor are almost unheard of."

If you are invited to someone's home, recognize it as an honor and a reflection of the depth of connection. No matter how curious you may be to see how your hosts live, don't look around or ask for a tour of the house. Enjoy the compliment of the invitation, and be sure to take a gift (see chapter 19).

We Welcome You Here: Toasts and Drinks

Dating back to the Greeks in the sixth century B.C., a shared drink and a raised glass have been considered signs of welcome. Originally the process served a pragmatic purpose. A host who drank wine poured from the communal bottle proved he didn't intend to poison his guests with the wine. Over time, the purpose of proving there was no poison vanished, but the sharing of drinks to mark friendships continued.

Offering a toast stems from the Roman practice of adding a piece of toasted bread to the wine. Given the poor quality of the wines of that time, the toast was thought to improve the taste. Possibly the charcoal of the bread diluted the acidity of the wine. Over time, wines improved, drinkers tired of crumbs in their glasses, and the practice disappeared. However, the word *toast*, derived from the Latin word *tostus* meaning "roasted," continues as the name for our offering of good wishes with a drink.[9] By the 1800s, offering a toast was part of a proper meal. A British duke wrote that "every glass during a dinner had to be dedicated to someone."[10] Today that edict is not generally followed. Most often, toasts occur at the beginning or end of a meal.

The purpose of a toast is to mark the importance of the gathering. It may be to celebrate a personal event or business achievement, welcome a guest, or express hopes for a future relationship. When giving a toast, a person stands, raises the glass, and gives a short, upbeat speech. Although tradition dictates that the glass contains wine, a toast may be offered with beer, liquor, or water. It is the raised glass as the signal of the toast and the words that are most important.

It's useful to prepare a toast or two in advance. It is, after all, a highly condensed, miniature version of a speech. Keep it simple and remember the purpose of the gathering. Avoid using a clever joke since humor has cultural limitations. However, if you're traveling to Central Asia, expect toasts that are far from brief. In that region, a long toast is considered a sign of intelligence.[11] One thing to remember is that the host must offer the first toast. No matter how much you want to make your statement, you must wait and follow the host.

Must I Clean My Plate?

Whether you eat everything that is served to you can be interpreted as a commentary on both you as the guest and your host. Are you greedy? Did you take too much and deny someone else an adequate portion? Was there sufficient food provided to assure that no one was left hungry? Was the meal tasty, good food to honor the guests? You want to achieve a balance that says you are reasonable in your choices and that the host generously provided for the guests.

Therefore, the answer as to whether you should clean the plate depends on where you are. In China if you empty your plate, it will be refilled over and over again. One visitor ate 6 helpings of fried rice, the eighth of 12 courses at a banquet. He believed that it was important to finish what was offered and fried rice (until then) was his favorite food. He finally was unable to eat any more and left a little in his bowl, providing the signal that he was done. Leaving some food on your plate is also important to indicate that your host offered enough food, provided for his guests, and that you, therefore, are no longer hungry.

At a banquet, especially in China, it's important to remember there will be many courses and to pace yourself when eating. No matter how delicious the first courses are, remember there will be more, and you are expected to eat some of everything. Although it may not seem important whether you eat all the things offered, that isn't true. The day after a banquet one of the members of the host committee commented about all the things the American visitors did not eat. He announced that he would not order such delicacies again since they weren't appreciated.

In France and South Africa, among other places, you are expected to eat everything. In Switzerland it's acceptable to ask for second helpings at someone's home. Before you ask, however, be certain you're still hungry because you will be expected to eat every bit that's served to you.

I Don't, Won't, and Can't Eat That

There are few reasons to decline food that is offered to you. You may decline something if you have a serious allergy or your religious beliefs include dietary restrictions. The idea of being a vegetarian as a personal choice is not always understood. Explain your dietary restrictions when you accept an invitation to a meal so that you will minimize awkward situations. However, realize that you may still be provided food that you don't normally consume. If you think there will be something presented that may make you uncomfortable, don't ask what you're eating. This may make it easier to follow the approach that you must taste everything. Remember, refusing the hospitality—the food—is akin to refusing the friendship of the host.

American businesspeople have a reputation for being difficult eaters. A woman in the apparel industry in Hong Kong confided that for most visitors there was only one restaurant where she would take them. The people who came from the United States had so many restrictions about what they were willing to eat and were so demanding that it wasn't a pleasant experience and had an impact on their business relationships.

Given the importance of a shared meal, creating an uncomfortable situation for the host is not a benefit. If you're flexible about what, where, and when to eat, your stature is raised in the eyes of your hosts. This isn't an issue limited to Asia. A very similar conversation took place in Paris. In this case, a Frenchwoman commented on the challenge of selecting a menu for Americans. "In a group of ten," she said, "there are only two who don't have some limitation on what they'll eat. It's a nightmare."

Remember that food, especially regional delicacies, is offered as a special gift, an honor. Try what is presented and be known as flexible and willing to experiment and therefore easy to work with.

While some requests and preferences can be annoying, as the host, you must attempt to fulfill them. It is especially important when there are practical reasons for the requests. Is the guest allergic to milk? Ask the staff to be sure there isn't cream in a dish being served. Similarly, you should respect religious prohibitions concerning certain foods. Two examples of the latter are that Hindus do not eat beef and Muslims do not eat pork. Order a special meal if necessary. This is both a courtesy and a necessity. Treat all requests seriously. Don't ask about the reasons, but simply take care of your guest. If they are allergic to something, let them know which dishes to avoid and offer a substitute. A host makes guests comfortable in many different ways.

Food Is a Trend

Throughout this chapter we've talked about meals and sharing food as a way people build connections. We've focused on the rules that give structure and predictability to those meals. But food can be more a part of a bonding ritual. Food and its importance have now emerged as an area of study as a lifestyle trend in contemporary society.

In the fall of 2004, trend forecasting services added food and wine as topics to be discussed. These companies are worldwide enterprises acting as consultants to a broad range of companies including apparel designers and automobile and mobile phone manufacturers.

The evolution of food as a lifestyle issue is evidenced by the new movement called Le Fooding. The name is a blend of *food* and *feeling* or the total experience of eating. The goal of the founders in 2000 was to "promote a new way of eating and cooking emphasizing quality, creativity, and ambience."[12] During the June 2004 Le Fooding there were weeklong celebrations in Paris, Rome, and Marseille. Watch the Web site (www.le-fooding.com) to see how this movement evolves and where and when the next event will occur.

Now We Know

Sharing a meal is a special activity that is less about the food consumed than the opportunity to spend time with other people. To help ensure a comfortable atmosphere, each culture and place has a set of protocols to create a predictable, safe environment for all who gather. Know the rules and fit into the environment so people will be at ease in your company. Along with your portfolio and resume, your ability with knives, forks, chopsticks, and napkins establishes your credentials as an experienced, knowledgeable professional. Be prepared because shared meals build the bonds that are critical to developing business relationships around the world.

I'm Glad I Know

In Asia it's disrespectful not to drink. The only two acceptable reasons for declining are if you're pregnant or it's a health problem. Otherwise you must taste the drinks even if you don't drink more than that. Prepare yourself by not drinking on the airplane!

> ✈ *Technology executive in San Jose*
> *who manages business relationships*
> *in Japan and Hong Kong*

CHAPTER 21

Travel

I Wish I'd Known

I wish I'd realized that travel had value beyond creating new business. If I'd known, I would have made travel part of my life sooner. We now do work in Madagascar, Vietnam, and India, as well as here in France. Travel has opened my mind, added to my creativity, and made me recognize the value of all that I have.

↠ *French fashion designer based in Paris*

I Wish They Knew

I wish that everyone could be more sensitive to other cultures. If I'd been more knowledgeable when my career began, I could have avoided many mistakes. It's hard to do business when people think we Americans are rather obnoxious. If we all knew a bit more, were more aware, that image would disappear.

↠ *Executive at a California technology company*
working in Asia and Europe

On the Road Again

Whether your trip is one day to a familiar place or three weeks on the road to a series of new destinations, travel is both exhilarating and stressful. Every journey includes moments of excitement and others of frustration. Each experience combines these elements in different proportions. The only certainty is that each of us will travel for business and pleasure as our careers evolve. As professionals in a global economy, travel, experiencing new places, and meeting new people are essential components of our lives. No matter how connected we feel by e-mail and conference calls, nothing replaces the experience of a face-to-face meeting. To make the in-person experience a reality, we travel near and far, crossing continents and time zones, to make day trips and quick visits to faraway places.

This chapter pulls together some ideas and advice from people who travel extensively for both business and pleasure. The goal is to provide insights and ideas that will help readers to create personal systems for planning and managing their travel experiences. All people have a special way to pack and different approaches to the experiences of a trip, but you can learn from others and adjust their ideas to suit your own situations.

Especially when you travel for business, it can be difficult to maintain a sense of adventure and pleasure. Your life is disrupted, you're trying to balance work in two places, and everyone thinks you're on vacation, especially if your destination is Paris. For you the ambience of the locale may not be apparent as you move from conference room to conference room in an office or hotel. Is this really Paris? It could just as well be Portland or St. Paul by the look of the conference room.

Creating your own approach to travel allows you to find out that *it is* Paris simply by exploring the magazine section of the hotel gift shop. What's on the front cover of a news or fashion magazine there? You have to experiment to find ways to create a connection with the place, no matter where you travel. Do you adapt more quickly if you change your watch to the local time upon arrival or if you never change it? Listen to the advice of others but create an approach for yourself. Knowing what works for you will enable you to adapt to events as they occur and find excitement in every destination.

Guides to Guide You

Guides for travelers aren't a recent invention. One of the oldest is a directory written by an Egyptian merchant dated sometime between A.D. 40 and 70. He included information about ports, landmarks, people to be encountered, and goods available for sale. This work can be considered the first business travel guide.[1]

Today there is an almost overwhelming choice of books and Web sites to guide you on your travels. For a business traveler it's easy to say, "I've no use for those guides. They're for tourists." But you may want to rethink that position. Even tourist guidebooks generally include some history of a destination and basic information regarding transportation and resources. One trick to make them useful is to copy the pages with pertinent information, or tear out the pages you want and leave the "tourist" section at home. Carry only what you need. You can also bookmark the Web site and check it as you go.

To get an idea of the types of guides available, visit the travel section of a local bookstore, look online for familiar names, or check the Get Lost Books Web site (www.getlostbooks.com). This San Francisco bookstore stocks 25 different series of guides. With such a wide selection, you, wonder how to choose from among them. One approach is to review a book in the series that covers the city where you live or one that you've visited. If you think the descriptions are good for a familiar destination, it may suit you for other places.

To be knowledgeable about a locale, a city, and the people, it's useful to read beyond standard guidebooks. If you have a special interest, such as sports, art, or wine, look for books and articles that link your interest to where you are traveling. Biographies of people from the town you'll visit, a history of the city, or fiction set in the region can all help you to understand the people you'll meet.

The Packing Challenge

No matter the reason or the destination, packing can be one of the most difficult aspects of planning any trip. You want to look as though you belong in the environment and be appropriately dressed for all occasions. Opinions on how to achieve that are many, but two pieces of advice are consistent throughout all the literature and personal recommendations. They are to take less than your first plan and make a list of what you think you need. Books and Web sites dealing with this topic are abundant and provide extensive advice. Here is a short and subjective list of key tips gathered from experienced travelers.

- Create a list not just of what to pack but things to do before you leave. Reminders range from canceling newspaper deliveries to drawing the drapes in the living room. Once you've prepared the list, put it in a place where you can easily find it, such as your PDA, a document file saved in your laptop, or a hard copy.
- Plan based on your itinerary and the weather (check online by setting weather alerts). Know your itinerary, and plan for what is required. Is the trip filled with business meetings in offices, conferences in hotels, golf outings, or beach volleyball?

- Take items that you can use multiple times. Before putting anything in a suitcase, make a list of everything you plan to take. See which items can be combined. One person's rule is to take three tops for each bottom (skirt or slacks) and to ensure they all mix and match. Can a sweater work as a jacket? Does your jacket dress up a pair of jeans and also go with wool slacks for a more formal gathering?

- Shoes, shoes, shoes: Comfortable shoes are a must. Take enough so that you don't wear the same ones every day. It's worth giving up the room in the suitcase to have the comfort of taking that spare pair. Pack them in shoe bags and fill them with socks, underwear, or miscellaneous items. No matter where you go (unless it's Los Angeles), the amount of walking will exceed your expectations. A change of shoes or even socks during a day will refresh your feet.

- Have garments cleaned just before a trip and pack them in the plastic covers from the cleaners, preferably on hangers. This makes it easy to unpack and reduces wrinkling.

- Pack sweaters, blouses, and trousers with tissue between the layers. Some people pack everything flat, others roll individual items, others are fans of packing systems that help you fold and stack your clothes. Plastic bags, the ones for food storage, are useful tools. It's easier to find your black socks in a hurry if you just have to grab a bag of socks rather than sort through an entire suitcase. Also, in a time when luggage is frequently inspected, plastic bags allow the inspectors to see what you have without touching your personal items.

- The most important element is to keep things simple. Take less than you think you'll need. If you forget something, chances are whatever you need can be purchased at your destination. If not, it can be sent to you quickly via FedEx, DHL, UPS, or a similar delivery company. Pack lightly, and don't panic.

Packing lightly helps to avoid problems with increasingly rigid weight restrictions. No longer can you be sure you'll be able to pay a surcharge and take your heavy suitcase. In some flights between countries in Europe, for example, if you exceed the limitation you simply empty part of the contents of your suitcase. Check with the airlines before departure. There is a possibility that carry-on luggage will also be weighed in the future. Keep abreast of developments by signing up for the frequent flyer newsletter at www.frequentflyer.oag.com.

Weight is a factor not only for the airlines but also for the traveler. As one executive said, "You never know when you end up being the porter with your luggage. I can't tell you how often I've heard, 'Oh, it's just a couple of blocks from the office to your hotel.' Suddenly, you're carrying your suitcase for what seems like miles! Pack light and be sure your bag has wheels."

Packing Is About More Than Clothes

Although it may not be obvious, your luggage is as much a part of your appearance as your clothes. At the end of a flight, when you board the hotel van with your colleagues, don't have your little brother's Winnie the Pooh duffel bag as your travel companion. Select your luggage as an accessory, one as important as your shoes.

Avoid oversized carry-on pieces. In small planes with limited space, the staff may require that they be checked. Nothing is as disconcerting as watching your carry-on that has your money, medicine, and precious documents disappearing into the hold of the plane rather than remaining with you.

The identification on your luggage is part of being safe on the road. Luggage tags should not have your full name and home address. Use an initial and last name and a phone number that will be answered 24/7. Luggage tags that have a cover over the space for identification are recommended for additional security. By using that style, your details are not readily observable. Place a copy of your passport and your itinerary inside the bag so that if it's lost you can be located. Plus, when the airline asks for a local number at your destination, provide one. That information can change a lost bag into one that is quickly found and returned.

In addition to the standard luggage tags, some manufacturers now use new technology to enable people to locate lost luggage. They include metal ID tags with specific numbers that can be registered. The same options exist through companies such as Globalbagtag and I-Trak.[2] They sell tags that can be registered and tracked, facilitating the return of lost baggage.

Certified locks that can be opened by the Transportation Safety Administration (TSA) personnel and you are the only types of locks that can be used for luggage going through screening in the United States. Otherwise, all luggage must be left open to facilitate inspections when required. To find a list of companies that have TSA-approved locks, consult the TSA Web site at www.tsa.gov.

Plan to Be Safe and Healthy

Creating a safe trip begins not when you arrive at the destination but when you start planning the journey. Whether for business or pleasure, once you know your destination, start gathering information. In chapter 18, we used research to come up with topics of conversation. In this section the focus is on how to stay safe and healthy.

Three Web sites top the list in this category. The first is www.travel.state.gov, the U.S. Department of State site that provides information on travel advisories, health, and safety. Its public announcements and travel warnings address the safety issues and link to consular information sheets that provide detailed information about countries throughout the world.

For information related to staying healthy consult the Centers for Disease Control Web site at www.cdc.gov/travel and the World Health Organization at www.who.int/en. These sites will enable you to determine what immunizations, if any, are necessary or recommended for your destination. Both sites should be reviewed as far in advance as possible and once again before departing to get the most current updates.

Be sure to get prescription medicines filled and to request copies of your prescriptions from your doctor. Taking that copy is a precaution in case the medicine is lost or if you're questioned. Take all medication in the original containers with the prescription information noted on the front. The cute containers you get in the travel section of a drugstore won't be helpful if you're stopped for inspection at customs. If you are questioned, the original container is more likely to be accepted as proof that the contents are the medicines that you claim are prescribed to you.

In addition to taking prescribed medicines, frequent travelers pack their favorite over-the-counter remedies for colds, upset stomach, and headaches. Depending on your destination, you may not be able to find comparable supplies. No matter where you are, if you feel miserable at midnight, it's easier to take familiar medication than to suffer and worry through the night. A small cold can become a major distraction if you have to focus on finding a decongestant rather than preparing for a presentation.

Along with medication, don't forget medical insurance. Check to see that your current insurance coverage will cover you at your destination. Consider a short-term travel policy that includes medical evaluation and referrals to doctors throughout the world. Whether you need to find a doctor to treat pinkeye in London or you need to be evacuated from Moscow because you broke your back, a travel insurance policy is a plus. You can search online to find companies that provide these policies. Three are listed in the Resources section of this book.

Please Call Home

For many businesspeople, a cell phone is literally attached to them. They wear them on their belts, hang them around their necks, or keep them in handbags or pockets. Making sure your cell phone is on you has become as much a part of getting dressed as slipping on a pair of shoes. While taking a cell phone with you when you travel is recommended so you can stay in touch and as a safety net, the one you use at home may not be the one to pack. Not all cell phones can be used around the world. Check with your mobile service provider to learn if yours is a tri-band model set for Global System for Mobile Communication. If so, be sure it is set for international calling.

If you don't have a tri-band phone, consider renting one for the trip. Arranging a rental is simple and can be done via a Web site; the phone is delivered to either your home or office. Even included in the rental materials is a return package, enabling you to return the phone easily. Phone rental kiosks are located in some airports around the world. Phones that work locally can be purchased in major cities. A cell phone is a useful way to ensure your safety.

If you prefer to not carry a phone, be sure you can call home or make the local calls that matter. For long distance, check the access numbers for your long distance provider. How do you get into the system from Dubai or Dalian? Remember that 800 numbers are free only within the United States. To access them from abroad, you'll need to go through a regular long distance provider. If you rely on prepaid calling cards, it is often best to purchase them at your destination. International calling cards purchased in the United States may possibly not be intended for calling the United States from another country. Be sure to check before you purchase one.

However you do it, call and check in with someone at regular intervals. Let people know when to expect your call, where you are, and what time it is at your location. Avoid surprises and confusion that can occur if someone thinks you are next door instead of across the globe. Calling regularly not only allows you to stay connected to projects at home but also helps to keep you safe. If you are expected to call and don't, someone can check to see whether there's a problem.

On the Plane and After

Dress for a flight remembering that your luggage may not arrive and you may have to go to a meeting. Balance comfort with the possibility that you will appear the next day in what you have worn on the flight. No matter how comfortable your oldest sweats, they may not feel as good if they become your attire for the meeting scheduled upon your arrival.

Shoes, as always, are an issue. Flight attendants advise you to leave them on during takeoff and landing. If there's going to be a problem on the flight, that's the most likely time it will occur. If you have to move quickly, you're better off with shoes on. Shoes also play a part when you go through security. To move through security easily, consider wearing slip-ons since you often have to take off your shoes. However, on a long flight where your feet swell, lace-up shoes can be adjusted and are thus more comfortable. Each traveler makes a different choice taking into consideration speed through security, safety, and comfort.

One traveler adamantly warns never, ever to get on a plane without water, food, and something to read. Meals on flights are vanishing. If served, especially on long trips, they may not appear when hunger strikes. Choices are limited, and you may even have to purchase your meals. Be prepared. Whether it's a power bar, a bag of candy, or a turkey sandwich, take something along. Food can also serve to help ward off a bout of motion sickness. A popular recommendation worth trying is a bag of salted potato chips.

During the flight remember the two W's: water and walking. Drink lots of water, and walk around the plane frequently. By bringing your own water, you can have it to drink even if the seat belt sign is on, limiting your movement. Doctors now recommend that travelers avoid sleeping pills, no matter how long the flight, because you don't move enough. The risk of blood clots is high, and walking, moving in your seat, and doing some stretching help to avoid that problem.

Given the prohibition regarding sleeping pills, each frequent traveler has a favorite aid for sleeping on a plane and for avoiding jet lag. There are those who advocate homeopathic aids such as pills called No Jet Lag. Others recommend not sleeping the night before a long flight, having a glass of wine, or taking a special pillow. Only personal experience can help you find the solution that's best for you.

Is It Dinnertime Yet?

Most people experience some form of jet lag ranging from a desire to nap at odd times for several days to upset stomach, headaches, and even depression. Everyone has a different pattern. For some, it's one day while for others it can last for three or four days. Everyone is a little fuzzy and forgetful the first few days. Adrenaline will often carry you through the day of arrival with ease, but the next day or so can be challenging.

One of the best ways to move through the process is to adapt to local time. If you arrive in Beijing at 1:00 A.M., go to bed. If you arrive in Paris at 2:00 in the afternoon, take a walk, unpack, and don't go to bed until evening. Eat well, drink lots of water, and realize that in a day or two the symptoms will pass.

Although it may not sound like a jet lag remedy, taking your own alarm clock can be a marvelous aid. Setting a familiar clock and not having to rely on the front desk for a wake-up call can improve your sleep. Security comes in many forms.

Don't forget that jet leg operates when you return, too. Coming to the West Coast from Asia is more difficult for most people than returning from Europe. The same symptoms and suggestions apply here. If possible, allow a day between the end of travel and returning to the office. Not possible? Drink water, eat well, and remember that the fuzzy feeling isn't permanent.

More Important Than Money

As long ago as 450 B.C. governments issued documents for use by travelers.[3] At that time the documents were letters from the king requesting safe passage for the bearer. The term *passport* dates back to the late seventeenth century and the court of King Louis XIV of France. His letters requesting safe passage were called *passe port*, reflecting that most travel was by ships that passed through various ports. The name stuck while the document evolved to the form it has today.

An executive order issued on December 15, 1915, required every person entering or leaving the United States to have a valid passport. Because one cannot enter or leave a country without a passport, it is the most important of all travel documents.

To obtain a U.S. passport follow the instructions on the U.S. government site www.travel.state.gov. In addition to a passport, some countries require visas for travelers. To determine whether one is necessary, check with the consulate or embassy representing your destination.

If you have an emergency situation and are required to make an unexpected international trip or if your passport is about to expire, check with the National Association of Passport and Visa Services (www.napvs.org). Some member companies of that organization specialize in expediting the processing of travel documents.

Once you have your passport, make copies to take with you and to leave at home or at your office. Some travelers now scan their passport and e-mail it to themselves so they can access it while traveling. When you are on the road, lock your passport safely away and carry a copy with you. Carry the original only if absolutely necessary. For example, if you have an appointment at a U.S. embassy or consulate, always take your passport. If you want to cash traveler's checks it's also a necessity. Otherwise, carry a copy. If it's lost, take two passport photos and the copy to the nearest embassy or consulate, and they'll help you get a replacement. When you have photos taken to apply for your original passport, take extra pictures. Then keep them with your travel kit and always take them with you, just in case. You don't want to walk the streets of Prague looking for a place to have photos taken when you should be attending a meeting.

In Case of Emergency

In addition to carrying a copy of your passport, your phone, and a map, create an emergency card to slip into your wallet containing the following information:

- name, address, and phone number of your hotel
- the number that is equivalent to 911
- name and number of your emergency contact (local and at home)
- phone number for the American embassy or consulate
- number for your insurance company

An alternative choice is to simply write the information on the copy of your passport that you carry with you. However you do it, keep the information handy, just in case.

Money, Money, Money

Another component of preparing for an international trip is to obtain currency for your destination. What will it look like, where do I get it, and how much should I take? Try always to arrive in and leave a country with local money in your wallet.

Banks and foreign exchange companies in your city can provide currency for your destination, allowing you to arrive without worry as to how to pay for a cab or buy something to drink. While you can exchange money at the airport, why worry about an extra task in the last minutes before a flight? Be sure you still have adequate local currency at the end of the trip, too. Don't end up in the same situation as an American banker in Colombia, who had to borrow money from a stranger at the airport to pay the departure tax.

When you arrive at your destination, you'll find that you can exchange money at hotels, airports, or train stations. Other choices include banks and currency exchange operations, which are often located in tourist areas. The rate of exchange will be most favorable at a bank and least advantageous at a hotel, airport, or train station. Rates at ATMs, even with the service fee, are closest to bank rates and thus favorable.

Using an ATM is probably the easiest way to obtain local currency; however, there are a few points to note. They are as follows:

- If you don't use your card regularly, try it before you go away.
- Check your pin (personal identification number). Make sure it's only four digits and that the first one is not zero.
- If your card is also a charge card, check the expiration date. There's nothing as frustrating as being unable to access your account because your card expired in the middle of your trip.
- Know your daily limit for withdrawals. Make certain that it's high enough so that you can take out enough to cover your expenses for a day or two.

Remember the 24-hour rule. The withdrawal limit is enforced within a 24-hour period. If you take out the equivalent of your $200 limit at 2:00 P.M. Tuesday, you can't take out any more money at noon on Wednesday. The system will deny you access until after 2:00 P.M., the 24-hour limit.

Know how you'll get money and what to do if the machine inhales your card. For example, carry an extra ATM card, or have some travelers checks or another source of cash. If it's during business hours, go into the bank and report what happened. If it happens late in the day, go back to the bank where your card disappeared the next morning and re-trieve your card.

Think about your planned withdrawal amount both in local cur-rency and in U.S. dollars. Know the current exchange rate so that you stay within your limits. How many Hong Kong dollars can you obtain and still stay below your maximum?

Keeping track of the exchange rate is important for purposes other than using an ATM. Most often it's an issue when you contemplate making a purchase. Rather than having to take out a calculator every time, learn to estimate based on the rate. This way you can quickly esti-mate the cost of a purchase or fee for a service. If a sweater is 77 euros, is that the equivalent of $77 or $97? A fast calculation will often show you whether that perfect souvenir is really the one you want.

Sometimes, when you look at money that isn't your own, it's diffi-cult to remember it's truly money. It is. No matter how pretty, how un-usual, or how worn it may be, it's money to be spent, saved, or turned back into your own currency at the end of the trip. Currency isn't the only way to make purchases when you travel. Most travelers rely on their credit cards for most of their purchases. Although using a credit card to buy a coffee at Starbucks isn't a common practice as it is at home. For small purchases, currency is still best. If you plan to use a credit card, it's helpful to have two in case one doesn't work. Check the expiration dates, and notify the credit card company of your travel des-tinations. Otherwise, when they see a charge from Sydney, Australia, they may assume your card has been stolen and deactivate it.

Never Leave Without

Comfort from home (snacks; pillowcase; and photos of family, friends, and pets)

Passport, visa, itinerary, insurance cards

Currency of the countries you'll visit

Credit card, ATM card (and numbers to call if they are lost)

List of important phone numbers, contact information

Personal medical kit with medications and copies of prescriptions

Copies of passport and extra passport photos

Comfortable shoes

Umbrella

Laptop, cell phone, chargers, and adapters

Before You Depart

Register with the U.S. embassy, and know the emergency numbers

Leave copies of your passport, credit cards, itinerary with family, friends

Leave behind anything that will cause you great pain if it's lost (jewelry, precious photos, or favorite tie)

Bring lots of lively curiosity, humor, and flexibility

Women on the Road

A recent survey revealed that women do almost 50 percent of the business travel in the United States, spending $175 billion annually on 14 million trips.[4] They travel for business and for pleasure in the United States and abroad, in groups and alone. The issues of importance for women who travel are generally the same as they are for men. However, female travelers frequently mention two topics of discussion. These are eating alone at restaurants, especially dinner, and personal safety.

Although the reasons that shape the experience are not clear, women say they feel uncomfortable eating alone in a restaurant, especially for dinner. Men who travel are more likely to check the restaurant reviews, select restaurants in advance, and enjoy the dining experience even on their own. However, few women adopt this approach. Their uneasiness may relate to fear of venturing out at night or fear of reflecting an old stigma of women eating alone. Whatever the reasons, women are more likely than men to order room service and stay in their hotel rooms. While at times staying in is the perfect choice, dinner in a restaurant can refresh the spirit and bring delightful surprises. In one such occurrence, a traveler engaged in conversation with a couple in a small French restaurant. Imagine their surprise when they discovered they would be part of the same meeting the next morning. To find a restaurant that is known to treat single diners well, you can check the recommendations on the Journey Women site (www.journeywoman.com). This Web site was created for women who travel. It includes advice on restaurants as well as other aspects of travel.

Safety is really an issue that applies to men as well as women. One of the most common pieces of advice given to single female travelers is never to return to their hotel rooms alone. They should have a member of the hotel staff escort them. But this is an issue that is not reserved solely for women, as illustrated by the following story. A group of managers from a technology company traveled to Thailand. After dinner, one of the men in the group returned to his room alone and was taken captive in the elevator by three men. He was robbed and tied up in his room, but otherwise unharmed.

Safety begins with common sense, paying attention to where you are and who is around you. The following are some recommendations:

- Know the areas of a city that are safe and those that are risky.
- Ask for information before you go for a walk.
- Believe the bus driver if he or she says the area isn't safe.
- Have the hotel or restaurant call a cab for you, especially in the evenings.
- No matter how much you love to run outside in the morning, don't do it if your colleague tells you there are snakes in the area.
- Don't use the room service door hanger menus to order breakfast. You have to indicate how many people are in the room.
- Select small hotels where the staff know who is a guest and who isn't.
- If you travel to the same city frequently, stay at the same place. It's wonderful to be addressed by name when you arrive even after a year's absence.
- Schedule a time to call home, or your office. Be sure someone expects to hear from you and will be aware if you don't check in.
- Leave your cell phone number so people can call you (remember to charge the phone and leave it on).
- Remember that women as well as men can be dangerous. Be cautious about new friends.

This Trip's for Me

Up to this point, we've viewed travel mainly as a part of a person's professional life. Examples have focused on travel for the purpose of meeting clients and suppliers, attending conferences, and checking out the competition. But trips for personal reasons are equally important. The key to planning a successful trip is to know why you're going and what you hope to accomplish. What will make this trip a success for you?

The words *goal* and *success* are usually associated with business plans and assessment but are equally valid in connection with your leisure travel. Why this trip? Why now? The responses will shape your plans. The more clarity you can bring to the process, the better the plan and the travel. Every trip is a balance among time, budget available, and purpose. We automatically recognize these constraints for business travel, but they are equally true for personal travel.

Is there a city you've dreamt about visiting since you were a child? Is this the trip that will satisfy the goal statement, "Before I die/turn 40/retire/get married, I want to see the Eiffel Tower/backpack through the Rocky Mountains/see a lion/taste wine in Chile?" Do you simply have a friend who had fun in Brazil, so now you want to go? Knowing what the parameters are for time and budget will guide you along the way.

Once you've decided where, when, and how much is available to fund the vacation, another series of choices emerges. What's the best way to make the practical arrangements: booking hotels, flights, trains, and cars? Will you take a tour and let the operator handle the details, including the museums and meals? Then you need only send payments on a set schedule and meet the group at a certain date and time.

Will you use an online site? You can book hotels, flights, and rental cars all at your leisure. You can get information and make reservations on sites such as Expedia.com, Orbitz.com, and Travelocity.com. These are not the only sites to check. Hotels and airlines, American Express, and others provide services for travelers. It's often wise to check multiple sites before making a final decision.

There are also the traditional providers: the travel agents. While a simple trip from Seattle to London or Rio may be easy to book online, multiple cities in multiple countries may be easier to book with the help of an agent. Additionally, having a phone number to call and a person to talk to can be extremely useful when sorting out changes in schedules. To find an agent, ask your well-traveled friends or consult the Web site of the American Society of Travel Agents (www.astanet.com).

A buyer for a specialty retail chain travels frequently and has used the same travel agent for a dozen years. The advantage, she says, is that the travel agent knows exactly what kinds of hotels and restaurants she and her husband like. She adds, "I can make suggestions, but he knows the areas. I love doing research, but when all is said and done, he always finds us something or someplace I never read about."

The choice is yours. You may want to select different options for different trips. But one bit of advice comes from all the travelers. Even if you are adventurous and plan to create your itinerary as you go, book a hotel for the nights of arrival and departure. When you are jet lagged upon arrival and rushed and tired at the end of a trip, you'll reduce the stress by knowing where you'll sleep.

Travel for yourself can have unexpected benefits in addition to satisfying a personal desire. A French executive observed that most successful people have traveled and that conversation about travel opens up new connections. An American corporate director is certain that a trip to Poland helped clinch her current position. Not that Poland related directly to the job, but it was meaningful that she'd taken an unusual trip on her own. The benefits of travel are often unpredictable.

Today It's Not Fun

Remember as you embark on a trip that travel is both exhilarating and stressful. No matter how perfect the destination, at some point, people want to go home, even if it's only to check the mail. The stress of a trip comes from lack of control and uncertainty. Flights may be cancelled or delayed. Connections may be missed, or crying children may fill the flights. Moving from hotel to hotel, one has to repeatedly figure out how to turn on the lights and flush the toilets. Nothing is as simple as being at home.

While it's impossible to eliminate all the uncertainties of a trip, you can do a few things to mitigate some of them.

- Try not to drive in a strange city. Take a cab, ride the subway, or hire a car and driver. Although the latter may seem extremely expensive, consider the work that can be done and calls that can be returned while someone else does the driving. Know a service in each city. It's amazing how much longer a meeting can last if you don't have to add time in your schedule to search for a cab to get to the airport.

- If you are traveling with children or lots of luggage, you may want to send your bags ahead. Services such as Luggage Express, Skycap International, Virtual Bellhop, or even FedEx deliver your luggage for you. Suddenly, all you have is a small carry-in and your laptop, and check-in is easy.

- A bit of the right food can brighten a day. Don't laugh when you find out that a person on an extended stay in Paris had Spaghetti O's and Pop-Tarts delivered to her to lift her spirits. A trip to McDonald's can be a touch of home; peanut butter crackers can be a perfect antidote to weeks of restaurant food. Pack something in your suitcase and avoid spending a day in Rome searching for something familiar to eat.

- Travel is tiring, no matter how exciting, so it's important to know your own rhythm. How much rest do you need, and where does it fit in? Do you want to be up and out and see every monument or are you content to sleep in, read, eat breakfast, start at 11, have lunch, nap, and take a stroll before dinner? When the trip is for you, set a schedule that is yours.

Now We Know

Travel is exciting, interesting, exhausting, and challenging. Plan carefully before you depart. Learn not only about the place and the people but also the practical aspects of the journey. As soon as you plan where and when to go, begin planning how to be safe, stay healthy, and keep financially prepared, and what to do when problems occur. Be sure to know how to stay in touch. Don't forget planning for the journey itself. Think about the airport, train station, bus, and car. What should you expect, and what should you take with you? Plan ahead and remember, most of all, to take your curiosity and sense of humor. They don't add to the weight of your luggage, but they are the keys to a successful trip whether it is personal or professional.

I'm Glad I Know

You have to expect the unexpected and consider everything an adventure. Without a doubt, airport schedules change, luggage is lost, and you can't be in control all the time. In the midst of a trip things can be extremely frustrating. However, when I looked back, those were the occurrences that proved most interesting. You can't get upset, annoyed. I learned that you just need to adapt and move forward.

→→ *Former State Department staff member,*
now executive director of a nonprofit
whose mission is to improve
the perception of Americans abroad

While reading through this book, subjects may catch a reader's interest, pique their curiosity, or raise a question. This section is presented to offer possible responses. Listed below are some of the resources and references that provided information for this book. This is a small sampling of the sources available. No endorsement is intended for any of the commercial sites nor is this presented as a definitive list.

Among the items listed, people will find their favorites. Each person's quest for information, his or her goals and requirements, is unique. The hope is that the following choices will help the reader begin their exploration.

The Big Picture

Aveni, Anthony, *Empires of Time: Calendars, Clocks, and Cultures*, New York: Kodansha Inc., 1995.

Dalton, Maxine; Ernest, Chris; Deal, Jennifer; Leslie, Jean; *Success for the New Global Manager*, San Francisco: Josey-Bass, 2002.

Foster, Dean, *The Global Etiquette Guide to Europe*, New York: John Wiley & Sons, Inc., 2000.

Friedman, Thomas L., *The Lexus and the Olive Tree*, New York: Anchor Books, 2000. A contemporary look at globalization.

Gundling, Ernest, *Working GlobeSmart*, Palo Alto: Davies-Black Publishing, 2003.

Hall, Edward Twitchell and Hall, Mildred Reed, *Understanding Cultural Differences*, Yarmouth: Intercultural Press, 1990.

Harrison, Lawrence E. and Huntington, Samuel P., editors, *Culture Matters*, New York: Basic Books, 2000.

Hodge, Sheida, *Global Smarts*, New York: John Wiley & Sons, Inc., 2000.

Hofstede, Geert, *Cultures and Organizations*, New York: McGraw Hill, 1997.

Hopkins, A. G., editor, *Globalization in World History*, London: W. W. Norton & Co. Ltd, 2002.

Irwin, Douglas A., *Against the Tide: An Intellectual History of Free Trade*, Princeton University Press, 1996.

Landes, David S., *The Wealth and Poverty of Nations*, New York: W.W. Norton & Company, 1998.

Levine, Robert, *A Geography of Time*, New York: Basic Books, 1997.

Lewis, Richard, *When Cultures Collide*, London: Nicholas Brealey Publishing Limited, 1996.

Micklethwait, John, and Wooldridge, Adrian, *A Future Perfect*, New York: Crown Business, 2000.

O'Hara-Devereaux, Mary, and Johansen, Robert, *Global Work*, San Francisco: Jossey-Bass Publishers, 1994.

Rosinski, Philippe. *Coaching Across Cultures*, London: Nicholas Brealey Publishing, 2003.

Tannahill, Reay, *Food in History*, New York: Crown Publishers, Inc., 1988.

Trompenaars, Fons and Hampden-Turner, Charles, *Riding the Waves of Culture*, New York: McGraw-Hill, 1998.

Visser, Margaret, *Much Depends on Dinner*, Toronto: McClelland and Stewart Limited, 1986.

Visser, Margaret, *The Rituals of Dinner*, Toronto: HarperCollins Publishers, 1991.

History, Culture, Business Etiquette, and More

Books That Cover Multiple Countries

Morrison, Terri, Conway, Wayne, and Borden, George, *Kiss, Bow or Shake Hands*, Holbrook: Bob Adams, Inc., 1994. A concise view of the history and culture of 60 countries.

Training Management Corporation, *Doing Business Internationally: The Resource Book to Business and Social Etiquette*, Princeton: Princeton Training Press, 1997.

Atkinson, Toby D., *Merriam-Webster's Guide to International Business Communications*, second edition, Springfield: Merriam-Webster, Incorporated, 1996. A guide to phone numbers, addresses, names, and forms of address in multiple countries.

Book Series

Bosrock, Mary Murray. *Put Your Best Food Forward series*. (St. Paul: International Education Systems). Titles include Asia, Europe, Russia, South America, or Mexico/Canada.

Culture Shock! series published by Graphic Arts Publishing Company in Portland, Oregon. Each book covers a specific country. Books are written and edited by people who are knowledgeable about an area. There are more than 50 countries in the series including South Africa, Singapore, France, Italy, China, and Morocco.

Axtell, Roger E., editor, *Do's and Taboos Around the World*, second edition, New York:

John Wiley & Sons, Inc., 1990. (Other titles include *Dos and Taboos for Hosting International Visitors* and *Dos and Taboos for Women in Business*.)

Web Sites

Intercultural Press (www.interculturalpress.com). Publishes a wide variety of books addressing business cultures throughout the world.

Executive Planet (www.executiveplanet.com). Provides information about culture in a variety of countries.

Regional Focus

Adams, Jerome R., *Latin American Heroes*, New York: Ballantine Books, 1991.

Asselin, Giles, and Mastron, Ruth, *Au Contraire! Figuring out the French*, Yarmouth: Intercultural Press, Inc., 2001.

Batey, Ian, *Asian Branding*, Singapore: Prentice Hall, 2002.

Blackman, Carolyn, *China Business*, Crows Nest: Allen & Unwin, 2000.

Denoon, Donald, and Mein-Smith, Philippa, with Wyndham, Marivic, *A History of Australia, New Zealand and the Pacific*, Oxford: Blackwell Publishers, 2000.

Fowler, Will, *Latin American 1800 – 2000*, London: Arnold, a member of the Hodder-Holder Group, 2002.

Knightley, Phillip, *Australia: A Biography of a Nation*, London: Johnathan Cape, 2000.

Leppert, Paul, *Doing Business with Koreans*, Sebastopol: Patton Pacific Press, 1991.

Lewis, Flora, *Europe: Road to Unity*, New York: Simon & Schuster, 1992.

Mole, John, *Mind Your Manners: Managing Business Cultures in Europe*, London: Nicholas Brealey Publishing Limited, 1995.

Nnadozie, Emmanuel Arthur, *African Culture & American Business in Africa*, Kirksville: Afrimax, Inc., 1998.

Pineau, Carol, and Kelly, Maureen, *Working in France*, Vincennes: Frank Books, 1991.

Philip, George, *Democracy in Latin America*, Cambridge: Polity Press, 2003.

Reader, John, *Africa: A Biography of the Continent*, London: Penguin Books, 1997.

Richmond, Yale, *From Da to Yes: Understanding the Eastern Europeans*, Yarmouth: Intercultural Press, 1995.

Seligman, Scott D., *Chinese Business Etiquette*, New York: Warner Books, 1999.

Street, Nancy Lynch, and Matelski, Marilyn J., *American Businesses in China*, London: McFarland & Company, Inc. Publishers, 2003.

Stewart-Allen and Denslow, Lanie, *Working with Americans*, London: Prentice Hall Business: 2002.

Stuttard, John B., *The New Silk Road*, New York: John Wiley & Sons, Inc., 2000.

Wilen, Tracey, and Wilen, Patricia, *Asia for Women on Business*, Berkeley: Stone Bridge Press, 1995.

Yamada, Haru, *Different Games, Different Rules: Why Americans and Japanese Misunderstand Each Other*, New York: Oxford University Press, 1997.

Etiquette Basics

Baldridge, Letitia, *Complete Guide to the New Manners for the '90s*, New York: Rawson Associates, 1993.

Baldridge, Letitia, *New Complete Guide to Executive Manners*, New York: Rawson Associates, 1990.

Craig, Elizabeth, *Don't Slurp Your Soup*, St. Paul: Brighton Publications, Inc. 1991.

Spade, Kate, *Manners and Occasion*, New York: Simon & Schuster, 2004.

Tell Me About Where I'm Going

Federation of International Trade Association (www.fita.org). Provides a newsletter with country-specific information plus links to other sources.

The CIA World Factbook (www.cia.gov). Provides country history, geography, and economic data.

U.S. State Department site (www.travel.state.gov). Gives insight to security situation in various countries.

We Know the World

Links to newspapers around the globe (www.ceoexpress.com).

Get news from a country that interests you (www.google.com).

Travel Guides for Business and Pleasure

Online or actual bookstores provide a wide variety of travel guides. Guidebook series include those by Fodor's, Frommers, Rick Steves, Lonely Planet, Rough Guides, Cagon, and more.

Booksellers to find these series include Amazon.com (www.amazon.com). Barnes and Noble and Borders offer both brick-and-mortar locations and Web sites, www.bn.com and www.bordersstores.com. There are independent specialty bookstores in many cities. Two that have Web sites and extensive selections are Get Lost Travel books in San Francisco (www.getlostbooks.com) and Globe Corner Bookstore, Boston (www.globecorner.com).

Tips for Travelers

Information for the frequent flyer (www.frequentflyer.oag.com). Newsletter available.

National Association of Passport and Visa Services site (www.napvs.org). Find resources to assist with obtaining a passport in a hurry.

Site for women travelers covering both business and pleasure (www.journeywoman.com).

Transportation Security Administration site (www.tsa.gov). Provides latest security information and estimate of time to get through security process at airports, as well as regulations relating to travel by air.

What shots may I need? This is the Center for Disease Control site and offers advice for staying healthy while traveling (www.cdc.gov/travel).

Where's my seat on the plane? Provides rating of specific seats on the planes for a variety of airlines (www.seatguru.com).

Please Call Home

Cell phone rental companies (www.cellhire.com, www.mobalrental.com, www.worldcell.com). This is not a complete list but a starting point.

Travelers Health Insurance

HTH Travel insurance (www.hthtravelinsurance.com), Medex International (www.medexassist.com), and Worldwide Assistance (www.worldwide-assistance.com) are three companies that offer medical and/or evacuation and emergency services for travelers.

Products for Travelers

Two companies that provide an extensive variety of products to outfit a traveler, whether the voyage is for business or pleasure, are Magellans and Flight 001. Both have brick-and-mortar locations as well as Web sites, www.magellans.com and www.flight001.com.

Globalbagtag (www.globalbagtag.com) and I-Trak (www.i-trak.com) offer metal tags with special numbers that can be registered with the airlines to help track lost luggage.

Notes to Chapter 1

1. Gary Ferraro, *The Cultural Dimension of International Business* (Prentice Hall, New York, 1994): 91.

2. Anthony Aveni, *Empires of Time: Calendars, Clocks, and Cultures* (Kodansha Inc, New York, 1995).

3. Robert Levine, *A Geography of Time* (Basic Books, New York, 1997): 76.

4. Levine: 60.

5. Edward Hall and Mildred R. Hall, *Understanding Cultural Differences* (Intercultural Press, Yarmouth, 1990): 13.

6. Hall and Hall: 13.

7. Richard D. Lewis, *When Cultures Collide* (Nicholas Brealey Publishing Limited, London, 1996): 55.

8. Donald A. Ball and Wendell H. McCulloch, Jr., *International Business: The Challenge of Global Competition* (Irwin McGraw-Hill, New York): 257.

9. Fons Trompenaars and Charles Hampden-Turner, *Riding the Waves of Culture* (McGraw-Hill, New York, 1998): 130.

10. Christopher Engholm and Diana Rowland, *International Excellence* (Kodansha New York): 78.

11. Trompenaars and Hampden-Turner: 133.

12. Trompenaars and Hampden-Turner: 132.

Notes to Chapter 2

1. Charles W. L. Hill International Business, *Competing in the Global Marketplace*, fourth edition (McGraw-Hill, New York 2003): 4.

2. Gary Ferraro, *The Cultural Dimension of International Business* (Prentice Hall, New York, 1994): 45.

3. Hill: 6.

4. Christopher Engholm and Diana Rowland, *International Excellence* (Kodansha International, New York, 1996): 76.

5. Ferraro: 45.

6. Hill: 104.

7. Engholm and Rowland: 72.

8. Ball and McCulloch: 284.

9. Ball and McCulloch: 287.

10. Story at Women in International Trade Meeting, Oct. 2003.

11. Haru Yamada, *Different Games, Different Rules: Why Americans and Japanese Misunderstand Each Other* (Oxford University Press, New York 1997): 41.

12. Tracey Wilen and Patricia Wilen, *Asia for Women on Business* (Stone Bridge Press, Berkeley, 1995): 27.

13. Fons Trompenaars and Charles Hampden-Turner, *Riding the Waves of Culture* (McGraw-Hill, New York, 1998): 70.

14. Trompenaars and Hampden-Turner: 72.

15. Philippe Rosinski, *Coaching Across Cultures* (Nicholas Brealey, London, 2003): 165.

16. Engholm and Rowland: 76.

17. Trompenaars and Hampden-Turner: 77.

18. Ferraro: 63.

19. Roger E. Axtell, editor, *Do's and Taboos Around the World, second edition* (John Wiley & Sons, Inc., New York, 1990): 47.

Notes to Chapter 3

1. 2001 World Christian Trends, www.gem-werc.org/gd/gd23.pdf.

2. Geert Hofstede, *Cultures and Organizations* (McGraw Hill, New York, 1997).

3. Maxine Dalton, et al, *Success for the Global Manager* (San Francisco: Josey-Bass, 2002).

4. Dalton, et al: 52.

5. 2001 World Christian Trends, www.gem-werc.org/gd/gd23.pdf.

6. Hill: 103.

7. Lawrence Harrison and Samuel P. Huntington, editors, *Culture Matters* (New York: Basic Books, 2000): 11.

8. Luigi Zinglaes, "Beyond the Protestant Work Ethic," *Capital Ideas*, Winter 2004, gsbwwww.uchicago.edu (accessed Nov. 23, 2004).

9. *The Futurist*, Jan./Feb. 2004: 98.

10. Hill: 111.

11. John Micklethwait, and Wooldridge, Adrian, *A Future Perfect* (New York: Crown Publishers 2000): 225.

12. Philip Longman, "The Land of the Parasite Singles," *Business 2.0* (Sept. 2003): 105.

13. Evelyn Iritani, "Loving the Little Emperor," *Los Angeles Times*, Aug. 2, 2003: A1, A5.

Notes to Chapter 4

1. Jean-Louis Barsoux and Peter Lawrence, *French Management* (London: Cassell, 1997): 98.

2. Fons Trompenaars and Charles Hampden-Turner, *Riding the Waves of Culture* (New York: McGraw-Hill, 1998): 83.

3. Roger Baumgarte, et al, "Friendship Patterns Among University Students in Five Cultures," *The International Scope Review*, vol. 3 (2001): 3.

4. John Mole, *Mind Your Manners* (London: Nicholas Brealey Publishing Ltd., 1995).

Notes to Chapter 5

1. Stephen Green, et al, "In Search of Global Leaders," *Harvard Business Review* (Aug. 2003): 39.

2. Merriam-Webster Dictionary, www.m-w.com/cgi-bin/dictionary (accessed Dec. 28, 2003).

3. Merriam-Webster Dictionary, www.m-w.com/cgi-bin/dictionary (accessed Dec. 28, 2003).

4. Christopher A. Bartlett and Sumantra Ghoshal, *Managing Across Borders* (Boston: Harvard Business School Press, 1998): 15–20.

5. Bruce Mazlish, *The New Global Economy*, www.web.mit.edu (accessed Dec. 28, 2003): 8.

6. Green, et al.: 42.

7. Bartlett and Ghoshal: 17.

8. Nancy J. Adler, *International Dimensions of Organizational Behavior*, fourth edition (Cincinnati: South-Western, Cincinnati, 2002): 66.

9. Mary O'Hara-Devereaux & Robert Johansen, *Global Work* (Jossey-Bass, Inc. Publishers, San Francisco, 1994): 31.

10. Stephen Green, et al: 43.

11. Stephen Green, et al: 40.

12. Eamonn P. Sweeney and Glenn Hardaker, "The importance of organization and national culture," *European Business Review*, 1994, vol. 94, http://proquest.umi.com, document 4689377 (accessed Dec. 14, 2003).

13. "Culture and Status – the Perils and Pitfalls," www.global-excellence.com/articles/text10.html (accessed Dec. 29, 2003).

14. Trompenaars and Hampden-Turner: 121.

15. www.global-excellence.com/artiles/text10.html (accessed Dec. 29, 2003).

16. www.global-excellence.com/artiles/text10.html (accessed Dec. 29, 2003).

17. O'Hara-Devereaux and Johansen: 54.

18. Donald W. Hendon, et al, "Negotiation Concession Patterns: A multi-country, multiperiod study," *American Business Review* (Jan. 2003): 3.

Notes to Chapter 6

1. Allyson Stewart Allen and Lanie Denslow, *Working with Americans* (Prentice Hall, London, 2002): 151.

2. McGiffert, Carola, "Bottom Up Legal Reform." *China Business Review* (May/June 2003): 38.

3. *China Business Review*: 38

4. The Timetable of World Legal History, duhaime.org, www.dhuhaime.org/Law_museum/hist.htm (accessed Dec. 26, 2003).

5. www.dhuhaime.org/Law_museum/hist.htmm (accessed Dec. 26, 2003).

6. Ricky W. Griffin and Michael W. Pustay, *International Business: A Managerial Perspective,* third edition (Prentice Hall, Upper Saddle River, 2003): 61.

7. www.dhuhaime.org/Law_museum/hist.htm (accessed Dec. 26, 2003).

8. Interview with author Dec. 15, 2003.

9. *The China Business Review*: 38.

10. Charles W.L. Hill, *International Business: Competing In the Global Marketplace,* fourth edition (New York: McGraw-Hill, 2003): 87.

11. Foreign Corrupt Practices Act Antibribery Provisions, www.bisnis.doc.gov/bisnis/fcp1.htm (accessed Dec. 30, 2003).

12. www.bisnis.doc/gov.

13. Roberto Ceniceros, "U.S. Multinationals likely to volunteer information on violations of Corruption," *Business Insurance* (2003) 3 pages. Proquest 384422131 (accessed Dec. 31, 2003).

14. Ceniceros: 2.

15. Quick Compliance, www.quickcompliance.net (accessed Dec. 31, 2003).

16. www.transparency.org (accessed Dec. 31, 2003).

17. Simon London, "Climate Change: Corporate Scandals Push the Need for Ethical Standards to the Top of the Business Agenda," *Financial Times* (Dec. 31, 2003): 9.

18. Socially Responsible Investing, Historical Background, www.ucalgary.ca/MG/inrm/finplan/investment/history.htm (accessed Oct. 2, 2004).

Notes to Chapter 7

1. Alison Maitland, "It's death if you stop trying new things," *Financial Times,* (Nov. 20, 2003): 8.

2. G. Hofstede, *Cultures and Organizations* (New York: McGraw Hill, New York, 1997): 110.

3. Nancy J. Adler, *International Dimensions of Organizational Behavior*, fourth edition (Cincinnati South-Western, 2002): 66.

4. Philippe Rosinski, *Coaching Across Cultures.* (London: Nicholas Brealey Publishing, 2003): 129.

5. Rana Foroohar, "Outsiders In," *Newsweek International,* Oct. 20, 2003, www.msnbc.com/news (accessed Oct. 17, 2003).

6. Maxine Dalton, et al, *Success for the New Global Manager* (San Francisco Josey-Bass, 2002*)*: 53.

7. Aaron Marcus, "Are you cultured?" *New Architect,* San Francisco, March 2003, http://proquest.umi.com, (accessed Dec. 21, 2003).

8. Thomas L. Friedman, *The Lexus and the Olive Tree* (New York: 1999): xv.

9. ExecutivePlanet.com, BizCulture Newsletter (accessed Dec. 8, 2003).

10. Hofstede: 116.

11. "Reinventing Europe," *The Economist,* Sept. 6, 2003 page 2, http://proquest. umi.com, (accessed Dec. 14, 2003).

12. Carol Craig, *Scot's Crisis of Confidence* (Big Thinking 2003).

13. Yasheng Huange and Tarun Khanna, "Can India Overtake China?" *Foreign Policy* (July/Aug. 2003).

14. Yinka Degoke, "It takes an entrepreneur to catch an entrepreneur," *Financial Times* (Nov. 7, 2003): 10.

15. *Wired* (Sept. 2003): 40.

Notes to Chapter 8

1. Thomas L. Friedman, *The Lexus and the Olive Tree* (New York: Anchor Books: 2000): 7.

2. www.imf.org.

3. Bruce Mazlish, "The New Global History," web.mit.edu/newglobalhistory/doc (accessed Dec. 2003).

4. A.G. Hopkins, editor, *Globalization in World History* (London: W. W. Norton & Co. Ltd, 2002): 5.

5. Jared Diamond, "Globalization, Then," *Los Angeles Times*, Sept. 14, 2003: M1.

6. Mazlish, "Quick Guide to the World History of Globalization," www.newglobal history.com.

7. "History of the Global Corporation," www.bigpicturesmallworld.com.

8. Flora Lewis, *Europe: Road to Unity* (New York: Simon & Schuster, 1992): 22.

9. The Ottoman Empire, www.planetexplorer.online.discovery.com (accessed Dec. 20, 2003).

10. "History of the Global Corporation," www.bigpicturessmallworld.com (accessed Nov. 29, 2003).

11. Lewis: 24.

12. William Dodson, "It's About Time," www.amamebers.org/global/2002/nov_01.htm (accessed Nov. 4, 2002).

13. Roger Thurow, "Ravaged by Famine, Ethiopia Finally Gets Help from the Nile," *The Wall Street Journal*, (Nov. 26, 2003): A1.

14. Landes: 46.

Notes to Chapter 9

1. Irwin A. Douglas, *Against the Tide: An Intellectual History of Free Trade* (Princeton: Princeton University Press, 1996).

2. Irwin: 12.

3. Irwin: 20.

4. Irwin: 21.

5. Irwin: 75.

6. John Heilemann, "Gearing Ouselves for Globalization," *Business 2.0* (Aug. 2004): 34.

7. James Flanigan, "The Global Economy's 2-Way Street," *Los Angeles Times*, Aug. 29, 2004: C1.

8. Alan Beattie and Frances Williams, "WTO says freeing trade is not cure-all," *Financial Times* (Sept. 17, 2004): 6.

9. Bernard K. Gordon, "A High-Risk Trade Policy," *Foreign Affairs*, (July/Aug. 2003): 105.

10. CIESIN Thematic Guides General Agreement on Tariffs And Trade, www.ciesin.org.

11. Foreign Policy, www.foreignpolicy.com (accessed Dec. 8, 2003): 5.

12. Larry Rother, "New Global Trade Lineup: Haves, Have-Nots, Have-Somes," *The New York Times* (Nov. 2, 2003): 3.

13. Bruce Berton at China Briefing, Feb. 28, 2004.

14. Ahmed Rashid, "The Great Trade Game," *Far Eastern Economic Review* (Jan. 30, 2003): 18.

15. World Trade Organization, Regional Trade Agreements, www.wto.org (accessed Oct. 16, 2004).

16. Koopmann, George, "Growing Regionalism – a major challenge to the multilateral Trading System," *Intereconomics* (Sept./Oct. 2003): 237.

17. "The Americas: Recruitment Drive; Trade in South America," *The Economist*, (Aug. 30, 2003): 41.

18. Koopmann (Sept./Oct. 2003).

19. "Seven Asian Nations Agree on Trade Zone Idea," *The New York Times* (Jan. 3, 2004): A5.

20. G. Feller, "Trade route of the future?" *Journal of Commerce* (May 26, 2003): 1.

Notes to Chapter 10

1. Nationmaster.com, Geography: Area (land), www.nationmaster.com (accessed Nov. 7, 2004).

2. Jose Azel, and David DeVoss, "Divided Loyalties," *Smithsonian* Jan. 2004, Vol 34, issue 10 (http://web15.epnet.com/citation).

3. J. Azel, et al.

4. J. Azel, et al.

5. Allyson Stewart-Allen, and Lanie Denslow, *Working With Americans*, (London: Prentice Hall Business, 2002).

6. Canada "Origin of Name" Wikipedia, http://en.wikipedia.org (accessed Nov. 7, 2004).

7. "New Scotland," *Maclean's* Feb. 2, 2004, vol. 117, issue 5, http://web15.epnet.com, Ebscohost, item 12060584 (accessed May 15, 2004): 55.

8. CultureGrams World Edition 2004, Canada-Quebec: 118.

9. http://encyclopedia.thefreedictionary.com/Canada (accessed May 15, 2004).

10. Pete Born, "Retailing for the New America," *Women's Wear Daily*, June 4, 2004: 11.

11. David Brooks, "Refuting the Cynics," *New York Times*, Nov. 25, 2004: A 29.

12. www.encyclopedia.thefreedictionary.com/Canada (accessed May 15, 2004).

13. Keith Orndoff, "Assessing American Diversity," *The Futurist*, Jan/Feb. 2003: 24.

14. Doris Montanera, "Tale of Three Cities: What is Canadian Style?" *Flare*, Oct. 2003, http://gateway.proquest.com.

15. Orndoff.

16. Holly Yearger, "American's Latino Market Makes the News," *Financial Times*, May 18, 2004: 9.

17. www.international-business=etiquette.com/besite/canada.htm.

18. www.state.gov/r/pa/ei/bgn/2089.htm.

19. *Foreign Trader*, Vol. 10, No. 18, May 6, 2004.

20. "Cities in a state," *The Economist*, Jan. 24, 2004: 32.

21. "The Canadian Way," *MacLean's*, July 1, 2000.

22. Jeffrey E. Garten, "At 10, NAFTA Is Ready for an Overhaul," *Business Week*, Dec. 22, 2003, http://69.0.144.8.

23. Peter Newman, "Why I'll Fight FTAA," *MacLean's*, April 30, 2004: 20, www.69.0.144.8 (accessed May 14, 2004).

24. European Union On-line, Europa site: www.europa.eu.int.

25. "It's a Grande-Latte World," *Wall Street Journal*, Dec. 15, 2003: B1.

26. Henry Cisneros, "Extra Spice for American Culture," *Financial Times*, May 24, 2004: 12.

27. "American Narcissism," *International Herald Tribune*.

28. Jonah Goldberg, editor, "The Specter of McDonald's," *National Review*, June 5, 2000, www.nationalreview.com/05june00/goldbergerprint060600.html.

29. Maxine Dalton, Chris Ernst, Jennifer Deal, and Jean Leslie, *Success for the New Global Manager* (San Francisco: Jossy-Bass) 2002: 53-54.

30. *Jungle* Oct./Nov. 2003: 52.

31. www.infoplease.com/ipa/A0781359.html.

Notes to Chapter 11

1. Rand McNally, *Atlas of World Geography* (New York: McGraw Hill Higher Education, 2000): 98.

2. Alonso Martinez, Ivan DeSouza, and Francis Liu, "Multinational vs. Multilatinas: Latin America's Great Race," *Strategy and Business*, www.strategybusiness.com, (accessed Sept. 6, 2003).

3. Will Fowler, *Latin America 1800-2000: Modern History for Modern Languages* (London: Arnold, a member of the Hodder Headline Group) 2002: 2.

4. Fowler: 5.

5. Culture Grams World Edition 2004 (Lindon: Axiom Press, Inc.).

6. Fowler: 114.

7. www.cnn.com/2004/TRAVEL/02/09/cuba.travel.ap.

8. Martinez, et al.

9. "New Latin Economic Rival: Eastern Europe," *Miami Herald*, May 17, 2004.

10. Warren Vieth, "U.S. Reaches Central American Trade Deal," *Los Angeles Times* Dec. 18, 2003: C1.

11. Thomas L. Friedman, "Beyond NAFTA, Mexico and the U.S. need to think big," *International Herald Tribune*, April 5, 2004: 8.

12. Maxine Dalton, Chris Ernst, Jennifer Deal, and Jean Leslie, *Success for the New Global Manager* (San Francisco: Jossey-Bass) 2002: 51.

13. John Cavanagh and Sarah Anderson, "Happily Ever NAFTA?" *Foreign Policy* Sept./Oct. 2002 (accessed May 29, 2004): 58–65.

14. www.businessweek.com.

15. Sarah Anderson, "A decade of NAFTA in the United States and Mexico," *Canadian Dimension* (March/April 2004), (accessed May 29, 2004).

16. "Sure Things in Mexico: Death, Taxes and Evasion," *Los Angeles Times*, May 16, 2004: C1

17. Geri Smith, and Cristina Lindblad, "Mexico: Was NAFTA Worth It?" *Business Week*, Dec. 22, 2003 (accessed May 29, 2004):34.

18. Tom Nevin, "Under Construction: Africa's Economic Highway to Brazil," *African Business*, April 2004: 38–39.

19. Jordan Karp, and Jonathan Karp, "Machines for the Masses," *Wall Street Journal*, Dec. 9, 2003: A19.

20. Jordan, et al: A19.

21. Lara Sowinski, "30 Top Countries for Trade and Expansion," *World Trade*, June 2004: 32–40.

22. Brian Ellsworth, "In Latin American a Cellular Need," *New York Times*, May 26, 2004: W1.

23. "The Americans: A stubborn curse; Inequality in Latin America," *The Economist*, Nov. 8 2003, Proquest ID 440338381, http://gateway.proquest.com: 60.

24. Marla Dickerson, "They May Protest Too Much," *Los Angeles Times*, May 24, 2004: A1/A4.

25. Fowler: 128.

26. Fernando Casares. *Business Credit*, Sept. 2002, Proquest ID 187624621, http://gateway.proquest.com.

Notes to Chapter 12

1. "Ambassador Monnet," Europa site, www.europa.eu/int.

2. John Pinder, *The European Union* (New York: Oxford University Press, Inc.) 2001.

3. Europa history of the EU, Europa site, www.europa.eu/int.

4. Robert Cohen, "America Has Second Thoughts About a United Europe," *New York Times*, May 2, 2004: 3.

5. www.europa.eu.

6. Internet Use in the European Union 2004, www.internetworldstats.com/stats4.htm (accessed Aug. 3, 2004).

7. Alan Riding, "Babel, a new capital for a wider continent," *New York Times*, May 2, 2004: 3.

8. Brandon Mitchener and Hannah Karp, "Europe's Parliament Puzzle," *Wall Street Journal*, June 9, 2004: A11.

9. Grzegorz Ekiert and Andrew Moravcsik, "At Last, Enlargement Day Has Come," *Newsweek*, May 20, 2004: 18.

10. Personal conversation with P. Kenneth Ackbarali, *International & Financial Economist*, Glendale, CA., Oct. 2004.

11. Michel Kwiecinski and Thomas Rudel, "Poland's Investment Challenge," *The McKinsey Quarterly*, 2004 Number 3, (accessed June 6, 2004).

12. "Turkey's EU accession in interest of Europe, say British FM," March 3, 2004, www.eubusinessw.com/afp/04030314331.rc8hwc95 (accessed Aug. 12, 2004).

13. Stefania Bianchi, "Europe: Turkey's Bid for EU Membership Still Gets a Way Response," Global Information Network, June 15, 2004, Proquest 651293171 (accessed July 30, 2004).

14. BBC News: Q&A: EU-myths and realities, http://newsvote.bbc.co.uk/ mpapps/pagetools/pirnt/new.bbc.co.uk/1/hi/world/europe/382 8/5/2004.

15. Cohen: 3.

16. Renee Cordes, "Changes Aim to Keep EU Competitive," *Women's Wear Daily*, Oct 29, 2003: 9.

17. David Murphy, "Best Friends," *Far Eastern Economic Review*, May 6, 2004, Proquest 629187981 (accessed July 30, 2004): 30.

18. IBID.

19. "Coming Soon," *Financial Times*, Sept. 2, 2004.

20. Scott Miller, and Guy Chazan, "EU Nears Accord to Back Russia in Bid for WTO," *Wall Street Journal*, May 14, 2004.

21. Andrew Jack, "Uneasy Russia guards its Interests," *Financial Times*, April 29, 2004.

22. HRI Survey 2004.

23. Marcus Walker, "Banking on Europe's Frontier," *Wall Street Journal*, Nov. 25, 2003: A14.

24. Scottish executive News, www.scotland.gov.uk/pages/news/2004/03/ SEFD371.aspx.

25. Kevin J. O'Brien, "For Jobs, Some Germans Look to Poland," *New York Times*, Jan. 8, 2004: W1.

26. Andy Reinhardt, "Forget India, Let's Go to Bulgaria," *Business Week*, Proquest 645322721, Mar 1, 2004 (accessed June 3, 2004): 93.

27. David Brooks, "Refuting the Cynics, " *New York Times*, Nov. 25, 2003: A 29.

28. Stuart Crainer, "And the new economy winner is … Europe," *Strategy and Business*, second quarter 2001: 43.

29. Jeffrey Pfeiffer, "All Work, No Play? It Doesn't Pay," *Business 2.0*, Aug. 2004: 50.

30. Mark Landler, "Western Europe slowly comes to grips with Working," *International Herald Tribune*, July 8, 2004: 1.

31. Brooks: A 29.

32. Phillip Longman, "The Global Baby Bust," *Foreign Affairs*, May/June 2004: 64–79.

33. World Internet Stats (updated July 26, 2004).

34. Estonian Embassy in Washington, "Information Society" Jan. 16, 2004, www.estemb.org (accessed Feb. 1, 2004).

Notes to Chapter 13

1. Interstate Statistical Committee of the Commonwealth of Independent States, www.cisstat.com/eng/cis.htm (accessed Feb. 20, 2004).

2. CIA – The World Factbook 2003, www.cia.gov/cia/publications/factbook.

3. CultureGrams, World Edition 2004 (Lindon: Axiom Press. Inc.): 529.

4. CultureGrams World Edition 2004: 420.

5. CultureGrams World Edition 2004: 345.

6. Alena Ledeneva, Commonwealth of Independent States, Global Corruption Report 2003: 166, www.grc@transparency.org.

7. Ledeneva: 166.

8. John B. Stuttard, *The New Silk Road* (New York: John Wiley & Sons Inc. 2000): 25.

9. "Strategic Focus: Food Retailing in Central & Eastern Europe," *Retail Forward*, Aug. 2003: 15.

10. CIA The World Factbook 2004, www.cia.gov/cia/publications/factbook.

11. McDonalds, www.mcdonalds.com/countries/russia.html.

Notes to Chapter 14

1. European Union online, www.europa.eu.int.

2. A. Humphreys, et. al, *Middle East* (Melbourne: Lonely Planet Publications 2003).

3. CultureGrams World Edition 2004 India.

4. Jonathan Fowler, "The Sound of Scotland in Eastern Pakistan; Out of Another Time, Fourth Generation of Bagpipe Makes Plies Its Trade," *the Washington Post*, Feb. 1, 2004, http://proquest.umi.com (accessed Feb. 7, 2004): A21.

5.   A. Humphreys, et al.

6.   Sally Jones, and Carla Anne Robins, "Tokyo Signs Oil-Development Deal with Tehran," *Wall Street Journal*, Feb. 19, 2004: A3.

7.   CultureGrams World Edition 2004.

8.   Hofstede, www.cyborlink.com/besite/mideast.htm.

9.   T. Morrison, W. Conaway, and G. Borden, *Kiss, Bow or Shake Hands* (Holbrook: Bob Adams, Inc., 1994): 167.

10. The CIA World Factbook 2005, www.cia.gov/cia/publications/factbook/geos.tu.html.

11. www.census.gov/cgi-bin/ipc/idbrank.pl.

12. CultureGram Egypt.

13. James Flanigan, "The Global Economy's 2-Way Street," *Los Angeles Times*, Aug. 29, 2004: C1.

14. Martin Baily and Diana Farrell, "Exploding the myths of offshoring," *the McKinsey Quarterly*, Web exclusive, July 2004, www.mckinseyquarterly.com, (accessed Nov. 2, 2004): 5.

Notes to Chapter 15

1.   "Malay Archipelago." *Encyclopedia Britannica*. 2004. Encyclopedia Britannica Premium Service. July 14, 2004, www.britannica.com/eb/article?eu=51514.

2.   Caroline Hsu, "The Chinese Columbus?" *U.S. News & World Report*, Feb. 23/March 1, 2004: 57.

3.   Kathy Fowler, *Culture Smart! China*, (Graphic Arts Center Publishing Company, 2003).

4.   Patsy Moy, "Flocking to a City of Dreams," *South China Morning Post*, April 29, 2004: A18.

5.   Landes: 381.

6.   Onishi: A4.

7.   Bertil Lintner, "Taste of Change in North Korea," *Wall Street Journal*, May 11, 2004: A16.

8.   Andrew Ward, "Fear and hate loosen grip on South Korean Young," *Financial Times*, July 22, 2004: 5.

9.   Ward: 5.

10. Carolyn Whelan, "Developing countries' economic clout grows," *International Herald Tribune*, July 10–11, 2004: 14.

11. Evelyn Iritani, "New Trade Pact Could Cut Clout of U.S. in Asia," *Los Angeles Times*, Nov. 30, 2004: C1.

12. "China Becomes South Korea's Number One Investment Target," *China Daily News*, Feb. 6, 2002, www.china.org.cn/english/26559.htm (accessed Dec. 18, 2004).

13. David Murphy, "Chinese Construction Companies Go Global," *Wall Street Journal*, May 12, 2004: B10.

14. Paul Gao, Jonathan R. Woetzel, and Yibing Wu, "Can Chinese brands make it abroad?" *The McKinsey Quarterly, 2003 Special edition: Global directions*, www.mckinseyquarterly.com (accessed July 19, 2004).

15. Whelan: 14.

16. Ian Batey, *Asian Branding* (Singapore: Prentice Hall, 2002): 204.

17. Interview with Sibylee Klose in Shanghai, April 2004.

18. "Japan's population shows lowest-ever increase," *Mainichi Daily News*, Mainichi Interactive, Aug. 5, 2004, http://mdn.mainichi.co.jp/news/200 40805p2a00m0dm0030000c.html (accessed Aug. 7, 2004).

19. Jayanthi Iyengar, "Of aging societies, Lost women, Lost consumers," *Asian Times Online*, Aug. 5, 2004, www.atimes.com/atimes/pint.html.

20. Andrea den Boer and Valerie Hudson, *Bare Branches: The Security Implications of Asia's Surplus Male Population* (Cambridge: MIT Press, 2004).

21. Jim Rogers, *Adventure Capitalist*, (New York, Random House, New York, 2003).

22. Mary Murray Bosrock, *Put Your Best Foot Forward, Asia*, (St. Paul, International Education Systems, 1997): 56.

23. Culturgram World Edition 2004, Japan: 326.

24. Ken Belson, "Japan's Samurai Past Thunders into the Present," *New York Times*, Dec. 7, 2003: 5.

25. Jon P. Alston, "Wa, Guanxi and Inhwa: Managerial Principles in Japan, China, and Korea," *Business Horizons*, March/April 1989: 26–31.

26. Transparency International Corruption Perceptions Index 2004, www.transparency.org (accessed Nov. 10, 2004).

27. Internet World Stats, Top 20 Countries with the Highest Internet Penetration Rate, Feb. 3, 2005, www.internetworldstats.com (accessed Feb. 21, 2005).

28. Tom Zeller, Jr., "Beijing Loves the Web Until the Web Talks Back," *New York Times*, Dec. 6, 2004: C15.

29. James L. Watson, Professor of Chinese Society and Anthropology at Harvard, www.rnw.nl/special/en/globalisation/html/hongkong020318.html (accessed June 12, 2004).

30. Leslie Earnest, "Catching a Wave of New Consumers," *Los Angeles Times*, May 16, 2004: C1, C4.

Notes to Chapter 16

1. Richard Lewis, *When Cultures Collide* (London: Nicholas Brealey Publishing Limited, 1996): 181.

2. Lewis: 181.

3. Terri Morrison, Wayne Conaway, and George A. Borden, *Kiss, Bow or Shake Hands*, (Massachusetts: Bob Adams, Inc., 1994): 8.

4. Donald Denoon and Philippa Mein-Smith with Marivic Wyndham, *A History of Australia, New Zealand and the Pacific* (Oxford, Blackwell Publishers, 2000): 32.

5. Denoon, et al: 162.

6. Denoon, et al: 162.

7. www.cyborlink.com/besite/hofstede.htm (accessed May 8, 2004).

8. Terri Morrison, et al: 247.

9. Dean Foster, The Global Etiquette Guide: Australia "Where Jack's as Good as His Mater," Monster Work Abroad, Dec. 19, 2003, http://workabroad.monster. com/articles/australian (accessed Dec. 19, 2003).

10. Phillip Knightley, *Australia: A Biography of a Nation* (London: Jonathan Cape, 2000): 35.

11. Denoon: 41.

12. Interview with Tim Walsh, May 27, 2004.

13. Global Entreneurship Monitor 2003, www.gemconsortium.org.

14. Nick March, New Zealand Management, "Opinion Reflections of a Returning Kiwi," May 2003, Proquest ID 334887531, http://69.0.144.9 (accessed May 8, 2004).

15. Wendy Guillies, Press Release, Global Entrepreneurship Monitor 2003, www.gemconsortium.org.

16. "Cities Guide Sydney, Business Etiquette," Economist.com, www.economist. com/cities (accessed May 22, 2004).

17. www.europa.eu.int/comm/trade/issues/bilateral/countries/newzealand/ index_en.htm.

18. www.dfat.gov.au/geo/china/proc_bilat_fs.html.

19. Peter Hendy, On-Line Opinion, "A trade agreement with China could bring big rewards for Australia," Nov. 17, 2003, www.onlineopinion.com/au (accessed May 9, 2004).

20. www.europa.eu.int/comm/trade/issues/bilateral/countries/newzealand/ index_en.htm.

21. Kim Griggs, "New Zealand Seeks Tolkien Dividend," BBC News (Dec. 6, 2001), www.news.bb.co.uk.

22. Simon Canning, "The Great Southern Brand," *The Australian*, (May 19, 2004), www.theaustralian.news.com.au.

Notes to Chapter 17

1. John Reader, *Africa: A Biography of the Continent* (London: Penguin Books, 1998): 1.

2. Reader: 1.

3. "How African is North Africa?" BBC News, http://news.bbc.co.uk/go/pr/fr/-2/hi/africa/3421527.stm, Jan. 23, 2004 (accessed Jan. 24, 2004).

4. Reader: 195.

5. Maxine Dalton, et al, *Success for the New Global Manager* (San Francisco Jossey-Bass, 2002): 51.

6. Geert Hofstede, *Cultures and Organizations* (New York: New York, 1997).

7. AfroBarometer Briefing Paper No. 1, April 2002, www.afrobaromter.org.

8. www.internetworldstats.com/stats1.htm, update Feb. 3, 2005 (accessed Feb. 21, 2005).

9. Population Reference Bureau, www.prb.org (accessed June 5, 2004), Human Population: Fundamentals of Growth, Population Growth and Distribution.

10. Lester R. Brown, "HIV Epidemic Restructuring Africa's Population," *World Watch*, Oct. 31, 2000, www.globalpolicy.org.

11. Tony Hawkins, "Economic Rankings Highlight Africa's troubles," *Financial Times*, June 3, 2004: 5.

12. "Emerging Deals," *The Economist*, Feb. 21, 2004: 73.

13. "Public Opinion in Africa, Confused democrats," *Economist.com*, April 1, 2004.

14. "Trade in Africa and Civil Society's Responsibility in the 21st century," Thompson Ayodele, Coordinator, Institute of Public Policy Analysis, Lagos, Nigeria, Jan. 13-17 2003, "AGOA: The NGO Perspective presentation," www.ippanigerial.org (accessed May 29, 2004).

15. Tony Hawkins, "Economic Rankings Highlight Africa's Troubles," *Financial Times*, June 3, 2004: 2.

16. Emad Mekay, "Economy: US-Africa Trade Rises, Falls Under New Deal," Global Information Network. New York. Jan. 29, 2004: 1, Proquest ID 599932951, http://69.0.144.8 (accessed May 29, 2004).

17. "African Growth and Opportunity Act (AGOA) Begins to Pay Off," *World Trade*, May 2004: 14.

18. Janet Jere, "Economy on the Up," *New African*, April 2004: 27, Proquest ID 620648591, http://gateway.proquest.com.

19. AGOA.info, Country Information – Mauritus, www.agoa.info (accessed June 1, 2004): 1.

20. Wyger Wenhtholt, "The Real Dutch Wax: the company that clothes Africa," *New African*, March 2003: 28, Proquest ID 50848432, http://gateway.proquest. com (accessed Nov. 21, 2003).

21. Elsa Artadi and Xavier Sala-I-Martin, "The Economic Tragedy of the Twentieth Century: Growth in Africa," World Economic Forum, Executive Summary Africa Competitiveness Report, 2004.

22. Tom Mbakwe, "Lesotho: No business as usual," *New African*, Dec. 2003: 26, Proquest ID 504177251, http://69.0.144.8 (accessed May 29, 2004).

23. Susuanne Baillie and Sarah Lisi, "High 5," *Profit*. Toronto. May 2004: 19, Proquest 623068411, http://gateway.proquest.com.

24. Culturegram 2004 South Africa: 593.

25. www.agoa.gov.

26. Africa: South Africa, "USAID's Strategy in South Africa," www.usaid.gov/locations/sub-shaharan_africa (accessed May 29, 2004).

27. Baillie, et al.

28. Matthew Garrahan and John Reed, "World Cup 2010," *Financial Times*, May 14, 2004: 11.

29. Jere Longman, "Awarded 2010 World Cup, South Africa is Celebrating," *New York Times*, May 16, 2004: 1, Sports Sunday.

30. Frank J. Prial, "10 Year Past Apartheid, Wine Industry Thrives," *New York Times*, May 12, 2004: D1.

31. Calvin Reid, "Digital Bookmobile Prints books for the Poor," *Publishers Weekly*, March 22, 2004: 14, Proquest ID 590853301, http://gateway.proquest.com.

32. Joseph Kony, "No respite; A massacre in Uganda," *Economist*, Feb. 28, 2004, Proquest ID 552262771, International: 61.

33. www.ugandaexportsonline.com/eac.htm.

34. Women of Uganda Network, www.wognet.org (accessed June 1, 2004).

Notes to Chapter 18

1. Toby D. Atkinson, *Merriam-Webster's Guide to International Business Communications*, second edition (Springfield: Merriam-Webster, Incorporated, 1996): 300.

2. Atkinson: 278.
3. Conway, et al: 327.
4. Major League Baseball (www.mlb.com), National Basketball Association (www.nba.com).
5. Executive planet online.

Notes to Chapter 19

1. Ramadam on the net, www.holidays.net/ramadan, May 15, 2005.
2. Morrison, et al: 143.
3. Christobel Williams-Mitchell, *Dressed for the Job – The Story of Occupational Costume* (Bland Press, 1982): 29, 102.
4. Josh Sims, "Spinning a New Yarn," *Financial Times*, Nov. 30, 2003: W11.
5. Seth Feman, "My, What a Stunning Coat!" *Wired*, Sept. 2003: 38.
6. Terri Morrison, "Fashion Faux Pas," Global Attitudes, Frequent Flyer online, Aug. 6, 2003.

Notes to Chapter 20

1. Margaret Visser, *The Rituals of Dinner* (Toronto: HarperCollins Publishers Ltd., 1991): 86.
2. M.M. Bosrock, *Put Your Best Foot Forward, Asia* (St. Paul, International Education Systems, 1997): 65.
3. Visser: 91.
4. Visser: 121.
5. Visser: 183.
6. Tannahill Reay, *Food in History* (New York: Crown Publishers, Inc., 1988): 131.
7. Visser: 72.
8. Alexandra Harney, "Coming soon to a tourist attraction near you: 100m Chinese holiday makers," *Financial Times*, Sept. 2, 2004: 11.
9. A Guide to Toasting @ Into Wine, www.intowine.com/wine-toasts2.html (accessed Sept. 12, 2004).
10. Harney: 11.
11. Terri Morrison and Wayne Conway, "Unusual Toasts & Celebrations," www.frequentlfyer.oag.com/stories/08162004/Global_Attitudes.asp (accessed Aug. 23, 2004).
12. Clotilde Dusoulier, "Wine and dine free in Paris," *Los Angeles Times*, www.latimes.com/travel (accessed Sept 12, 2004).

Notes to Chapter 21

1. John Reader, *Africa: A Biography of the Continent* (London: Penguin Books, 1998): 196.

2. Jesse Freund, "Finding Your Luggage in a Sea of Samsonite," *Business 2.0*, Sept. 2004.

3. Doreen Steiddle, History of Passports, www.ppt.gc.ca/passport_office/history_e.asp (accessed Aug. 13, 2004).

4. www.womentraveltips.com/tips3.shtml (accessed Aug 7, 2004).

INDEX